KYOTO ANIMATION

ALSO BY DANI CAVALLARO AND FROM MCFARLAND

CLAMP in Context: A Critical Study of the Manga and Anime (2012)

Art in Anime (2012)

The Fairy Tale and Anime: Traditional Themes, Images and Symbols at Play on Screen (2011)

The World of Angela Carter: A Critical Investigation (2011)

Anime and the Art of Adaptation: Eight Famous Works from Page to Screen (2010)

Anime and the Visual Novel: Narrative Structure, Design and Play at the Crossroads of Animation and Computer Games (2010)

Magic as Metaphor in Anime: A Critical Study (2010)

The Mind of Italo Calvino: A Critical Exploration of His Thought and Writings (2010)

Anime and Memory: Aesthetic, Cultural and Thematic Perspectives (2009)

The Art of Studio Gainax: Experimentation, Style and Innovation at the Leading Edge of Anime (2009)

Anime Intersections: Tradition and Innovation in Theme and Technique (2007)

The Animé Art of Hayao Miyazaki (2006)

The Cinema of Mamoru Oshii: Fantasy, Technology and Politics (2006)

Kyoto Animation
A Critical Study and Filmography

Dani Cavallaro

McFarland & Company, Inc., Publishers
Jefferson, North Carolina, and London

LIBRARY OF CONGRESS CATALOGUING-IN-PUBLICATION DATA

Cavallaro, Dani.
    Kyoto animation : a critical study and filmography / Dani Cavallaro.
        p.   cm.
    Includes bibliographical references and index.

    ISBN 978-0-7864-7068-6
    softcover : acid free paper ∞

    1. Kyoto Animeshon Kabushiki Kaisha. 2. Animated films — Japan — History and criticism. I. Title.
NC1766.J32K963 2012
791.43'340952 — dc23   2012031704

BRITISH LIBRARY CATALOGUING DATA ARE AVAILABLE

© 2012 Dani Cavallaro. All rights reserved

No part of this book may be reproduced or transmitted in any form or by any means, electronic or mechanical, including photocopying or recording, or by any information storage and retrieval system, without permission in writing from the publisher.

Cover art © 2012 Hemera/Thinkstock

Manufactured in the United States of America

McFarland & Company, Inc., Publishers
  Box 611, Jefferson, North Carolina 28640
    www.mcfarlandpub.com

*To Paddy, for providing me with
the inspiration to journey in
more ways than one.*

Contents

Preface 1

1 • Kyoto Animation in Context 3
2 • Science Fiction Reimagined 24
3 • Crossing Worlds 78
4 • Art and Play 119

Filmography 175
Bibliography 185
Index 191

With a gust of wind
Fall scarlet leaves;
So clear the waters that
Those unfallen cast their shadows too
Upon the pond-bed.

—*Kokinshuu* (古今集, Heian poetry anthology, 920)

Preface

Creativity comes from looking for the unexpected and stepping outside your own experience. — Masaru Ibuka

Choose a job you love, and you will never have to work a day in your life. — Confucius

Having risen from humble beginnings to become the creator of some of the most acclaimed titles in the history of contemporary anime (as well as their beautifully designed spin-offs), Kyoto Animation has gained recognition the world over as a uniquely inspired and inventive creative enterprise. This factor may be sufficient unto itself to warrant the desire to produce a monograph devoted to the studio and its works. No less stimulating, however, is the recognition that in its unmatched sensitivity to the wonders and quandaries of ordinary life, Kyoto Animation has consistently proved able to yield special syntheses of stylization and realism by capitalizing to great effect on a quintessentially Japanese aesthetic formula: the galvanizing blend of elegance, refinement and gentleness.

The book comprises four chapters. Chapter 1, "Kyoto Animation in Context," examines the studio's philosophy and creative vision vis-à-vis a range of concepts drawn from both traditional and contemporary culture, seeking to highlight its distinctive production values and thematic priorities. Chapters 2, 3 and 4 are devoted to close analyses of Kyoto Animation's anime, including TV series, OVAs, ONAs and feature length movies. These chapters focus on the studio's choice of genres, themes and imagery while also commenting on its approach to the production process. Chapter 2, "Science Fiction Reimagined," focuses on Kyoto Animation's adventurous take on classic sci-fi formulae by recourse to unprecedented generic blends and provocative storytelling. The titles examined in depth in this chapter include *Munto, Munto 2: Beyond the Walls of Time, Full Metal*

Panic? Fumoffu, Full Metal Panic! The Second Raid, The Melancholy of Haruhi Suzumiya (2006 and 2009 versions), *The Melancholy of Haruhi-chan Suzumiya, Nyoron churuya-san* and *The Disappearance of Haruhi Suzumiya*. With Chapter 3, "Crossing Worlds," the discussion concentrates on the studio's varied portrayal of the infiltration of everyday reality by parallel realities imbued with mythological, mystical and speculative connotations. This chapter focuses on *Air, Kanon, Clannad* and *Clannad: After Story*. Chapter 4, "Art and Play," addresses KyoAni's enthusiastic endorsement of the principle that creativity, and hence the practice and performance of art, should never be totally divorced from an element of fun even in the face of unavoidable technical priorities and the rigors of training. *Lucky☆Star, K-ON!, K-ON!!, K-ON!* the movie and *Nichijou* (a.k.a. *My Ordinary Life*) constitute this chapter's key titles.

1

Kyoto Animation in Context

> *Imagination is more important than knowledge. For while knowledge defines all we currently know and understand, imagination points to all we might yet discover and create.* — Albert Einstein
>
> *Creativity is allowing yourself to make mistakes. Art is knowing which ones to keep.* — Scott Adams

Held in high esteem worldwide for its exceptionally refined production values and animation quality, Kyoto Animation (京都アニメーション) — a.k.a. KyoAni — is one of the most imaginative, ingenious and widely acclaimed studios in the history of modern anime. Established in 1981, KyoAni became a limited company in 1985 and then a corporation in 1999. (Please note that the studio will hereafter be referred to as KyoAni throughout the book.) The company is affiliated with the distinguished studio Sunrise (whose achievements include the hugely popular anime *Gundam, Vision of Escaflowne, Cowboy Beebop, InuYasha, Mai-HiME* and *Code Geass: Lelouch of the Rebellion*) and the studio Animation Do. As well as creating its own anime series, OVAs and ONAs in tandem with multifarious ancillary merchandise, KyoAni has been involved in the production of several well-known titles released by other studios, such as the aforecited *InuYasha, Kiddy Grade* (GONZO) and *Tenchi Universe* (AIC), alongside game openings and endings. This chapter seeks to situate these achievements contextually by examining KyoAni's philosophy and creative enterprise with reference to salient aspects of both traditional and contemporary Japanese culture.

Anime studios which, like KyoAni, enjoy both local and international prominence, often adopt an approach to production which prioritizes volume and hence a steady flow of releases. In order to meet their challenging deadlines, these studios frequently rely on freelance assistance drawn from disparate quarters, which entails that they are not always in a position to guarantee quality control. KyoAni, conversely, has regularly tended to give precedence to quality over quantity, making the pursuit of artistic excellence and technical experimentation its principal goals. Striving to achieve these objectives, the studio has relied on the imagination and expertise of in-house staff, thereby ensuring the communication of a coherent vision and the maintenance of high production values throughout each release. In this fashion, KyoAni continues to achieve remarkable results not simply by preserving the high quality of its animation, but also by building upon its previous accomplishments so that virtually each of them appears better than the last. A further factor distinguishing KyoAni from many other popular studios lies with its thematic preferences. Aiming to produce works endowed with overtly impactful dramatic qualities in order to secure immediate (though not automatically enduring) appeal, several studios of the volume-oriented variety have favored stories which focus on extraordinary events on an epic scale. KyoAni, by contrast, has increasingly sought to concentrate on seemingly ordinary occurrences, and delivered a distinctive and thought-provoking world picture by instilling the ordinary with an ironic sense of the absurd.

KyoAni's work ethic is economically encapsulated by the set of fundamental precepts outlined in the company's official website, which are intended to guide its day-to-day operations no less than its overall productive venture. Literally translated, these include: embracing challenges; doing one's best; creating animations that people need; being a human company. Concurrently endeavoring to make much of others and to help people develop in their own terms, KyoAni aims to be an entertainment company which focuses on animation with utter sincerity (*Kyoto Animation*). As they unremittingly endeavor to stretch both their purview and the boundaries of their art, KyoAni's directors, animators and artists appear to abide by the traditional principle of *kaizen*, which Boyé Lafayette De Mente succinctly describes as "continuous improvement" or the "process of striving for perfection ... in all fields of endeavor" (De Mente). Relatedly, the studio's philosophy finds expression in all areas of its productivity, not only in its anime. Thus, in order to understand fully KyoAni's philosophy, it is important to take into consideration the entire spectrum of its ongoing activities. At present, these encompass animation production (with an increasing focus on the perfection of digital techniques); goods planning and sale intended to reflect fans' expectations and preferences while capitalizing on resources unique to KyoAni as an animation company; publishing (especially of art books) grounded in a deep respect for the book as an object and cultural entity; original character design meant to work synergistically with merchandise design; and academic instruction. KyoAni's CM Library beautifully complements its cognate design and publishing initiatives.

As the section of the studio's site devoted to its animation school explains, this venture is designed to provide both advanced professional training and classes meant to foster the emergence of new talents within a stimulating environment. Working under the direct supervision of experts who are regularly engaged in anime creation, students are given the opportunity to acquire the real techniques necessary to their advancement in the profession as they are actually employed in the context of hands-on production (*Kyoto Animation*). KyoAni's studio, therefore, approaches teaching as a mission involving not merely the communication of theoretical material, valuable as this undeniably is in the development of a student's conceptual range, but also active participation and practical experience. At the same time, KyoAni's methodologies echo the approach to artistic training embedded in Japanese culture since ancient times. As Sarah Lonsdale observes, "the traditional way of learning a craft has always been one of emulation: an apprentice observing a master, learning through osmosis as the student becomes familiar with the materials. Perfection for the master was traditionally more about enhancing the natural beauty of a material rather than asserting the individual ego" (Lonsdale, p. 147). This contention is epitomized by the formative experience of one of the most widely acclaimed Japanese artists of recent decades, the architect Tadao Ando. As Sunamita Lim explains, "this introspective architect mastered the traditional art of Japanese wood designing and building first.... In the time-honored tradition of studying from the masters, he learned the precision techniques required in building with wood joinery, sans hardware" (Lim, p. 20).

According to De Mente, the training methods based on the "*meisho* (master) and *deshi* (apprentice) approach to arts and crafts" have proved so influential over time as to affect virtually all levels of Japanese existence by "permeating the culture from top to bottom. The teachings of the masters incorporated philosophical and ethical factors as well as precise *kata*, or 'way of doing things.' Masters in every art and craft used precise steps or processes in the training of their apprentices. Deviations from the *kata* were absolutely taboo" (De Mente). Although the old rules have somewhat relaxed today, their legacy is still palpable, and KyoAni's activities certainly do not fail to honor their lessons. Most vitally, the studio's staff are eager to ensure that enjoyment is never entirely superseded by technical or commercial objectives. As its own anime consistently intimate, creativity amounts to precious little without at least a modicum of fun. The classes run by KyoAni's instructors are therefore meant to provide contexts in which students can experience the pleasure of creating drawings and animated images, and learn to refine that pleasure by honing their vision and skills. A frank desire to share their expertise with future generations of artists and animators fuels at all times the approach to teaching and the pedagogical enthusiasm characteristic of the studio's instructors. Their lectures and practical classes, in other words, are lessons taught by established anime practitioners to prospective anime practitioners — and, no less vitally, by anime lovers to anime lovers (*Kyoto Animation*).

At the same time, attentive inspection of the sample images accompanying the description of the principal tasks designed for both prospective animators and background artists demonstrates a desire to inculcate not only specific skills but also a philosophical lesson of critical significance to Japanese thinking at large: the imperative to adopt a deeply respectful attitude toward one's materials and tools. *Ki* (wood), *ishi* (stone), *wara* (straw) and *take* (bamboo) are amongst the most eminent items, and are consistently allowed to guide the conception and execution of the objects of which they are made alongside the instruments which enable their manufacture. In Kyoto, it is worth noting, funerals are still held today for needles which are no longer functional as a means of expressing one's gratitude to their services. This world view underscores the corporeal dimension of life. The same essential message is conveyed by the indigenous writing system as a cultural construct whose ideographic (and latently pictographic) principles strike their roots in nature and the mechanism of metaphor governing nature's internal correspondences. A defining component of its culture, Japan's writing system deserves attention in the present context due to its ancestral relationship with anime. The connection is thrown into relief in the writings of the seventeenth-century Japanese calligrapher Ojio Yuushou. Proceeding from the assumption that "characters were first created in the image of a human figure," Yuushou maintains that the proficient calligrapher must be able to handle the brush in such a way as to evoke the movements of an animate human body (cited in Ueda, p. 176). In Makoto Ueda's words, "every student of calligraphy must strive to produce living characters" endowed with numerous attributes meant to denote not only their intrinsic aliveness and dynamism but also their ethical values.

Hence, Yuushou argues that a competently executed calligraphic character must be seen to have a "soul," "individuality," "force," "morals," "ardor," "nobility," a "voice" and a "spirit" (Ueda, pp. 177–178). The twelfth- and thirteenth-century pictures known as *Chōjū-jinbutsu-giga* (literally, "animal-person caricatures") — a.k.a. *Scrolls of Frolicking Animals* or *Scrolls of Frolicking Animals and Humans* — recall the graphic terseness of Japanese calligraphy at its best with their fluid, elegant and entertaining rhythms while also standing out as forerunners of modern manga and anime. Thus, they stand out as memorable embodiments of the contention advanced by Yuushou that the graphic sign can be regarded as fundamentally *animate*. The passion for characters capable of exuding an aura of aliveness can also be traced back to the tradition surrounding the execution of the portraits of illustrious Zen masters meant as inspiration for their pupils. As Tze-yue G. Hu comments, this art "demanded acute observational skills of the painter…. From background setting to posture, dress details to facial expressions, each portrait painting depicted a powerful psychological presence which could be regarded as the early genealogical images of manga/anime characters" (Hu). Both Yuushou's reflections on the art of calligraphy and key developments in scroll painting and portraiture could therefore be said to foreshadow the vital mechanisms guiding the creation of anime: namely, methods to which KyoAni's works adhere to a paradigmatic degree.

In both the creative and the educational arenas, KyoAni's modus operandi is underpinned by an ethical and creative approach which places the collaborative spirit at the forefront of its priorities, as concisely borne out by the physical layout of its main studio. This is predicated on the division of labor within an integrated structure, and hence seeks to foster the values of proximity and privacy at once by maximizing the scope for concentration without condemning the individual creators to isolation. The same basic layout is employed for the top floor (which houses the workstations used by the directors and the key animators alongside a flexible area serving by turns as a meeting room, a common room, a kitchen and a reference library); the middle floor (where the in-between animators and background artists undertake their tasks); and the bottom floor (reserved for the staff responsible for production overview, editing and recording). The managers, in this context, fulfill an essentially coordinating function in the light of the studio's objectives for both each production and the company's overarching vision. The studio's mission statement, outlined in its official website, further emphasizes its eminently corporate vision and collaborative ethos. The statement's key sentence declares that with its logo, based on the *kanji kyō*, KyoAni seeks to communicate the extent to which the company draws on a pool of all of its members' ideas in the production of its moving images. Thus, the studio's works must be seen as a product of the creativity and imagination of each of its members (*Kyoto Animation*). The *kanji kyō* to which the statement makes reference is the first character in the word Kyoto — i.e., 京 — which designates the city's status as "capital." The logo's resemblance to a sun or flower emanates directly from that *kanji*. This particular meaning of *kyō* will be revisited later in the discussion. It is first desirable to examine some additional *kanji* with the same pronunciation which are specifically relevant to KyoAni's context.

Given the studio's emphasis on the collaborative spirit, it is especially notable that one of the many homophones of the *kanji kyō* used in the word Kyoto is 協, which means "to cooperate." It is also worth remembering that a further available spelling of *kyō* is 狂, which translates literally as "mad." In the philosophical framework of Zen, this word has been used to designate the state of spiritual ecstasy induced by total absorption in the gardens designed to capture nature in a conceptual and stylized fashion — the very gardens, in other words, one still has a chance to experience in contemporary Kyoto. A comparable feeling of sensory inebriation is conjured up by KyoAni's stupendously detailed and glowingly colored settings, and especially those which aim to capture in a metaphorical form the dynamic emotions of the characters whose actions they accommodate. At the same time, however, KyoAni's background art and related locations embrace quite a different experience which is also traditionally associated with the atmosphere fostered by classic Japanese landscaping: *seijaku*. This concept describes an entity's power to evoke a feeling of energized quietness. According to Patrick Lennox Tierney, *seijaku* is epitomized by "the calming influence one feels on entering a Japanese Garden.... Silence and tranquillity prevail and all sense of disturbance is absent. Reflections on water often express this principle. Its opposite is noise and disturbance. An old proverb says stillness is activity, therefore *seijaku* is thought of as an active state though its effect is one of calm and unruffled solitude. Its timely and seasonal character has to do with late autumn or early spring, and it is evident at dawn and dusk, in the moonlight and in snow-covered gardens" (Tierney). The affects described by Tierney are characteristic of the particular brand of Zen Buddhism which took root in Kyoto over time. This doctrine cultivated eminently introspective tendencies, and therefore tended to focus on private reflection, solitary effort and individual responsibility rather than on the priorities of the state and political integrity (which had been the main concerns of Buddhism in the form in which it had first entered Japan from China). The perspective delineated above is relevant to the project in hand, even though it is neither explicitly nor implicitly referenced by KyoAni's mission statement, by virtue of its artistic significance. The concepts of spiritual ecstasy and energized quietness, in particular, find expression on numerous and often memorable occasions in the context of the studio's productions vis-à-vis the representation of the natural environment. Indeed, this is consistently portrayed as a reality pervaded by a beauty so sublime as to hold the potential to engender feelings of intoxication, while concurrently exuding a sense of peace which belies its inexhaustible energy.

The instances of semantic richness thrown into relief by the use of *kyō* emphasize the passion for wordplay, punning and double meanings inherent in the Japanese language, and continually encouraged by its composite writing system. Also worthy of special notice, in assessing the company's mission statement, is its use of the word 創造 (*souzou*), which translates literally as "to create" but is also homophonic with a word which means "to imagine."* This element highlights the inextricability of the interdependent concepts of imagination and creativity in the context of Japanese philosophy at large. Within this perspective, the process of creation is characteristically invested with greater importance than the artifact created. This tenet is central to any artist's search both for fresh expressive vehicles and for adventurous blends of novel ideas and long-established traditions. In both cases, the quest for a harmonious relationship between human beings and the natural environment is tirelessly promoted. Concomitantly, even the most repetitive everyday actions and rituals are respected, and even the humblest of objects are ascribed social worth. Emancipated from the destiny of utter anonymity to which persistent reiteration would otherwise doom them, such actions, rituals and objects are actually acknowledged as the mundane counterparts of the cyclical rhythms through which nature goes on regenerating itself and the *ki*, the energy coursing through all things, manifests itself as a forever astounding, albeit understated, life spirit. Working together, the abstract ideals and the concrete practices encouraged by this world picture offer an enticing vision

---

*The translation of this part of the KyoAni mission statement has benefited from the advice of Dr. Jonathan D. Mackintosh of the Department of Media and Cultural Studies at Birkbeck College, University of London.

of art as a semiotic dance wherein fantasy colludes with reality, and new life stories are incessantly made and unmade.

In order to grasp the full scope of KyoAni's activities not only within but also around animation per se, it should also be noted that since 2009, KyoAni has been running an annual Kyoto Animation Award competition for creators of original novels, manga and story scenarios. The winning entries have a chance to be animated by the studio. To date, no grand prizes have been awarded in any of the three categories but some of the more impressive entries have been accorded extensive visual treatment on the KyoAni website. Moreover, in December 2011, KyoAni announced that it had started working on an anime adaptation of the romance novel *Chū-2 Byō Demo Koi ga Shitai!* ("I Have Adolescent Delusions, But I Want to Love!"), a recipient of an honorable mention in the first Kyoto Animation Award. Given this prospective work's somewhat peculiar title, it seems worth mentioning, with the assistance of *Anime News Network*, that "the comedian Hikaru Ijūin coined the term '*chū-2 byō*' (literally, 'middle-school second-grade disease') for adolescent thoughts that teenagers commonly have — especially delusions of grandeur or the belief that one is special compared to everyone else ("Kyoto Animation Plans *Chū-2 Byō Demo Koi ga Shitai!* Anime"). In 2010, the company imaginatively extended the scope of its activities with the launch of the KyoAni Original Character Series. The key idea underlying this project is that all of the studio's creators should feel free to come up with an original character inspired by a basic theme, and to submit it for consideration. Entries are posted on the KyoAni website, and visitors have a chance to vote for their favorite work, thus determining the submissions' final ranking. The works published and ranked on the studio's site evince refreshing variety, and include the following sets: "KyoAni Sisters" (based simply on the theme of "four sisters"), "KyoAni Kids" (based on the ever popular motif of the "cute or dreamy" character), and "KyoAni Boys" (based on a mix of humorous and "cool" types). Although the initiative is not (at least yet) harnessed to the achievement of any ulterior objective, its main function apparently consisting of the provision of an arena for the expression of unfettered talent and creativeness, there is no doubt that it has the capacity to consolidate the studio's philosophy — and hence its corporate image — to great effect.

In this respect, the KyoAni Original Character Series bears affinities with a broader cultural project embraced in various parts of Japan over the past few years, whereby popular figures of a cartoon-like nature have been utilized as a means of capturing and preserving regional identities.

As Hannah Fearn explains, "recent schemes to connect local residents to their communities in Japan have sought to exploit regional strengths to create a new identity — including designing pop art characters to represent the area. It has been a success, with residents reporting a sense of ownership and pride in their city." A paradigmatic instance of this trend is Nerima City (Tokyo): an area whose cultural and historical significance appears to have been forgotten by its current inhabitants even though, strictly speaking, it is "the birthplace of Japanese animation." As Fearn points out, "in an attempt to revitalise the area through its biggest industry, the local authority launched an official anime homepage in 2010, describing the history of the industry and showcasing interviews with designers. It was so popular the council commissioned the design of a new anime character, named Nerimaru, as a city mascot." Analogous initiatives were subsequently launched in Iwate, whose local authorities have begun to publish a "manga anthology ... drawn by local artists to cover local issues" and meant "to showcase the region's most attractive features." Hence, various parts of Japan are now associated with "their own character, or pop culture identity, and the process of designing the character has involved residents"— in much the same fashion as the design of figures for the KyoAni Original Character Series seeks to involve the entire community of the studio's creators outside the boundaries of activities geared specifically toward the production of titles intended for commercial release. The idea that cartoonish characters may act as potent vehicles for the communication of regional identities has recently received considerable interest outside Japan. In the United Kingdom, for example, "local authorities are taking lessons from Japan on how to use popular culture, regional history and local produce to promote regions across the country" (Fearn).

Returning to the *kyō* on which KyoAni's logo is based, it is now useful to assess its relevance as a specific signifier of the city of Kyoto. Yoko Hatta, the studio's co-founder with her husband Hideaki Hatta (KyoAni's current president) hails from Kyoto but neither she nor her associates are driven by the desire to make the studio's works intimately associated with the city. In fact, KyoAni has assiduously endeavored to establish an identity which can transcend the geographical and cultural boundaries of its place of birth to reach out to broader audiences. This does not preclude the possibility of the "Kyoto" component of the designation Kyoto Animation from striking particular chords with non–Japanese viewers, who will feasibly often tend to associate the city with certain established images and with a long history of artistic excellence reaching back to the Heian Period, when Kyoto itself was founded. Hence, it is useful to bear in mind, in exploring the studio's oeuvre, that Kyoto might still carry subliminal connotations for some strata of the viewing public. This contention will be revisited later in this discussion. What must be emphasized at this point is the fact that if the Kyoto element carries implicit connotations for non–Japanese audiences, this is a "virtual" significance, not the result of a self-conscious effort on the studio's part to establish any specific reputation (or evoke any specific set of associations) in non–Japanese viewers. Its priority is actually the pursuit of modest goals, even as it constantly strives for artistic improvement and for ways of reinvigorating well-tested formulae and familiar genres alike: the very goals which underpin its unwavering experimentative vigor. Commercial success with indigenous audiences is absolutely necessary for the studio to pursue its agenda, yet this prerequisite has never been conducive to its pandering to vapid entertainment for its own sake. In fact, KyoAni has never relinquished its desire to convey a message—a distinctive philosophy which, in a nutshell, consists of the belief in the paramount value of ordinary life, and has increasingly led the studio to focus on everyday matters instead of exceptional events. However, the quotidian dimension is not dealt with in a soap-operatic manner, since its portrayal characteristically incorporates a tendency to impart the mundane with a peculiar twist. Thus, KyoAni's appetite for fantasy has been progressively translated into a taste for the absurd, the grotesque and the uncanny, and into a tendency to highlight the wacky undercurrents which course ordinary existence as relentlessly as motion itself. This vision is communicated through a sustained use of humor, exaggeration, distortion, unexpected modulations of perspective and dislocations of the sense of proportion. With their idiosyncratic take on ordinary life, KyoAni's works can help people relate to reality via fiction, and even discover feelings of connection and continuity (if not exactly stability) vis-à-vis both social atomization and disruptions unleashed by nature's terrifying powers.

Stylistically, the effectiveness of KyoAni's proposition regarding the importance of everyday life typically depends on a subtle interplay of distillation (fostered by a penchant for minimalism and stylization) and realism (borne out primarily by a preference for vivid details and a pervasive atmosphere of immediacy). These factors are smoothly blended through what the Japanese term *yuga*: a sense of "gracefulness and refinement that is strongly infused with gentleness" (De Mente). *Yuga*, in KyoAni's case, is not necessarily conveyed by people's behavior per se but rather emanates from the qualities of the image, line and motion: the animator's alchemic mix. Minimalism and stylization are at times so refined as to verge on the surreal, yet the visuals never lose contact with realism altogether insofar as impeccable stylishness and painstaking attention to minutiae infuse them at all times with a strong sense of verisimilitude. This art yields a graphically realistic chart of the hypothetical: it translates what ought to be considered impossible or implausible into a virtually real (or potentially viable) world. Its effects are most striking when elements drawn from tradition and lore coalesce with advanced digital technology: in such instances, we are offered worlds which are patently unreal, yet exude a sense of not only realism but even hyperrealism by virtue of the delicious intensity of their details. In this respect, KyoAni's works could be said to epitomize Hu's conception of anime. According to the critic, "the visual functions of animation fulfill a reality, a reality that may not be rational, structured, stable, or even highly visible or audible ... anime is laden with energy which flows from the hand that draws the frames and that meticulously tailors the pre-calculated movements. Equally energy-driven is the creative flow of stamina that visualizes the aesthetic background and an imagined subjective abode" (Hu).

KyoAni's ability to evoke images which are patently artificial but feel consummately real is memorably demonstrated, in all of its productions, by a tendency to use real-life locations as the bases of its settings, to pay homage to their distinctive features with naturalistic punctiliousness, and yet immerse them in a magical atmosphere which places them well beyond simple photojournalism. This effect is accomplished by treating the materials gleaned through fieldwork as sources of inspiration, and as springboards to autonomous artistic expression and creative experiment, not as fixed templates to be robotically reproduced. Among the many real-world places featuring in KyoAni's anime as luminously transfigured settings are Jindai High School in Chōfu, Tokyo Metropolis (*Full Metal Panic? Fumoffu* and *Full Metal Panic! The Second Raid*); Nishinomiya Kita High School in Hyōgo Prefecture, Kansai (*The Melancholy of Haruhi Suzumiya*); Kounan Hospital in Central Tokyo (*The Disappearance of Haruhi Suzumiya*); the fishing village of Kasumi (a.k.a. Kami) in Hyōgo Prefecture, Kansai (*Air*); the towns of Moriguchi in Osaka Prefecture, Yokohama in Kanagawa Prefecture, Tachikawa in Western Tokyo and Sapporo in Hokkaido (*Kanon*); Komaba Junior-high and High School (affiliated to the University of

Tsukuba) in Setagaya, Tokyo (*Clannad*); Kasukame School in Saitama Prefecture, Kantō (*Lucky☆Star*); Toyosato Elementary School in Shiga Prefecture, Kansai (*K-ON!*, *K-ON!!* and *K-ON!* movie); Kyoto Tower, Kinkakuji, Kitano Tenmangu Shrine, Arashiyama and Hanazono Kaikan Hotel in Kyoto (*K-ON!!*); London, UK (*K-ON!* movie). Some of these places will be revisited in later chapters in greater detail. Interestingly, *Nichijou* dies not seem to contain any recognizable references to real-world locations, which could be interpreted as a way of emphasizing the anime's desire to capture the rhythms of everyday life — which is exactly what its title signifies — in a universal sense instead of becoming enmeshed with local specificities. However, this has not hindered the show from accommodating a stupendous range of more or less overt allusions to various facets of both traditional and contemporary Japanese culture.

If it is the case, as suggested earlier, that Kyoto is liminally relevant to the experience of non–Japanese audiences as an ensemble of cultural symbols and icons, it is worth looking at the specific area in which KyoAni's main studio is located. This is the district of Momoyama-cho in Fushimi-ku, one of the eleven wards in Kyoto Prefecture, and is nested within the southernmost hills of the Higashiyama Mountains in southern Kyoto, with the Uji River flowing to the south. Fushimi-ku's principal landmark is undoubtedly the Fushimi Inari Taisha: the head shrine of all the shrines devoted to the figure of Inari, the fox spirit honored by Shintō as the god of rice, of which over 30,000 are reputedly scattered throughout Japan. Regarded as the patron of business and commerce since ancient times, Inari is worshiped most alacritously by merchants and manufacturers (as well as virtually anyone seeking good fortune), who have been donating for centuries the *torii* (red gates) which line the shrine's footpaths and form the four-kilometer-long tunnel-like passage leading to the top of Mount Inari. Alongside Fushimi Inari Taisha, the next most eminent cultural fulcrum of the Fushimi Ward is Fushimi-Momoyama Castle. Built from 1592 to 1594 by the warrior and diplomat Toyotomi Hideyoshi, who is credited with the unification of Japan's political factions, the edifice was destroyed twenty years later by Tokugawa Ieyasu, the Tokugawa shogunate's first ruler responsible for shifting political power to the city of Edo (thereafter Tokyo). In the aftermath of the Tokugawa assault, many peach trees were planted among the ruins of the castle, thus inspiring the designation of the local hills as Momoyama, or "Peach Mountains." The castle itself was not properly rebuilt till 1964, at which point it came back to life as a concrete replica destined for use as an amusement park.

The radical reconfiguration incurred by the illustrious edifice brings to mind Jean Baudrillard's observations concerning the character of postmodern culture in its entirety as a hyperreal Disneyland of sorts (Baudrillard). Fushimi-Momoyama Castle is also a good example of what Regina Dahmen-Ingenhoven, following the sociologist Gerhard Schulze, describes as an experiential, adventure-driven society. In the kind of postmodern social environment posited by the critic, architecture does not depend exclusively on buildings specifically designed for leisure, such as amusement parks, to kindle the appetite for adventure. In fact, all sorts of edifices lend themselves to adaptation as vehicles for the stimulation and provision of supposedly exciting interactive experiences: museums, shopping malls, department stores, banks, train stations, airport lounges — and ancient castles are clearly not to be exempted. Since the shared goal pursued by these disparate architectural constructs is to enliven the emotions of their users by immersing them in a stirring ambience, they often rely on the semiotic conventions of comics and animation in order to accomplish their effects, and hence bear a direct connection with the art form pivotal to this study (Dahmen-Ingenhoven).

Japanese culture is by no means resistant to postmodern options of the kind described by Baudrillard and Dahmen-Ingenhoven — nor should the image of the ancient castle turned fairground, accordingly, strike us as an anomaly. In fact, Japan yields an eminently prismatic and composite cultural formation: a cauldron in which tradition and modernity, East and West, indigenous preferences and foreign influences have been meeting and blending for time immemorial, and thereby yielded truly unique artistic results. Moreover, as Mitsukuni Yoshida emphasizes, the study of Japan's cultural history shows that from an early stage in the country's development, "the Japanese taste for foreign things helped broaden their limited horizons with tangible proof that other cultures besides their own existed. It also nurtured an openness and flexibility toward the artifacts of other cultures completely independent of the people or the historical backgrounds of the places from which they came" (Yoshida, p. 40). This tendency is largely responsible for the seemingly effortless flair and creativity with which Japan has been able to reconceptualize its borrowings without having to worry inordinately about their provenance. The imported materials are not regarded as unassailable monuments but rather as pliable and endlessly transformable resources akin to Surrealist *objets trouvés*. Most importantly, Japanese culture has consistently demonstrated a discerning attitude toward the imported items — abetted by an intuitive grasp of their structural cores — which has enabled it to adapt them so as to ensure their relevance to its own specific needs. Consequently, the collusion of sundry elements can be seen as a fundamental facet of Japan's everyday creativity, which characteristically manifests itself as a tendency to experiment assiduously with combinations and juxtapositions of disparate materials and images. Flamboyantly syncretic structures like Fushimi-Momoyama Castle vividly encapsulate this idea. The same vision is evoked — less spectacularly, yet effectively — by the (sub)urban context of KyoAni's first studio. Although Fushimi-ku itself is pregnant with historical connotations, the studio's immediate location reminds us above all of Japan's cultural hybridity through its topographical and architectural identity. The studio itself is a modern building, akin to a relatively small apartment block, and is placed in a close which leads through a narrow passage to a street lined with dwellings built in a predominantly old-fashioned townhouse style (*machiya*), and is abutted by portions of an extensive housing estate explicitly indebted to the style used in contemporary England for suburban constructions of that kind.

Moreover, much as KyoAni is by no means indissoluble from the city whence it derives its designation, it is important to recognize that contemporary Kyoto itself epitomizes Japan's penchant for hybridity by fostering a tantalizing coalescence of the old and the new, tradition and innovation, local customs and global trends, the popular arts of anime and manga and time-honored arts of both indigenous and Western derivation. Kyoto is a city in which the country's tradition, history, artistic heritage and lore are more palpably manifest than in any other major Japanese city, yet fluidly intersect with the forces of modernity and postmodernity. This proposition is corroborated by the portrayal of Kyoto presented in the context of the Japan Media Arts Festival Entitled "Parallel World, Kyoto," and held at various major venues throughout the city from 29 October to 23 November 2011. The festival's objectives ask for close attention insofar as they felicitously complement the argument here pursued by underscoring Kyoto's hybridity not only as a salient characteristic of the city per se but also as an indirect commentary on a philosophical condition of global relevance. "'Parallel world' is a term often used to describe another world existing in parallel with this world," the festival's official website points out, "and this is the theme for this year's Media Arts Festival in Kyoto. Kyoto is a parallel city where historical time and cultural influence coincide. The idea that various worlds cross over and coexist without conflicting with each other cultivates a rich and supple mind and leads to the charm of a city. Also, in this era, when it is easy for us to shift among the layers of different realities thanks to technologies such as computers, mobile phones and the Internet, we are beginning to realize that even we ourselves are layers of various different 'selves.' That likely leads to a supple sense of reality adequate for this new era." The Media Arts Festival in Kyoto has sought to give these messages visible and tangible shape by showcasing a wide range of art works executed by recourse to a stunning variety of media, and cumulatively pointing to the emergence of "new ideas and expressions" from the "development of technology." This is not, however, the sole objective pursued by "Parallel World, Kyoto." More memorable still is its employment of that body of works as a means of drawing attention to the losses which have inevitably accompanied the gains brought about by progress. To this extent, the varied material on display "reminds us of the things that have become needless and forgotten due to the development of technology. The exhibition gives us the opportunity, through experiencing these works, to think about today's media art and our way of being" (*Japan Media Arts Festival in Kyoto*).

As argued in more detail in the pages to follow, KyoAni's anime embrace cultural polyphony in an inimitable fashion by discreetly harking back to tradition through several of their recurrent topoi, yet also striking very contemporary notes or even venturing into futuristically speculative scenarios. The material interplay of diverse reality levels finds a correlative in a philosophical perspective which has consistently pervaded Japanese mythology, literature and popular culture: the conception of the boundaries supposedly separating reality from fantasy and facts from dreams as tenuous, capricious and ultimately unreliable. In artistic terms, this stance has typically resulted in a distinctive integration of serenity and turbulence, harmony and strife, playfulness and belligerence as interpenetrating processes rather than mutually incompatible states.

KyoAni's anime deal with a wide variety of genres, ranging from romance to comedy, from action adventure to the ghost story, from the supernatural mystery to domestic drama, and from school drama to the bildungsroman — alongside several hybridizations of these and other forms along the way. As hinted, in practically all of the generic categories upon which they draw, KyoAni's works tend to adopt a deliberately — and tantalizingly — ambivalent perspective on their materials. On the one hand, they abound with varyingly explicit allusions to indigenous myth, tradition and lore and even occasionally employ figures such as spirits, demons and monsters as pivotal cast members, while also incorporating curses, transfigurations, miracles and visions into their narrative repertoire. On the other hand, they no less frequently engage in the depiction of futuristic scenarios sustained by sophisticated worldbuilding techniques. KyoAni's proclivity to hark back to ancient materials while simultaneously experimenting with speculative universes is undoubtedly one of its output's most distinctive attributes. However, no less defining a facet of the studio's cachet consists of its capacity to bring together those two alternate dimensions by evoking the inexhaustible energies which permeate everyday reality. Thus, KyoAni proposes that while the extraordinary worlds conjured up by both mythology and futuristic yarns may seem extraordinary, the world we experience in our ordinary lives may ultimately constitute the greatest marvel of them all, despite its ostensible monotony, as long as its unfolding is candidly and conscientiously attended to. Relatedly, even when KyoAni's yarns venture into the realms of mysticism, mythology or science fiction, their events are not seen to emanate from a transcendental dimension but rather from the urge to reimagine the here-and-now from within its very fabric. All of the studio's anime variously corroborate this message by means of sensitive storylines and psychologically nuanced character portrayals, which are unfailingly abetted by stunning background art.

 The ability to recognize the specialness of the quotidian is therefore pivotal to KyoAni's vision even when its stories venture most boldly into sci fi territory or down the winding trails of fantasy. In fact, the studio's imaginary scenarios would not achieve the impact for which they are justly renowned were it not for its ability to interleave them with both perceptive and amusing portraits of the everyday lives which they variously disrupt, complement or compete with. From a philosophical point of view, KyoAni's tendency to present its hypothetical otherworlds as realities enmeshed with ordinary existence rather than as unearthly dimensions finds a close correlative in a propensity which Japanese art has consistently exhibited over the centuries. This is economically encapsulated by the concept of *geidō*, which indeed designates, as Leon explains, "a way of working and a way of treating everyday actions as an art form. Every art form—from painting, sculpture, dance, tea ceremonies to Kabuki—all of these not only have an end result but they also have a process/method in which they are created. *Geidō* is a celebration of the discipline involved in the process of the artform," warning us against the widespread temptation to dismiss the "importance" of that process "in view of the final result" (Leon).

KyoAni's celebration of the quotidian dimension is consistently bolstered by the studio's celebration of the unsurpassed value of simplicity. This quality should not be carelessly confused with insipidity or dullness insofar as it is accomplished through studious dedication, just as the state of childlike innocence fostered by Zen requires mindfulness and perseverance. By paying homage to the everyday in preference to extraordinary occurrences, KyoAni's works are able to immerse even the thorniest of situations in a delicate atmosphere of spontaneity, and to screen all traces of toil behind a semblance of graceful effortlessness. Simplicity is an accomplishment requiring great skill, yet bound to be effective only as long as it appears absolutely unforced. Accordingly, KyoAni assiduously channels rare talent and labor-intensive practices into the evocation of scenes meant to seem quite uncontrived. Most commendable, in this respect, is the studio's thorough integration of all components of the production process from conception to completion. The first stage consists of the translation of the source material (e.g., a manga, a computer game) into a scenario through the collaborative input of the director and the scriptwriter. It is at this seminal stage in the production process that the narrative skills of the director and the his or her team come vitally into play. On the basis of the scenario, the staff member responsible for overviewing the creation of the storyboards sketches out the anime's general flow, thereby detailing "how a scenario should be turned into pictures" ("A Close Look at an Anime Production House Part 2"). The storyboards also supply the bases upon which the layouts for the various scenes are designed. These represent "the blueprints of the scene cuts," and require the production team to devote its creativity to the integration of separate visual and dynamic elements into a coherent whole ("A Close Look at an Anime Production House Part 3"). Once the layouts have been completed, the team's concretization of the actual story finally begins. It is indeed on the basis of those templates that the drawings showing the "key points in the flow of actions," as well as their "timing," are created ("A Close Look at an Anime Production House Part 4"). While the key animation itself is drawn according to the layouts, the in-between animation is drawn with reference to the key drawings. Backgrounds are also painted while the key and in-between frames are being executed. Color is then added to the pictures by the finisher or colorist. The scanned key and in-between drawings are amalgamated with the background art, and the assembled frames are then shot. Once the connections between individual shots have been thoroughly checked, consolidated and smoothed out, the anime is ready for the conclusive photography stage.

KyoAni's grasp of the paradoxical nature of simplicity as a hard-won achievement gains further substance when one takes into consideration its own history as a creative cluster. Much as KyoAni might stand out today as the protagonist of an uplifting success story, it would be erroneous to assume that the path conducive to its current standing has constituted an unproblematically spectacular ascent to fame. In fact, the studio's history features the humblest of beginnings, its initial commitments consisting of the undertaking of in-between animation work for already established companies, such as Studio Sunrise and Studio Ghibli. The capacity to deploy highly sophisticated strategies to surround even the thorniest situations with a delicate aura of spontaneity and candor is largely inspired by KyoAni's own learning curve. This stands out as a lesson in the importance of developing one's abilities unassumingly and patiently over an appropriate period of time without aspiring to immediate sensation, let alone instantaneous recognition. No less importantly, KyoAni has learned from its own experiential trajectory that virtually any activity requiring direct and diligent engagement with the materials and tools characteristic of one's art harbors endless opportunities for the most honest and unadorned pleasure at the same time as it inevitably entails hard work and painstaking dedication to the tiniest detail. It is also worth noting, in this context, that when KyoAni first started producing full-fledged anime, it did not attempt to deliver any obviously groundbreaking products, focusing instead on artistic refinement, formal consistency, and the thematic synthesis of realistic slice-of-life elements with intimations of the supernatural: a thematic blend which still plays a part in the studio's works today. It is with the OVA *Munto* (2003), specifically, that KyoAni made its first independent contribution to the anime world by releasing an intriguing, yet quite inconspicuous, blend of fantasy and everyday experience. However, to say that KyoAni has tended to pursue modest goals is not to say that it has never taken risks — in fact, it is by daring to go where other studios had not gone before that it has not only delivered appealing shows but also set trends for other studios to follow. This is eloquently attested to by its utterly original take on the adaptation to anime of the visual novel form — specifically with *Air* (2005), *Kanon* (2006), *Clannad* (2007) and *Clannad After Story* (2009) — and by its bold reinvention of many of the structural and generic parameters characteristic of both school comedy and the bildungsroman tradition with the likes of *The Melancholy of Haruhi Suzumiya* (in its various configurations), *Full Metal Panic? Fumoffu* and *Full Metal Panic! The Second Raid*.

The studio's history could be regarded as an important model for prospective animators and artists insofar as it offers an implicit invitation to embark on the road to independent creativeness equipped not only with talent and vision, vital though these are, but also a good supply of unpretentiousness and an enthusiastic attitude to even the apparently most menial of tasks. It is, after all, on the strength of its humble beginnings and cautious rise to distinction that KyoAni can now afford to create an anime like *Nichijou* (2011), where the studio's desire to have fun with a series is clearly a priority and contributes to its overall charm no less than the phenomenal quality of it animation. KyoAni's most recent creation to date, the TV series *Hyouka* (2012), offers the latest evidence of the studio's unabated desire to explore new grounds and, in the process, open up original perspectives and develop fresh strategies. In this instance, by choosing a mystery novel as its source text, and by engaging with a wide range of subtly nuanced emotions in the dramatization of its elaborate plot, KyoAni has chosen to confront unprecedented challenges in the areas of genre and characterization with both courage and playfulness. The freedom to give full rein to the experimental drive is a luxury which KyoAni has undeniably earned, and is most likely to disclose exhilarating developments as the studio, having primarily served as an assistant to other companies in the early stages of its life, and having subsequently focused on adaptations, may soon be ready to enter a new phase marked by the emergence of its own autonomous creations. A step in this direction is signaled by the forthcoming *Chū-2 Byō Demo Koi ga Shitai!* as a work which, though not actually conceived by a KyoAni member, has nonetheless emerged from a studio-sponsored initiative, and can therefore be considered the fruit of a talent fostered by KyoAni "in house." All in all, one thing is clear: no contemporary anime studio offers a more faithful embodiment of the expression "learning never ends" than KyoAni.

Where mood is concerned, KyoAni's most distinctive feature could be simply described as a firm eschewal of extremes. This propensity should not, it must be stressed, be mistaken as artistic cowardice as it actually requires more skill, commitment, poise and creativeness than out-and-out audaciousness. KyoAni's avoidance of extremes entails that its anime are able to engage with quite serious situations and topics, to push their grimness as far as this is feasibly possible, and yet refrain from plunging into the depths of downright tragedy at the last possible moment. At this crucial point of balance, the mood often lightens in the direction of humor. Once again, the tone is not allowed to run its course in an unbridled fashion to the limit, and the action's comical connotations are therefore held in check exactly at the point where they could dive into undiluted farce. The gravity-to-humor trajectory just outlined may in fact unfold in the opposite direction: in both cases, the anime's emotional and psychological substance is proficiently maintained through the achievement of a delicate equilibrium. KyoAni's penchant for debunking the potentially more stereotypical moments of emotion-laden situations works by morphing gravity into fun and comedy into somberness without ever leading to sheer cynicism. In fact, romantic scenarios abound across the studio's repertoire and are often treated with uncommon sensitivity to their intricacies and mysteries with no trace of clownishness for its own sake. What does happen time and again, however, is that the more serious affects traversing such scenes are instilled with a hint of the absurd, and thus observed with ironic distance. This serves to enliven their emotive import, not to cheapen it or to render it grossly risible.

The principle of irony courses KyoAni's oeuvre, enabling its productions to come across as palpably credible, yet so elegantly refined as to border on abstraction. The broad philosophical implications of that irony deserve consideration at this juncture. In this respect, the words of the Japanese seventeenth-century thinker Tosa Mitsuoki are especially useful to the extent that they make it possible to interpret KyoAni's irony as a product of the coexistence of two alternate ways of approaching creativity. "If ... there is a painting that is lifelike and that is good for that reason," the philosopher opines, "that work has followed the laws of life. If there is a painting which is not lifelike and which is good for that reason, then that work has followed the laws of painting" (cited in Richie, p. 89). According to Donald Richie, by contrasting the type of work which follows the laws of life with the type of work which follows the laws of painting, Mitsuoki is pointing to two ways of creating images: "to imagine is to form a notion or an idea, a mental image.... In response to stimulus — words for example — a mental image is constructed for the individual doing the imagining. To create an image is both to amplify and to short-circuit this process. Mitsuoki thus distinguished between two kinds of images. Those that mirror the object and those that mirror the mechanisms of the means through which the image is made. This latter concern has been one of the richest sources of Japanese aesthetics —

respecting the artistic means. This would retain the grain of the wood, the strata of the stone, the limitations of black ink on white paper" (p. 88). The tendency highlighted by Richie constitutes a fundamental element of KyoAni's vision: as argued earlier in this discussion, this is clearly shown by the attitude to matter underlying the studio's approach to training. It is from its unwavering love of the raw materials and instruments sustaining the animator's art (conventional or digital as these may be) that KyoAni's anime have persistently derived their special verve.

The trenchant reflections on Mitsuoki's argument offered by Ueda offer a felicitous way of bringing the present discussion to a close. "It should be noted," the critic maintains, "that Mitsuoki ... conceives of the laws of nature and art not as mutually exclusive or contradictory, but as complementary. The artist must first observe the laws of nature before he comes to cope with the laws of art; otherwise his work would not resemble life but become lifeless" (Ueda, p. 131). KyoAni's artists, by analogy, create works which are capable of following the rules of their own art — and thus of reinforcing them and challenging them by turns — precisely because they have studied nature with painstaking care, yet also know how and where to deviate from nature in the service of their art. Without a deep knowledge of their initial model, or matrix, they could never presume to fathom where nature ends and their art begins. Without an exhaustive grasp of their art, however, they would have no means of transposing their experience of nature into one of the most inspired portrayals of ordinary life ever to have regaled the anime screen.

Homage to Kyoto Animation

> "It's all about Teamwork. In a recent statement by a KyoAni staff; 'In Kyoto you won't get business unless you do the work yourself. We cooperate as we're in Kyoto ... I don't mean to criticise Tokyo, but they use a lot of freelancers so it can't be helped. As for us, we do things together as company employees. This injects an energy into our products which just isn't there in other works. We have passion. Maybe that's why they sell. Games can't beat us with mere CG — character is what moves animation. Human feelings move characters.'"— Hideaki Hatta, Kyoto Animation

> "The production team CARES about its product. A LOT. They make every effort to make the show appealing. They pay a lot of attention to backgrounds. They come up with innovative and attractive screen wipes. They animate hair, fabric and hand gestures with every little thing in mind.... For that, I tip my hat off to you, Kyoto Animation. Truly you are masters of your craft."— The Captain

2

Science Fiction Reimagined

In all affairs it's a healthy thing now and then to hang a question mark on the things you have long taken for granted.—Bertrand Russell

Everything that is new or uncommon raises a pleasure in the imagination, because it fills the soul with an agreeable surprise, gratifies its curiosity, and gives it an idea of which it was not before possessed.—Joseph Addison

As anticipated in Chapter 1, *Munto* marks KyoAni's debut as an independent anime producer. This consists of a two-episode OVA comprising the initial *Munto* itself, released in 2003, and the follow-up *Munto 2: Beyond the Walls of Time*, released in 2005. The original two-episode OVA was remade in 2009 as a nine-episode TV series entitled *Sora o Miageru Shoujo no Hitomi ni Utsuru Sekai* (i.e., *The World Reflected in the Eyes of the Girl Looking at the Sky*). This includes a restructured director's cut of the original OVA as well as new animation and footage. The *Munto* epic reached its grand finale in 2009 with the theatrical release of the movie *Tenjou-nin to Akuto-nin Saigo no Tatakai* (i.e., *Last War of the Heavenloids and Akutoloids*), a compilation encompassing the director's cut of the series' climactic moments interspersed with some new footage. *Munto* is certainly not unique in its employment of a supernaturally gifted schoolgirl as its protagonist. Nor does it develop a first-time dramatic premise in positing its heroine as the sole means of preventing the onset of apocalyptic disruptions. On both counts, in fact, it can be seen as heir to a long and proud tradition. What distinguishes KyoAni's OVA from many anime dealing with analogous themes, and thereby lends its sci-fi scenario an utterly special twist, is its frank emphasis on the ordinary. Thus, despite its ostensibly average (or indeed even formulaic) attributes, it cumulatively comes across as unexpectedly and refreshingly original. Yumemi Hidaka, the protagonist, does become increasingly enmeshed in an epic plot rife with extraordinary occurrences and otherworldly characters of mythological stature. Yet, she never loses touch with her everyday reality, and indeed remains sincerely concerned about her family life and about her friends' welfare even as the grandiose omens presaging the end of the world crowd upon her from all sides. Therefore, *Munto* as a whole never relinquishes the candid tone of a down-to-earth slice-of-life drama of the finest quality.

Although Yumemi's greatest wish is to be just a normal teenager like her friends, she has been cursed since childhood with the preternatural ability to perceive floating islands in the sky without the slightest inkling of their nature or significance. It is only when Lord Munto descends to Earth from his Magical Kingdom in a desperate effort to save his doomed people that Yumemi finally learns the meaning of those bizarre apparitions — and, more crucially, is apprised of the role she is expected to play in rescuing Lord Munto's world from certain annihilation. With Yumemi, we thus discover that the floating islands constitute a parallel world driven by fear and discord as a result of its reckless exploitation of the special power on which its existence depends. Known as "Akuto," this is a form of energy which was originally derived from the emotions and dreams of human beings, and may now be restored only through Yumemi's miraculous intervention. On the surface, Yumemi's superhuman abilities may appear to constitute *Munto*'s main source of wonder but the story gracefully reveals that more marvelous still are the entirely human affects sustaining its dramatic unfolding from start to finish: most vitally, the unconditional trust which her loyal schoolmates Ichiko and Suzume accord Yumemi in the face of her ostensible madness. The OVA's overall tenor is economically encapsulated by a cinematographical ruse worthy of much more ambitious productions: namely, the juxtaposition and intercutting of sequences recording Lord Munto's fight with a titanic automaton, on the one hand, and the "test" undertaken by Suzume and her boyfriend Kazuya, on the other. The former focuses on a martial exploit of epic magnitude, regaling the eye with an assortment of special effects matched by vibrant colors and stirring music. The latter, conversely, depicts a boy and a girl facing a comparably prosaic challenge — crossing a river — in the most discrete and mellow of tones. Ironically, the more low-key of the two sets of sequences ultimately comes across as the more dramatic, its positive take on the wonder of the quotidian enabling it to impart those seemingly sedate moments with greater pathos. On the whole, instead of foregrounding the extraordinary elements of its heroic adventure, *Munto* chooses to abide in memory primarily as a personal, even intimate, record of a young girl's efforts to bear an intolerable destiny.

At the same time, the OVA strikes some humorous chords in its portrayal of Lord Munto. When the Magical Kingdom's ruler is not actually engaged in some grand battle, he comes across as rather immature and petulant by comparison with the terrestrial characters. His risible insistence on being addressed as "Lord" in the most preposterous circumstances succinctly sums up the character's foibles. More amusing still is the indication, proffered in the 2009 film, that Lord Munto harbors a fetishistic attraction to cute female clothes: although his world is on the brink of collapse, this does not stop him from lingering, as he prepares for the climactic events, to deck out Yumemi and her friends in some enticing and tactfully revealing girly outfits. This is indubitably a passion which implicitly equates Lord Munto to the kind of anime viewer for which many studios (KyoAni included on occasion) are known to provide the dubious joys of "fan service." At the same time, this detail demonstrates that even a marginal facet of character portrayal can be astutely deployed by an ingenious creator to provide an entertaining snippet of self-reflexive metacommentary.

Although Yumemi and her friends remain central to *Munto*'s remakes, *Sora o Miageru Shoujo no Hitomi ni Utsuru Sekai* and *Tenjou-nin to Akuto-nin Saigo no Tatakai* often seem to posit as their real protagonists the visual techniques deployed to bring what is an otherwise fairly obvious story to resonant life. This may come as a bit of a surprise for those who have watched the original OVA but have not yet sampled the remakes. Indeed, in the OVA, it is not technology but the natural environment that stands out as a non-human protagonist of rare caliber. This contention is especially true of the scenes portraying Yumemi's world in the aftermath of copious rain, when myriad reflections of the sky — as sensed both by common humans and by the psychic heroine — glide over the sprawling paddles on the streets below, thus opening up a shimmering liquid world of truly magical beauty. However, the first OVA's nature-inspired scenarios and the remakes' technology-centered visions turn out to be not so much conflicting agents as complementary factors when their respective roles are evaluated in the light of the lessons of Shintō. Within that philosophical perspective, nature and technology alike can be regarded as the receptacles of animate forces — as alternate incarnations of the all-pervasive life energy which flows through the entire cosmos in all of its multifarious manifestations. In contemporary Japan, it is by no means unusual for even a person without marked spiritualist leanings to approach both nature and technology as inherently alive. An old tree bearing upon its very surface the vestiges of time and an industrial robot designed to abet efficient manufacture, for instance, may be considered equally worthy repositories of the world's spiritual substance. Concurrently, through its articulation of the theme of animate technology, *Munto* points to a further philosophical argument of great topical relevance. It alerts us to the idea that if for Descartes the phrase "the ghost in the machine" referred to the state of the mind encased in a physical shell, in the age of the internet and related technologies, it more accurately designates the spirit coursing those technologies, the communication networks which these technologies inaugurate, and attendant modes of interaction and embodiment. Moreover, the spirit animating the new technologies is in a sense comparable to the energy which has enabled the medium of animation itself from its very dawn to generate dynamism from stillness — and hence give life to the inert and the stagnant. Animation, in this respect, could be said to fulfill the ancestral aspiration to simulate life in a symbolic defiance of death.

―✺―

With *Full Metal Panic? Fumoffu* (TV series, 2003) and *Full Metal Panic! The Second Raid* (TV series, 2005 and OVA, 2006), all of which were directed by Yasuhiro Takemoto, KyoAni embarks on an altogether more ambitious project. In so doing, it embraces the singular challenge of creating sequels for an already popular anime, the 24-episode TV series *Full Metal Panic!* (2002), directed by Koichi Chigira and produced by the animation giant Gonzo. The *Full Metal Panic* franchise as a whole, it should be noted, consists of a series of adaptations of the novels and manga by the prolific author Shouji Gatoh, who has also contributed to a few episodes of KyoAni's *The Melancholy of Haruhi Suzumiya* and *Lucky ☆ Star* in the capacity of anime scenarist, and been responsible for *Hyouka*'s series composition. In its *Full Metal Panic* TV series and OVA, KyoAni utilizes the original anime's characters and thematic hypotheses. At the same time, however, it imparts its distinctive signature on the *Full Metal Panic* universe, primarily through its treatment of the drama's mood and of the generic conventions underpinning its development. KyoAni's dedication to high production values instantly announces itself as one of the studio's principal contributions to the franchise. Both *Full Metal Panic? Fumoffu* and *Full Metal Panic! The Second Raid* exhibit top-quality animation and artistry across the board, excelling at the smooth integration of two-dimensional cel techniques and three-dimensional computer methodologies. This synthesis is consistently abetted by the employment of digital coloring reliant on a stimulating palette which manages to look vivid and bright without deteriorating into the garish. Combined with KyoAni's galvanizing explosion effects, these strategies impart the two series with an elegantly sharp cutting-edge feel. However, it is with the studio's proverbial flair for naturalistic background art that the anime reveal KyoAni's signature most compellingly. Even spectators who are not particularly used to appreciating visual forms of expression in a systematic manner will soon take notice of the exquisite backgrounds and settings flowing smoothly in and out of scenes. Autonomous works of art in their own right, visuals such as these require many hours of studious dedication even though their creators are aware all along that each painting is destined to grace the screen for no more than a few seconds before being replaced by another. Its is immediately evident that each of these visuals has been drawn for the purpose of expressing the distinctive atmosphere of a particular scene by capturing the spirit of its location — its *genius loci* so to speak — and thus complementing the action it accommodates.

A seventeen-year-old military expert employed by the secret antiterrorist organization "Mithril," Sousuke Sagara has been trained as a soldier practically from birth. As a consequence, he has a detailed knowledge of every conceivable weapon, explosive device and battlefield tactic, as well as an intuitive grasp of even the most intricate operation and of the methods most likely to lead to its satisfactory completion. However, Sousuke's legendary martial prowess and strategic acuity are matched by an equally exceptional ignorance of ordinary school life. This does not pose a problem for the valiant mercenary until the day he is enjoined to enroll in an ordinary school (modeled after Jindai High School, Tokyo) in order to protect Kaname Chidori: a spunky and beautiful girl reputed to harbor special gifts which would make her a "Whispered"— namely, an individual who is able to access "Black Technology." This term, in the franchise's idiolect, defines an ensemble of sophisticated procedures and instruments which surpass by far the level of technological competence achieved by common scientists and, being therefore bound to alter the world's military equilibrium, is avidly sought after by all manner of factions. Sousuke's efforts to guard Kaname's safety misfire to often ludicrous extremes as the youth, utterly unable to read and decode the everyday world around him, misreads ordinary occurrences as major threats to his protégée's welfare, and hence launches extreme military initiatives which inevitably lead to minor disasters — including classroom and lab explosions on more than one occasion.

The most eminent member of the Whispered cast is Mithril's head, Captain Teletha "Tessa" Testarossa, a teenage girl with outstanding strategic skills and military intuition, yet gauche and immature when it comes to negotiating her private emotions. This inadequacy manifests itself in Tessa's conduct vis-à-vis not only Sousuke, to whom she feels romantically drawn, but also several of her close associates and her brother, Leonardo, toward whom she harbors a dormant inferiority complex due to his reputation as the only known Whispered endowed with levels of mathematical and scientific adroitness which exceed the Captain's own gifts. Mithril's headquarters is a futuristic submarine conceived for deployment in aquatic and sub-aquatic warfare, and equipped with prodigiously advanced technology of which Tessa alone has an intimate (and barely communicable) knowledge. While the secret organization at the heart of the saga is named after a preternatural metal indigenous to Tolkien's cosmos, its HQ, the "Tuatha De Danaan" (or "TTD-1" for short), derives its designation from an ancient race in Irish mythology. These terms reflect a widespread tendency in anime to incorporate into its own lexicon vestigial allusions to time-honored Western texts and traditions as a means of adding a touch of what native audiences would feasibly consider exotic or vaguely mysterious. The actual meanings of the foreign words absorbed into an anime are relatively irrelevant, since their intended effect depends entirely on the impact produced by the sheer sounds attendant on their use.

The narrative and dramatic premises behind KyoAni's *Full Metal Panic* anime productions situate them in the realm of science fiction by positing an imaginary technology as the crux of an alternate reality. To this extent, the sequels continue in the tradition launched by the initial Gonzo series. Moreover, they emulate the first anime by consistently combining their SF motifs — with the employment of the awesome mecha known as "Arm Slaves" in pride of place — with action adventure and romantic comedy, making a few sorties along the way into the thriller genre, the bildungsroman and the psychological drama. Many of the familiar ideas conventionally associated with all of those typologies can be easily identified in both *Full Metal Panic? Fumoffu* and *Full Metal Panic! The Second Raid* by even a casual spectator. What invests the familiar with special appeal is KyoAni's decision to intensify its source's ironical stance by shifting the drama's sci-fi axes in such a way as to draw the audience's attention progressively away from the anime's futuristic substratum, with its predictable emphasis on the extraordinary, and to train it instead on the characters' struggle to negotiate the dilemmas which ordinary life keeps throwing into their paths regardless of the heroic magnitude of their extracurricular exploits. To foreground the significance of the everyday without sacrificing the series' humorous import, KyoAni resorts to a classic mock epic ruse: i.e., the depiction of actions and passions which are ludicrously disproportionate to their triggers, and rhetorically inflated to boot. Relatedly, the glee one experiences vis-à-vis the flurry of madcap chases and rapid-fire fight scenes which flood the screen at regular intervals is born mainly from a ridiculous sense of incongruity. It is quite astonishing, for example, to discover that retrieving a bunch of literature notes forgotten at home can turn into a major operation akin to the rescue of top-secret data from a fearful opponent. Thus, it could be argued that the key to KyoAni's displacement of emphasis from the extraordinary to the ordinary lies with its ability to imbue its vision of daily life with a decidedly barmy atmosphere.

Their unique taste for the ordinary with a wacky twist enables KyoAni's anime to yield top-notch entertainment which never ceases to feel fresh and spontaneous, and simultaneously exude a realistic ambience. It is therefore possible, when watching a KyoAni production, to sense in a genuine and palpable fashion the atmosphere which a visitor to an ordinary district of a Japanese city could experience on a regular weekday, as kids in their uniforms flock to and from school, eagerly purchasing their lunches from stalls and convenience stores, frantically rehearsing their notes in anticipation of a test, or texting their mates as they stream along pavements or through train stations and malls. On a more macrocosmic scale, the space evoked by KyoAni's well-defined urban settings conveys a tangible impression of the spirit of hybridity, discussed in some detail in Chapter 1, which characterizes Japan's main cities today. The swirling diversity of traditional and modern motifs, Eastern and Western influences, high culture and mass culture makes itself felt at every turn as the eye metaphorically roams that fictional, yet tangibly convincing, space.

As the foregoing remarks indicate, KyoAni's contributions to the peculiar metareality of the *Full Metal Panic* universe are eminently enjoyable unto themselves, despite their official status as sequels and their adoption of the source's foundational assumptions, insofar as they are handled mainly as valuable opportunities to articulate a different world view of KyoAni's own conception. Chigira's series asserted its creative originality by blending the staple ingredients of the classic high-school comedy with elements of the mecha war drama with a gritty edge. KyoAni's sequels take this synthetic approach to a new level, exuberantly pushing the clichés characteristic of both of those modalities to self-consciously parodic extremes. In the process, as Enoch Lau maintains, they offer a "cheeky look at the anime tradition of making mecha/military experts young teenagers and having them handle the trouble of integrating into a normal, peaceful society" (Lau) by juggling the established formula in a fashion never before attempted by any other studio. What renders Sousuke's modus operandi peculiarly absorbing, in KyoAni's specific approach to the saga, is the fact that despite its absurdity, it soon comes to feel strangely predictable. Yet — and this is where KyoAni's magic reveals itself at its best — even though one may know beyond doubt that Sousuke will overreact to a phantom threat in ways which are bound to make the situation infinitely more problematic, it is virtually impossible to anticipate from one scene to the next how exactly he will accomplish this perverse feat. At the same time, though one cannot foretell Sousuke's actions conclusively, one gradually comes to understand how his utterly methodical, though somewhat warped, brain functions, and hence to condone its strategies in spite of oneself. This is ultimately what makes the character so comically and endearingly unique.

Sousuke's futile efforts to fit in prove *almost* invariably hilarious insofar as the ridiculous enormity of his misapprehension of the regular human world is typically accompanied by straight-faced resolve, scrupulous professionalism and uncompromising pragmatism. The emphatic use of the word "almost" in the foregoing sentence requires elucidation. The reason for its use is that it might be tempting to assume that KyoAni's take on the *Full Metal Panic* world is so undilutedly comical as to preclude any concessions to anything other than the zany. In fact, Sousuke's failure to understand Kaname's reality and feelings is sometimes made so touching by its absurd insensitivity and clumsiness as to invite the type of sympathy which might warrant an affectionate smile but would render outright laughter quite tasteless. It is as though the young soldier's stunning agility (both mental and physical) in the face of even the starkest martial challenges were offset by a proportionately pathological ineptness when it came to coping with simple human situations and emotions. A case in point is the climax of the episode in which Kaname is harassed by a bunch of *yakuza*, and Sousuke comes to the rescue in disguise as the mascot of the amusement park Fumo Fumo Land, Bonta-kun — a costume destined to recur throughout the series and to give rise to the word "Fumoffu" itself, this being the sound repeatedly uttered by the massive teddy bear. From this point onward, whenever Kaname appears to get into trouble, Sousuke responds by adopting the guise of Bonta-kun with the addition of fearsome martial skills quite unknown to the originally peaceful and jovial teddy. He thus unwittingly gives birth to the one and only gun-wielding kick-ass giant mascot in the history of anime to date. When, at the end of the amusement-park episode, Kaname discovers that Sousuke has been secretly following her in the course of her date with a former classmate and admirer, which her bodyguard has misinterpreted as a potential trap, she entertains the thought that he might harbor romantic feelings toward her, and accordingly strives to communicate her own growing fondness for the awkward soldier. Sousuke seems entirely at a loss as he sits on a bench with the gorgeous girl, framed by the most glorious (and potentially inspiring) of sunsets. KyoAni's sensitive manipulation of character expressions manages to impart even the mascot's mask-like face with shifting emotional nuances, conveying the image of a creature so touchingly confused as to discourage the audience from responding to its absurd plight with sheer hilarity. At the same time, however, neither this nor analogous scenes punctuating KyoAni's *Full Metal Panic* productions allow the drama's affective import to degenerate into tacky sentimentalism since the studio, as argued in Chapter 1, never allows a scene's tone to become so extreme as to swamp altogether the possibility of a conflicting mood from emerging from its interstices to rebalance the situation's overall spirit.

 Delving deeper into *Full Metal Panic*'s eccentric reality, it is vital to appreciate that Sousuke's obsessive behavior does not actually mean that Kaname is not truly at risk. In fact, Mithril's hunches regarding the girl's identity as a Whispered turn out to be entirely accurate, and this makes her a desirable prey for the organization's enemies. In the original series, the drama's main events indeed ensue from Kaname's abduction, Sousuke's rescue mission, and their multibranching repercussions. In structural terms, the KyoAni anime themselves can be said to offer two alternate perspectives on the *Full Metal Panic* franchise, adopting a markedly episodic approach in the case of *Full Metal Panic? Fumoffu*, and a sequentially integrated narrative in that of *Full Metal Panic! The Second Raid*. While *Full Metal Panic? Fumoffu* has often been described as *Full Metal Panic!*'s second season, it would be inaccurate to regard it as a straightforward continuation of the Gonzo series. In fact, as Paul Fargo points out, it is "more akin to an alternate universe, or a collection of side stories taking place between story arcs of the first season" even though it pivots, like its predecessor, on Sousuke's vain attempts to blend into the day-to-day routine of Jindai High School and its civilian population. In keeping with this significant formal reorientation, the series "completely scraps the action and drama found in the first *FMP!* in favor of fast-paced comedic misadventure" (Fargo). This entails that *Full Metal Panic? Fumoffu* exhibits a consistency alien to its antecedent. Tian Ma advances a related argument, suggesting that KyoAni's first intervention in the franchise succeeds in establishing a tonal balance which the Gonzo series sometimes seemed to lack. "Showing the (relatively) ordinary life at Jindai High is a nice change of pace," argues the reviewer, "especially considering that *Full Metal Panic* wasn't completely successful at blending it in with military action. With a more focused intention, the story is much better able to expand on one of its strong points" (Ma). It would be arduous to refute that the original *Full Metal Panic* anime, though undoubtedly absorbing throughout its unfolding, occasionally appeared to have difficulty in achieving the required equilibrium of comedy and drama, and ended up juggling its clownish eruptions and its moments of stark drama with marginal uncertainty if not downright awkwardness. With its first foray into the *Full Metal Panic* world, KyoAni unsentimentally discards the first series' lingering gravity altogether to concentrate instead on what not only its staff but also the majority of fans around the globe saw as the most distinctive and engaging aspect of the original production: the peculiar chemistry released by Sousuke's aberrant responses to a non-military context, his relationship with Kaname, and the girl's own mixed feelings about Sousuke. The outcome is one of the most unswervingly amusing series to have visited the anime screen in decades. It is hard to imagine more enthusiastically persuasive an assessment of the comedic feat accomplished by KyoAni in *Full Metal Panic? Fumoffu* than the one proffered by Shadowmage in *The Nihon Review*. "Good comedy," the critic accurately avers, "can only be created by an appropriate chemistry of timing, wit, irony, presentation, stupidity and sheer luck. Misusing even one of these elements can bring an antic to its knees. Yet, despite all these hurdles, there still are a few shows [which] go above and beyond the call of duty and prove themselves to be nothing short of amazing. For all those who thought that the first *Full Metal Panic!* was hilarious, I present you the Holy Grail of comedy: *Full Metal Panic? Fumoffu*" (Shadowmage).

Full Metal Panic? Fumoffu consists of essentially standalone incidents, held together by their shared focus on Sousuke's irresistible tendency to impose his martial bias on every situation he encounters, regardless of whether this consists of an ordinary scholastic pursuit, such as an art lesson or a rugby match, or a not-so-ordinary complication, such as a kidnapping or an instance of gangster rivalry. At the same time, the separate incidents dramatized in *Full Metal Panic? Fumoffu* assiduously rely on the dramatic and psychological interaction between Kaname and Sousuke as the chief source of its swift-moving and meticulously scripted humor. In addition, even though the series tends to deliver its hilariously unholy marriage of school comedy and military drama mainly in the form of relatively autonomous extended vignettes and impressionistic mini-adventures, its contents are also periodically interconnected by means of retrospective allusions and discreet foreshadowings. Some of the installments echo the set pieces commonly found in standard anime fare of the episode-oriented ilk. Nonetheless, where more regular productions will probably provide a trip to the beach, a test-of-courage party, a visit to an *onsen*, a haunted-house mission and a date about town as its staple courses, *Full Metal Panic? Fumoffu* bears full witness not only to the intrinsically idiosyncratic character of the *Full Metal Panic* franchise in its entirety but also to KyoAni's keenness on experiment. Hence, its reconfigured version of the established repertoire delivers some inspiringly original scenarios. The beach-based set piece, for example, is morphed into a mock-romantic tale centered on Kaname's invitation to have tea with a wealthy boy in his palatial clifftop mansion, and on the extreme military tactics implemented by Sousuke when he suspects she has been kidnapped by the enemy. The *onsen* topos is likewise turned on its head in the episode where Sousuke, Kaname, Tessa and a bunch of their friends and associates visit a hot-spring resort in quest of some well-earned relaxation and rest, and the eternal warrior, for whom concepts such as recreation and leisure are simply unfathomable, instantly proceeds to devising an intricate defensive system replete with booby traps, surveillance cameras and explosives in order to protect the girls' privacy, and hence frustrate the other male characters' efforts to spy upon them. Another brilliant variation on a popular anime topos — in this instance, that of a boy and a girl being forced by peculiar circumstances to live together without adult supervision — occurs when Tessa, tired of her strict daily routine aboard the Tuatha De Danaan, decides to take a vacation from the Mithril HQ and to spend a couple of weeks as Sousuke's and Kaname's classmate while residing in the soldier's own apartment. As though Sousuke's efforts to live like a normal teenager were not enough to test his sanity, at this point he has to worry not only about protecting his superior officer without this resulting in any intimate contact with her but also about marginal fripperies such as transforming his monastically sparse premises into a warm and hospitable accommodation suitable for what is, after all, a sensitive teenage cutie.

In several instances, individual installments accommodate two distinct (or fortuitously linked) incidents. For instance, one episode devotes its first segment to Sousuke's confrontation of a secret admirer whose love letter he misreads as a death threat, and the second to the youth's chastisement of a street gang whose members, feeling unpardonably slighted, seek revenge by holding Kaname hostage. In another installment, the action's first portion is devoted to Sousuke's strategies to foil the physical education teacher's attempts to sabotage the merchandise to be sold at the school's bread stand, while the second turns to the incident, alluded to earlier, revolving around Sousuke's and Kaname's retrieval of a set of notes, followed by a frenzied dash to return to school before the end of the lunch break. Though late, the protagonists do manage to accomplish their goal but their heroic exploits ultimately turn out to have been a total waste of time since the literature teacher has meanwhile fallen ill. KyoAni's appetite for comically bathetic dénouements economically asserts itself at the close of this episode in its full dramatic glory. The adventure also offers a paradigmatic instance of KyoAni's aversion to unequivocal emotional extremes with the scene in which Kaname and Sousuke, confident that they have achieved their goal in good time, share a flash of rare harmony coursed by latently romantic connotations as they observe how well they are able to work as a team in stressful circumstances. This mellow moment of respite, appropriate though it is in the aftermath of a whirl of frantic action, could easily degenerate into cheesy sentiment were it allowed to dominate the mood uncontrasted, and is therefore swiftly disrupted in favor of a return to humor by the realization that due to Sousuke's misreading of the railway timetable, the couple will not make it back in time after all in spite of their apparent success.

In another episode, the first part focuses on a field trip to a park, where Sousuke's class chooses the young soldier as its model for an art project — hardly suspecting, of course, that Sousuke, having outrageously misinterpreted the art tutor's modeling guidance, will transform the assignment into a potentially lethal military operation. The second part of the same episode is devoted to the aforecited incidents set in Fumo Fumo Land amusement park. In a further felicitous instance of dramatic bipartition, Sousuke and Kaname take it upon themselves to investigate a chain of weird incidents involving a masked prowler notorious for attacking schoolgirls and for rearranging their locks into ponytails whether they like it or not. With the unplanned cooperation of a local policewoman whose law-enforcing zeal is no less fanatical than Sousuke's soldierly ardor, they set up a trap to capture the predator by using Kaname as bait. In the second segment, Kaname takes Sousuke into a supposedly haunted hospital in an effort to get him to sample the experience of fear, with which he appears to be totally unfamiliar, to discover that in spite of the baleful apparitions which infest its dismal rooms, the edifice is not in the least haunted, and that its baleful reputation had been purposely divulged by its inhabitants to guard their peace and quiet. As it strives to provide a full-rounded comedic experience, KyoAni does not demur from sporadic dips into the pool of dark humor. This is demonstrated in an exemplary fashion by the episode in which Sousuke and the captain of Jindai High School's karate club vie with each other to prove their physical and moral excellence by caring for the injured school janitor. Although the young antagonists' excess of zeal causes more discomfort than solace for the incapacitated man, he stoically manages to remain patient until the day they go as far as serving him his beloved *koi* for dinner — at which point, he gives vent to his ire to mock-apocalyptic extremes in a theatrical display which brings together diverse facets of indigenous mythology and lore, while also echoing the acting techniques associated with traditional Japanese theater at its most sensational. In addition, KyoAni's appetite for formal experimentation does not fail to include a generous dose of intertextuality, as borne out by the series' tongue-in-cheek allusions to films as diverse as the live-action productions *Full Metal Jacket* (dir. Stanley Kubrick, 1987), *The Last Starfighter* (dir. Nick Castle, 1984) and *Battles without Honor and Humanity* (dir. Kinji Fukasaku, 1973) as well as the anime series *Gundam SEED* (dir. Mitsuo Fukuda, 2002–2003).

KyoAni's flawless comic timing is certainly an aspect of its dramatic cachet which even fans usually indifferent to comedy would be quick to recognize. Throughout the series, the handling of pauses, rhythm and tempo serves to sustain the action's humor no less than Kaname's and Sousuke's assorted antics. It must also be noted, however, that much of the anime's funniness often lies with far less overt visual details which, being normally delivered without the backup of words, could easily go unheeded to a casual observer. A case in point is the visual refrain used in the seaside mini-adventure, where the teacher accompanying the protagonists and their friends never utters a single syllable for the entire duration of the outing, but is shown to be reading one book after another without ever relinquishing his distinctive poise and beatific smile. The sheer scope of the volumes which appear in his hands from one scene to the next is a source of humor unto itself, ranging as it does from Machiavelli's *The Prince* to Thomas Man's *Death in Venice*, from a textbook on elementary particles to a torrid romance and a gardening guide. The fun, in this instance, issues from the felicitous juxtaposition of the teacher's unruffled tranquility and the farcical complications swirling around him, the absurd variety of the tomes which elicit his attention enhancing the humor to great effect. Another memorable comic detail occurring in the same episode is the sudden appearance of Sousuke on the beach, again unaccompanied by verbal remarks of any kind, garbed in full military gear inclusive of a bullet-proof vest, even though only seconds earlier he has been wearing nothing other than his swimming trunks, in preparation for his self-appointed rescue mission. Arguably less original, yet immensely amusing, are the recurrent scenes in which the soldier extracts from his austere everyday clothing the heaps of weapons and explosives which he seems to be carrying around at all times but could never be logically accommodated within Sousuke's minimalistic combination of black trousers and white short-sleeved shirt.

Full Metal Panic! The Second Raid, KyoAni's second contribution to the popular franchise, could in many respects be regarded as the original series' direct continuation. Its opening episode is set just three months after the climactic fight presented in *Full Metal Panic!*, and follows so fluidly from its predecessor as to make one feel that the action has never actually halted. KyoAni's considerate pacing makes it possible for established fans of the franchise to dive straight into the story without their interest being slowed down by redundant introductions. Yet, viewers as yet unfamiliar with the saga's characters and themes are not plunged into a haze of enigmas insofar as, even without resorting to specific details, the anime succeeds in conveying its plot's central premise with unequivocal lucidity. As we have seen, the original Gonzo anime offered a blend of action, drama and humor whereas KyoAni's first contribution to the franchise chose to concentrate on comedy. With *Full Metal Panic! The Second Raid*, KyoAni takes an entirely different approach by prioritizing the action side of the story, by darkening its overall mood, and by intensifying the visuals' graphic component. This shift indicates that KyoAni is not content with testing its creative and technical resources in just one field but is eager instead always to explore new grounds, and hence set itself higher and higher stakes as it tirelessly proceeds along the challenging road of experiment. As Theron Martin explains, "the original *FMP* was very much a tactics–heavy action–oriented series, but *TSR* has outdone it both in quality and concentration of caliber action scenes. It seems to revel in its extensive use of military gadgetry, whether it's fantastical equipment like Arm Slaves and helicopters with cloaking devices or more conventional equipment like a gun which can shoot around corners." In addition, its alternate-history setting enables it to take an imaginative approach to political matters, as evinced by its presentation of "a China split north-south by a civil war, much like Korea in our world" (Martin 2006). At the same time, the anime devotes some of its most memorable moments of drama to the dramatization of Kaname's and Sousuke's developmental journey, which shows that the series' graver dimension does not manifest itself solely, or indeed most memorably, at the action level.

By contrast with *Full Metal Panic? Fumoffu*, *Full Metal Panic! The Second Raid* elaborates a continuous yarn, positing as its starting point Mithril's confrontation with a secret organization known as "Amalgam." Bound to prove Mithril's most determined and powerful adversary ever, Amalgam is in possession of Black Technology, having obtained it from the Whispered, as well as of a sophisticated means of countering Mithril's prized "ECS" (Electronic Conceal System) mode, the mechanism which enables Arm Slaves to assume temporary invisibility and thus facilitate enormously their pilots' moves, especially in densely populated areas. In *Full Metal Panic! The Second Raid* the saga's narrative basis is subject to radical redefinition as Sousuke's mission to protect Chidori is unexpectedly terminated by Mithril, and the girl is thereby left in the care of an anonymous agent dubbed "Wraith" whose abilities and credentials Sousuke finds highly questionable. Sousuke's decommissioning both triggers and encapsulates the drastic shift in tone characterizing *Full Metal Panic! The Second Raid* compared with its antecedents in the franchise. In his review of the second volume of the American DVD release, Martin persuasively describes this reorientation as follows: "no longer is the franchise using the standard 'as long as it's entertaining it doesn't need to make sense' logic to dodge the practical issues surrounding Sousuke personally protecting Kaname while still going on missions. Mithril has people in its organization suitably trained for such a guard job, and that isn't Sousuke, who has failed to integrate into normal society even after six months of effort and despite Kaname's help. Previously this has been a point ripe for humor, but now the serious side of it shows and delivers a full measure of dramatic intensity" (Martin 2007a). Another major factor distinguishing *Full Metal Panic! The Second Raid* from *Full Metal Panic? Fumoffu*, alongside its rejection of the former's episodic structure in favor of an integrated narrative with a somber bias, consists of its reintroduction as key actors of several key characters from the original series marginalized by *Fumoffu*'s comedic priorities. The dramatis personae engaged in *Full Metal Panic! The Second Raid* are so diverse, and its members' personalities so sensitively nuanced that it would be preposterous to presume to supply a comprehensive gallery of important actors in this context. It is worth observing, however, that in allowing ample room for characters which *Full Metal Panic? Fumoffu* had no choice but to marginalize in pursuit of its elating carnival, KyoAni's second contribution to the franchise is bound to satisfy fans of the original anime while also imparting the action as a whole with utterly novel plot twists of great dramatic intensity. Furthermore, as Jd Banks points out, the variety evinced by the series' characters extends innovatively to their sexual and ethnic representation: "unlike other anime, *The Second Raid* enlists female characters as strong and capable beings in tough, normally male-dominated roles without unnecessary sexualizing.... Adding more to the social openness is that the protagonists and villains are a fairly multicultural bunch.... It's refreshing to see non–Japanese characters play significant role" (Banks).

In *Full Metal Panic! The Second Raid*, a new and economical way of underscoring Sousuke's ordeal as he struggles to negotiate the incompatible demands of school life and military duty consists of recurrent sequences in which the young soldier confronts his homework. *Full Metal Panic? Fumoffu* already contains a few allusions to Sousuke's difficulties vis-à-vis his school-related duties — for instance, in the scene where he endeavors to explain to his classmates that his unfamiliarity with the texts of classical Japanese literature is due simply to the fact that there were no people in places such as Cambodia and Afghanistan who could even read those texts, let alone teach them. Moreover, the youth's one-track mentality is hilariously thrown into relief in the scene where, in trying to extract some sense from an episode in the *Manyoshu*, he visualizes a situation in which the characters, one of them injured, flee a war-torn area to seek refuge aboard the legendary Battleship Yamato. Sousuke has no idea, of course, that Yamato is actually Japan's ancient designation. The story he construes is as preposterous and as far from the truth as any of the fantasy scenarios he envisages in his protection of Kaname with astronomical financial repercussions for Jindai High School. In *Full Metal Panic! The Second Raid*, the boy's academic tribulations enter a more complex phase, and are accordingly accompanied by more extreme attitudes. There is little doubt that at this point in his career, Sousuke approaches his homework as a mission whose completion is a matter of life and death. Unwisely, in his older comrades' appreciation, he has a tendency to embark on his academic tasks in the immediate aftermath of major martial exploits when his mind should logically be least open to the absorption of fresh concepts and the memorization of data. Japanese history appears to be one of the many subjects he finds particularly impervious. At one stage, we are treated to a close-up of the line in Sousuke's test sheet which informs him of the date in which the capital was transferred to Heian-kyō—a hint at a seminal moment in the history of KyoAni's cultural cradle. In addition, Sousuke's scholastic obligations provide scope for some cameos of classic KyoAni humor. A paradigmatic example is the scene in which the youth rescues his closest comrades, Melissa and Kurz, from the Sicilian mafia just before launching into a *Bullit*-style chase through the picturesque town of Canicattì and its lush surroundings: as Kurz is about to board the vehicle provided by the rescuer for the occasion, he finds the time to observe, with uproarious incongruity, that Sousuke is expected to have tests the following day.

While it is important to appreciate that *Full Metal Panic! The Second Raid* is generally darker than either of the previous series in the saga, it is also noteworthy that the nature of the threats with which both the protagonists and Mithril have to contend has grown in both severity and magnitude. Among them is a deranged and indomitable agent by the name of Gates who appears to have brought back to life the fearsome "Venom" mecha from the Gonzo series: an Arm Slave which has given ample and devastating evidence of its ability to deploy a form of Black Technology known as the "Lambda Driver." This is a mechanism supposed to transform the emotional and nervous impulses emanating from the mecha's pilot into potent forces which can be used for both defensive and aggressive purposes. Its successful operation requires phenomenal powers of concentration and resolve, and since its functionings have not yet been scientifically fathomed to the last detail, neither its activation not its effective deployment can be dependably anticipated by even the most competent technician. Meanwhile, another formidable foe challenges Mithril from the wings as he lies dying while his acolytes, the sisters Xia Yu Lan and Xia Yu Fan, perpetrate a complex revenge scheme on his behalf. This adversary eventually turns out to be none other than Sousuke's archenemy from the original series, Gauron: a terrorist and warrior of the highest caliber. While Gauron himself has been rendered incapable of martial action by the injuries he incurred in his climactic confrontation with Sousuke in the first *Full Metal Panic!*, the blood-thirsty mercenaries at his service pose fearsome threats unto themselves with their unnerving display of speed, strength and uncompromising brutality.

In *Full Metal Panic! The Second Raid*, Sousuke is once again forced by his exceptional circumstances as a teenage mercenary to perform a delicate balancing act between attending Jindai High School as Kaname's overzealous bodyguard and honoring his contract with Mithril in his capacity as the designated pilot of the special Arm Slave "Arbalest." Kaname is quick to sense the stress engendered in her protector by this schizoid schedule. Her thoughtful responses to this worrying state of affairs clearly demonstrate the extent of this series' departure from its predecessors at the levels of both characterization and mood. It indeed creates precious opportunities for a dispassionate anatomy of the key characters' psychological makeup, and hence for a sensitive exploration of their complex relationship. This aspect of *Full Metal Panic! The Second Raid* finds memorable expression in the episode where Kaname cuts Sousuke's hair, the youth having shown himself incapable of tolerating contact with a stranger in possession of a sharp tool without instinctively resorting to lethal defensive measures. The charm of the sequence lies to a significant extent with its deliciously slow pace, which allows each frame to disclose in a gracefully understated style the true extent of Kaname's feelings for Sousuke. More notable still is the revelation that Sousuke himself has subliminally come to feel about Kaname in ways he has never felt about anybody else before: an idea which is wordlessly conveyed by his ability to relax sufficiently to go to sleep while Kaname carefully trims his locks. For a person who never lets his guard down lest some real or imaginary enemy should appear on the scene, the ability to unwind so totally in the presence of another human is practically tantamount to a declaration of love. In the home barber sequence, the close-ups focusing on the severed tresses as they land on the newspaper laid out on the floor to catch them speak volumes about the unparalleled delicacy of KyoAni's visual sensibility.

The full complexity of Sousuke and Kaname's convoluted relationship comes into focus in a more overtly dramatic fashion with a set of sequences indicating beyond doubt that Kaname does not only care for Sousuke but has also come to depend on him for a feeling of safety somewhat in spite of himself. The impact of this discovery is thrown sharply into relief by the installment in which the girl seeks out her loyal guard in a moment of crippling fear and finds, for the first time in many months, that Sousuke is simply not there. This is the kind of dramatic development which, in the hands of a truly proficient studio, has the power to characterize the spirit of an entire anime. The scenes in which Kaname first begins to sense the danger looming over her in Sousuke's sudden and inexplicable absence encapsulate KyoAni's ability to generate arresting drama even without recourse to electrifying action sequences. In the first of these scenes, Kaname arrives at school the morning following the hair-cutting episode, clearly looking forward to what will be her first meeting with Sousuke after a potentially crucial turning-point in the tortuous evolution of their relationship. Initially surprised to find that the youth has not yet taken his customary seat at the back of the classroom (a strategically selected place meant to abet his bodyguard role), she nonetheless manage to sit composedly at her desk. Only her acutely modulated facial expressions give away the tense expectancy with each she awaits Sousuke's arrival. When it becomes obvious that he is going to be absent for the day and, in addition, seems unable to pick up her calls to his cellphone, she decides to put on a brave face despite her disappointment, going out of her way to appear cheerful. In fact, her exaggerated jollity is in itself suspicious, insofar as it is not hard to tell that it merely belies Kaname's mounting anxiety. What the heroine cannot possibly guess, at this stage in the action, is that Sousuke has even been forbidden to say his goodbyes before returning to the Tuatha De Danaan to embrace his military duties on a full-time basis. In the next key scene, where the girl strives to bolster the optimistic façade by planning a ten-hour karaoke marathon, the drama abruptly shifts gears, and the inchoate feeling of apprehension which Kaname has thus far bravely managed to dissemble morphs into downright dread. This sudden change is triggered by her subliminal perception of the gaze of one of the Xia Yu sisters piercing through her as sharply as the direst blade, its bloodlust eyes licking at the periphery of her vision as though to give her a foretaste of the much more intrusive disruption of her safety and peace of which she is about to become the victim.

When Kaname returns to the uncertain security of her home, whence she again endeavors to contact her protector to no avail, a string of creepy noises and an anonymous phone call serve to fuel her uncharacteristic trepidation, as menacing shadows crowd around her loneliness with suffocating density. Even now, however, the indomitable Kaname does not surrender to panic but resolves instead to contact Sousuke by means of the transmitter installed in his apartment for the purpose of direct communication with the Tuatha de Danaan. The coup de grâce comes when Kaname enters the familiar room — only to find that in the space of a few hours, it has morphed into the most unfamiliar of spaces, all its furniture and equipment having mysteriously vanished, and all traces of its erstwhile occupier having been likewise erased, as though Sousuke himself had never existed. Adamantly resolved not to let her fear paralyze her, in the knowledge that a defeatist attitude would only serve to render her infinitely more vulnerable, Kaname soon takes her fate into her own capable hands — a tall order if there ever was one when we consider that she is hounded down not only by the lethal sisters but also by Tessa's hitherto absent sibling, Leonard Testarossa, who claims to be in love with Kaname, and seems determined to enlist her loyalty in the advancement of his own mysterious cause. Unfamiliar with sophisticated moves and unequipped with sophisticated weapons, Kaname only has her own ingenuity to rely on, and this simple but vital element contributes greatly to the action's overall impact by making the sense of danger tantalizingly palpable.

As for Sousuke, he is forced to face for the first time in his life a series of confrontations of a kind which cannot be handled on the battlefield insofar as their primary causes consist of emotional tensions and psychological frictions alien to the youth's soldierly makeup. Sousuke must first face Wraith, whose skills as Kaname's protector leave much to be desired. His later quarrel with Tessa presents even greater problem since the Captain's criticisms of his conduct reach straight to the heart of Sousuke's introverted personality by contending that his private attachment to Kaname has caused him to neglect his combat duties and hence to disrespect his allegiance to Mithril. It is at this point that Sousuke begins to suspect, albeit inchoately at first, that acting as the ideal subordinate and living as an ordinary teenager might ultimately prove to be irreconcilable tasks. Finally, the dispirited mercenary is challenged by Belfangan Clouseau, the Special Response Team's new commander, who defies Sousuke most unchivalrically by pretending to scorn his abilities. As it happens, the capable leader harbors a hidden agenda, his intention being to enhance Sousuke's chances of piloting the Arbalest successfully by helping him realize that his previous failures have not been caused by his lack of skill but rather by his resentment toward the mecha. Sousuke's ordeal reaches its nadir when, having placed his Mithril associates in danger as a result of his anxiety about Kaname's wellbeing, decides to desert the team altogether, and proceeds to roam Hong Kong's surreally deserted streets aimlessly until he is brought face to face for the last — and decisive — time with the diabolical Gauron. The confused and drifting Sousuke we see at this stage in the series offers a version of the character which departs quite drastically, even disquietingly, from the portrait to which we have grown accustomed. Unsettling though it is, Sousuke's psychological collapse serves to humanize his portrayal to an unprecedented degree. Moreover, it is depicted throughout in a flawlessly credible manner, which enhances the anime's affective import to a notable degree. If *Full Metal Panic? Fumoffu* demonstrates the impressive extent to which KyoAni is capable of tilting the generic axes of an existing franchise with both flamboyance and flair, *Full Metal Panic! The Second Raid* bears witness to the studio's exceptional sensitivity in the treatment of what is arguably the most challenging aspect of all drama in both its live-action and its animated expressions: human emotions.

One of the anime's greatest strengths indubitably resides with its both adventurous and proficient cinematography. The numerous fight sequences which punctuate the show gain considerably from KyoAni's cinematographical experiments, as borne out by their deft integration of close-ups of the pilots in the cockpits of their Arm Slaves, panoramic frames capturing the action in its full — and, at times, veritably epic — scale, and tableaux which focus on a specific portion of the landscape or townscape where a major incident is unfolding. In the latter instance, natural or architectural features of the scene are often constellated so as to replicate, by means of their shapes, proportions and relative positions in the overall arrangement, the rhythms of the human drama they accommodate. The battle sequences are not the only ones, however, to benefit from KyoAni's cinematographical flair. Several sequences set in the school or in residential areas (both indoors and outdoors) consistently draw energy from their agile intercutting with sequences concentrating on political, diplomatic or technological matters. It could be argued that in these cases, the camera enables the story's microcosmic and macrocosmic dimensions to intersect so intimately as to become virtually inextricable — as indeed are the private and public sides of the protagonists' quest as the yarn steers a course between the bildungsroman and the epic. The beauty of *Full Metal Panic! The Second Raid* can perhaps be summed up in one sentence: very few anime containing so much passion, action and thought would not merely get away with but actually resplend through a closing line as bathetic as "I see."

Based on a series of light novels penned by Nagaru Tanigawa and illustrated by Noizi Ito, *The Melancholy of Haruhi Suzumiya* develops on the basis of a superbly ironical narrative premise by capitalizing on the peculiar chemistry released by the collusion of two polar opposites. At one end of the spectrum stands Kyon, the most average high-school student imaginable; at the other, stands the titular heroine, the most eccentric of Kyon's peers. Whereas the boy resolutely refuses to believe in the existence of preternatural beings such as aliens, espers and time travelers, Haruhi appears to harbor no interest whatsoever in common humans. In fact, she openly despises anything even remotely ordinary as tedious and criminally uninspiring, and is therefore hell-bent on detecting enigmas and aberrations round every corner. As Carlos Ross colorfully puts it, "she clearly does not live in the same reality as the vast majority of humankind, and flatly refuses to conform to societal norms or even employ the least bit of tact.... The show's events are clearly driven by her whims and desires, and while at times it seems she can be a walking non-sequitur, Haruhi's actions have a bizarre sense of internal consistency to them. She knows what she wants, and she's not going to let petty things such as 'rules,' 'teachers,' 'feelings,' and 'morals' get in her way. She's brilliant, obnoxiously cheerful, and entirely heedless of how others think of her, and constantly willing to pat her own back in the process. I imagine a lot of people are going to come into this wondering what sort of crack Haruhi is on, because she will undoubtedly strike most audiences as strange, even for anime — most shows would not have the cojones to feature a character like this as the lead, but rather, as comic relief" (Ross). The clash between Kyon's blasé attitude, often fueled by a factual sarcasm, and Haruhi's unswerving determination to hunt for adventure at any price yields multifold opportunities for lively interaction. The irony at the heart of the two characters' association is compounded by the fact that it is Kyon who, in spite of his ordinariness, ends up indulging Haruhi's passion for the anomalous most liberally. Moreover, it is Kyon himself who inadvertently inspires the extravagant girl to establish one of the most unusual ventures ever witnessed in the history of their school, North High: namely, a school club dubbed the "SOS Brigade" ("Spreading Excitement All Over the World with the Haruhi Suzumiya Brigade") and dedicated to the detection of aliens, time travelers, espers and all manner of paranormal phenomena.

Kyon is suddenly asked to reassess radically his established views on the extraordinary from within the fabric of the seemingly ordinary reality of his daily routine. On the surface, he appears to endure this challenge with scarce enthusiasm, reacting to its implications with acerbic coldness, cynicism and apathy. Yet, there is reason to suspect that beneath that public façade, the youth harbors an intense — and ever-growing — fascination with the extraordinary which by and by both clashes and intersects with his likewise suppressed attraction to Haruhi herself. There are times when the youth's interior monologue, which defines the angle from which the story is experienced by the audience, intimates that he may subliminally long for the existence of the very sorts of beings he so resolutely dismisses as figments of the imagination. In fact, it could even be suggested that in generic terms, Kyon embodies a nostalgic longing for the fantasy plots regaled by classic magical-girlfriend anime (e.g., *Urusei Yatsura*, *Oh My Goddess!*, *Chobits*) in which the heroine would be a means for her human admirer to experience extraordinary events and meet preternatural entities. It is also noteworthy that even though it is repeatedly suggested that Kyon is the only normal human among Haruhi's associates, both the action and the script increasingly hint that no truly normal human would be not only willing but eager to have anything to do with the likes of Haruhi and her club. Haruhi herself, in this perspective, could be regarded as an irreverently postmodernist distortion of the magical-girl stereotype: although, like classic heroines in that mold, she is said to possess superhuman powers, her brass, aggressiveness, conceit and scornful dismissal of romance separate her conclusively from the conventional magical girlfriend.

Ostensibly drawn by chance, Kyon and Haruhi soon find themselves entangled in a concatenation of bizarre occurrences which progressively gel, in spite of their episodic nature, into an absorbing futuristic yarn which lends the concept of science fiction a very imaginative twist. This is incrementally emphasized as the series' comprehensive world view reveals itself step by step, thereby focusing on the age-old philosophical enigma surrounding the relationship between truth and make-believe: a conundrum which *The Melancholy of Haruhi Suzumiya* addresses by assiduously highlighting the baffling tenuousness of the boundary supposedly separating reality from fantasy, and empirical evidence from delusion. The cinematic experiments undertaken by Haruhi and her mates throw these preoccupations into relief most explicitly — and most absurdly — with their self-reflexive approach to filmmaking. Appallingly patched together by the SOS Brigade for the school's approaching cultural festival, *The Adventures of Mikuru Asahina* is effectively the outcome of Haruhi's presumptuous posturing as original creator, scriptwriter and director. More importantly, however, it is also a quintessentially metafictional product through which KyoAni indulges in a precious moment of pure play by poking fun at established formulae and stock characters. One of the anime's main personae, Mikuru, is cast in the role of a combat waitress from the future (a parodic adaptation of the titular heroine of Gainax's *Mahoromatic*) while the character of Itsuki assumes the part of a psychic kid whom Mikuru is enjoined to protect. The third key member of Haruhi's club, Yuki, features as an undefeatable witch and Mikuru's principal enemy. At the same time, the amateur movie supplies the studio with an exciting opportunity to comment on the filmmaking process (and, by implication, the anime-making process, too) in a gleefully unsentimental fashion. This is most explicitly borne out by the observations offered by Kyon in the capacity of narrator, in which he takes it upon himself to draw attention to each of the film's many inconsistencies and failings. In addition, Kyon occasionally takes part directly in the onscreen action in ways which any audience would deem inappropriate for a proper narrator to contemplate.

In August 2007, the magazine *Newtype USA* published an interview with the director of *The Melancholy of Haruhi Suzumiya*, Tatsuya Ishihara, provokingly entitled "The director was Haruhi," and handled so as to cast the character of Haruhi herself as the interviewer and Ishihara as the interviewee. In inviting the director to express his opinions on *The Adventures of Mikuru Asahina*, this unusual interview offers him a context in which he can indirectly voice his stance on KyoAni's own use of that bold metafictional flourish. A lot of the time, when directors are asked to talk about particularly contentious aspects of their work, they deliver views which can easily be misinterpreted as spurious lecturing or even as attempts to overinflate the significance of their gestures. The unorthodox format adopted by the *Newtype* conversation has the advantage of purging Ishihara's words of even the slightest trace of self-promotion. Prompted by "Haruhi" to comment on what she terms, with characteristic arrogance, "the blockbuster of the summer," the director states that although he found the film very funny, he "was worried that other people wouldn't get the humor behind its awkwardness," and that "the TV networks," in particular, would deem it unacceptable. Ishihara is also aware of the potential difficulties posed by the placing of *The Adventures of Mikuru Asahina* at the very start of the broadcast. The 2006 series' airing is deliberately based on the order used in the parent text in order to enable "both fans of the original novel series and newcomers" to "enjoy it." However, Ishihara and his colleagues were somewhat hesitant about "whether or not to throw such a wicked curve ball in the first installment." As to the reason proffered by Ishihara for eventually adopting the film as the series' entrée, this consists of a real gem of KyoAni humor: "in the end, I asked myself what Haruhi would have done if she had been in charge of the order, and went with that. So it's not wrong to say the first episode was directed by Haruhi" (Ishihara 2007).

In the course of the same conversation, we also get to sample KyoAni's distinctive take on the notion of quality. Where several other studios would have opted for the easy way out, and made the amateur film look flawed by simply putting it together in a slapdash manner, KyoAni honors its loyalty to high production values even in the execution of this intentionally deficient product. Storyboard artist and animation director Satoshi Kadowaki has commented as follows on this aspect of the studio's modus operandi: "the more handmade we tried to make it look, the harder it was to produce it. It takes more effort to make animation look like a poorly done live-action film than it does to make it look perfect. For example, the camera pans up occasionally, right? The camera we use for that is mounted on a guide to ensure that it moves smoothly, but we wanted it to look shaky, as if an amateur shot the scene. So we had to find a way to purposely jiggle the camera" (Kadowaki). Paradoxically, the visually and technically shoddiest portion of the series turns out to be the one which required greatest effort on the creative team's part. Color designer Naomi Ishida corroborates the point with specific reference to the chromatic level of the venture: "they had lots of difficulty choosing the right colors.... After all, they had to constantly make tiny changes in the color because it was supposed to look like they'd shot the different parts of the same scene at different times of the day. It was as detail intensive as a theatrical film!" (Ishida). As the series' director emphasizes, virtually all facets of Haruhi's messy metafilm required special care precisely because of its consummate trashiness. Hence, cinematography and voice recording also posed some unusual challenges: "we purposefully made the camera unstable, and even occasionally made it go out of focus. But I think the hardest task was getting the voice actors to act badly" (Ishihara 2007).

Situated at the start of the series in both the original broadcast and the DVD release even though the events it covers actually constitute episode 11, *The Adventures of Mikuru Asahina* constitutes the culmination of KyoAni's passion for a metafictional take on the art of anime as a whole which actually runs through the entire franchise. This proclivity informs the studio's audacious reconceptualization of well-tested codes and conventions characteristic of diverse genres, from school comedy to action adventure, from romance to the epic. Set pieces are also dramatized with some regularity — notable examples are the numerous sequences in which

Haruhi indulges her fetishistic urges by forcing Mikuru to don costumes worshiped by all self-respecting otaku with a bias for the *moe* category. Also remarkable, in this regard, are the installment devoted to the club's investigation of an apparent closed-room murder case and the one where the improbable baseball team haphazardly cobbled together by Haruhi with the intention of winning a tournament miraculously manages to win the game. However, these and other set pieces are introduced mainly as opportunities for debunking the clichés on which they have persistently depended and are accordingly defamiliarized, as though KyoAni were inviting us to consider what such occurrences would really look like if they were ever to take place in the actual world. Relatedly, the show initially appears to rely on general high-school stereotypes such as the dim-witted bimbo, the mysterious bookworm and the self-assured transfer student. Yet, it soon becomes evident that these characters have utterly unconventional parts to play in the larger drama of Haruhi's thirst for adventure. KyoAni's fascination with self-reflexivity contributes crucially to its unique approach to science fiction: a generic vessel in which many conventional tropes are revered and parodied by turns. When the story's sci-fi elements begin to pepper the screenplay and the visuals, it is immediately clear that KyoAni has no desire to handle the genre in a conservative style: there are no hints at spaceships zooming through the night sky and even when high-octane clashes finally take place, their start point and end point are ordinary and patently unglamorous school settings.

To begin with, there is nothing obviously "melancholy" about Haruhi. In fact, she is characteristically ebullient, hypercharged and stridently dictatorial. In advancing the quirky club she has created, there is no obstacle she is not prepared to bulldoze with no consideration for the victims of her abusive and prevaricating actions. The melancholy gradually insinuates itself into the drama as its more overtly science fictional elements begin to transpire. At this point, it becomes evident that Haruhi is not merely a self-inflated monomaniac but is *literally* larger than life insofar as her will power, moods and desires can have momentous repercussions for the fate of the entire universe. Were the girl to descend into a state of severe dejection, her frame of mind would affect so fatefully the delicate mechanisms on which cosmic balance depends as to precipitate its catastrophic annihilation or, in the best case scenario, its radical reconfiguration. In the logic of the series, the world as we know it — or rather *think* we know it — only exists in the particular form in which we experience it because that is how we are able to perceive it. Even a minuscule shift in the universe as a whole could in fact produce a situation in which there is simply no place for either the contingent world we perceive around us or indeed the human species itself. Haruhi, in this context is ascribed powers which exceed by far those of ordinary people to the extent that she is held capable of bringing into being just about anything she happens to long for, fantasize about, or simply envision as potentially desirable. There is danger, therefore, that whenever Haruhi feels emotionally unsteady or antagonized, her superhuman capacities might give rise to gaps between dimensions: namely, so-called "Closed Spaces." These anomalous areas look pretty much like the parts of the real world which they displace but are generally depicted as deserted and immersed in a dull and dreary light. When they do spring to life, they do so in the most calamitous of fashions, and become populated by gigantic fluorescent monsters known as "*Shinjin*" which personify Haruhi's inner turbulence, and seem eager to wreak havoc with their surroundings with no concessions to the laws of either physics or logic.

The characters whom Haruhi recruits as club members, briefly referred to in the discussion of the metafilm, soon turn out to be emissaries of various intergalactic agencies appointed to monitor her conduct. It is worth looking more closely at the individual members of the SOS club insofar as both their personalities and their sparkling interplay nourish the drama's soul to great effect. A demurely cute book junkie of the first water, Yuki Nagato is the first character to join the SOS Brigade — or rather, to be more precise, to be absorbed by Haruhi into her enterprise without so much as an invitation, let alone a polite request. In fact, the society of Yuki's own choice would initially appear to have been the now defunct Literature Club. It is not long before Kyon — and hence the audience alongside him — are informed by Yuki, who unexpectedly shelves the quiet bibliophile persona and becomes very eloquent when mindboggling explanations seem necessary, that she is actually a humanoid interface. Created by the Data Integration Thought Entity, Yuki is charged with the task of observing Haruhi and establishing the reasons behind the sudden explosion of data reputed to have taken place three years prior to the story, and to be inextricably connected with Haruhi's existence. Yuki is endowed with extraordinary faculties, including the ability to manipulate the data which form her environment. While ostensibly devoid of feelings in the human sense of the term, the alien creature is by and by shown to harbor the capacity to develop intense emotions — though within the theoretical framework and parlance of the agency which has produced her, this capacity is branded as a lamentable accumulation of erroneous data conducive to aberrant behavior.

If Yuki embodies the gentle bookworm typology, Mikuru Asahina typifies the more overtly sexy, yet disarmingly innocent, cutie. It is indeed on the basis of her looks that Haruhi, convinced that a charming female mascot is the sine qua non of any self-respecting club, forcibly recruits Mikuru to her ranks. More disturbing still is the stubborn insistence with which Haruhi decks Mikuru out in all sorts of stereotypically seductive costumes (including the Bunny Girl, the Victorian Maid, the French Maid and the Nurse), which the gentle girl finds infinitely embarrassing. In truth, there are times when viewers too may experience a subliminal sense of embarrassment in the face of her obvious, albeit not malicious, humiliation. Yet, Mikuru has no choice but to endure her penance insofar as she is also the envoy of an extraterrestrial organization — the "Time Traveler's Committee" — keen on monitoring Haruhi's moves. A lowly member of the organization barred access to countless items of "classified information," Mikuru is a time traveler from the distant future specifically appointed to explore the causes of the inability to journey in time to any moment prior to three years earlier. Mikuru's narrative, like Yuki's, foregrounds the three-year period as a detail of the utmost — though as yet mysterious — significance. Kyon is attracted to Mikuru but the charming time traveler repeatedly discourages him from giving vent to his interest in the belief that he has been somehow "chosen" by Haruhi. The subtext here entailed is that Haruhi is most likely to react quite negatively to any intimation that her right to control Kyon as though he belonged to her is being challenged, and that this would have inevitably detrimental effects for them all. Mikuru's message is so cryptically formulated that Kyon, initially at least, has no means of fathoming its exact import. Though tactfully handled throughout the show, this aspect of the character dynamics developing within the SOS Brigade imparts the drama with precious moments of both drama and humor.

Itsuki Koizumi, finally, is an esper from an organization known simply as the "Agency" who has acquired the power to perceive and explore the pockets of "Closed Space" which, as seen, appear connected with Haruhi. The crucial three-year spell supposed to have elapsed between the cosmic transformation putatively bound up with Haruhi and the present is once again thrown into relief by Itsuki as he discloses that both he and his colleagues within the Agency have possessed their unusual faculty for precisely this amount of time. As the epitome of bonhomie and a hassle-free disposition, the esper superficially comes across as the least problematic of the three characters invested with extramundane credentials. However, the youth's suave manners and almost constant smile belie a complex and unsettling mentality. This is patently borne out by his tendency always to offer contrasting interpretations of the events in hand: an attitude which more or less explicitly enjoins both Kyon and the audience to wonder how far appearances can be trusted and, by extension, how dependable people like Yuki, Mikuru and, ultimately, Itsuki himself truly are — or are meant to be.

While Haruhi's regular classmates only regard her oddity as annoying or offputting, these paranormal beings provide various — and more or less bizarre — explanations for her peculiar behavior and predilections, describing her as either some kind of deity or a product of a space-time warp or a form of human self-evolution. The different arguments advanced by Yuki, Mikuru and Itsuki have two things in common: their insistence on a phenomenon supposed to have occurred three years prior to the SOS Brigade's establishment, and the contention that Haruhi is somehow responsible for its occurrence. While endeavoring to keep an eye on the eccentric girl's unforeseeable actions, all three characters strive to prevent her lingering melancholy from overflowing by humoring her whenever necessary. Such strategies are the sole means of keeping at bay Haruhi's unwittingly lethal powers, at least until such a time as the precise extent and magnitude of the phenomena she might unleash have been reliably ascertained. Above all, it is crucial to prevent Haruhi from realizing her full abilities. While the girl's ignorance is safely maintained throughout, Kyon is let in on the critical secret and gradually discovers that the part he has to play in the world's preservation is by no means that of a casual bystander. Concomitantly, it becomes evident that he is the person with the greatest chances of holding Haruhi's dormant melancholy in check as a result of the feelings she gradually develops toward him — utterly human emotions which, with characteristic stubbornness, Haruhi is either unable or unwilling to recognize. The audience, however, cannot fail to detect the symptoms of a growing romantic attachment in her interaction with Kyon, especially in the scenes where his obvious fondness for Mikuru invariably ends up provoking a jealous fit, which she self-defensively disguises as an ironfisted managerial decision.

In one of its most adrenalin-pumping installments, *The Melancholy of Haruhi Suzumiya* gives us a great opportunity to sample KyoAni's ingenious approach to the subtle art of adaptation. The episode, titled "The Day of Sagittarius," dramatizes the SOS Brigade's battle with the Computer Research Society for the possession of a state-of-the-art PC — which Haruhi has in fact already extorted from the rival club by means of vicious blackmail — as well as additional laptops. The fight is conducted in ludic form by recourse to a computer game — the titular "Day of Sagittarius" — conceived by the Computer Research Society, and designed to allow them to cheat, thereby guaranteeing their victory and reappropriation of the purloined equipment. Unfortunately for them, in creating their weapon, the club's technowizards have not taken into account Yuki's immense computational skills, and hence her ability to neutralize the deceitful program and have it boomerang neatly on its inventors. Triple_R has usefully commented on KyoAni's treatment of its source materials in this installment by situating it in the broader context of the studio's approach to adaptation at large. "A complete pure translation from one entertainment medium to another is both unrealistic, and perhaps even undesirable," the critic reminds us. "Because a narrative that may work fine in a novel or a game may be a bit too slow (novel) or a bit too fast (game) in an anime format. Basically, what works in one entertainment medium may not work in another. Kyoto Animation, I think, are acutely aware of this." The game-centered episode discussed above fully corroborates this contention by infusing fresh materials into its novelistic model in an adventurous, yet conscientious, fashion. That is to say, KyoAni is not interested in twisting its sources for the sake of mere spectacle. In fact, it only modifies them through careful additions or elisions (when appropriate) in order to enhance their impact in the specific context of its own medium. Thus, "The Day of Sagittarius" features "grand creative flourishes" meant to impart it with additional "content" not included in the parent text. "This added content," Triple_R emphasizes, "suited the anime well, and made for a much more enjoyable viewing *without* detracting significantly from Kyoto Animation's faithfulness to the source material. The idea is to take a line of novel content, and expand upon it in a logical way. Viewing the video game battle between the SOS Brigade and the Computer Club from within the game itself ... does not alter the plot in any meaningful way, but it does make the anime episode more explosive, flashy, and theatrical.... So, Kyoto Animation typically does a superb job of *balancing* the desire of many anime fans for faithful adaptations with the realization that some novel scenes need to be spiced up to work in an anime format." The perspective adopted in this book is only too happy to embrace the critic's glowing appreciation of KyoAni's handling of adaptation as an achievement bordering on the sublime: "I very much like Kyoto Animation's approach to putting an added special dash of soaring sparkling *stupendousness* into the key scenes of the material that they adapt" (Triple_R).

A further aspect of the distinctive dramatic texture evinced by *The Melancholy of Haruhi Suzumiya* deserves close attention. This is an attribute which even casual spectators will be quick to note: namely, its capacity to produce spectacle out of apparent inertia. Despite the extraordinary dimension of the whole franchise, substantial doses of both its drama and its humor are actually evoked by the simple scenario of a bunch of people sitting around a room, often in total silence. Although the anime contains many memorable instances of intense action, not least courtesy of its female lead's hyperactive disposition, much of its distinctive charm could therefore be said to lie with its treatment of the quieter moments — the scenes, sequences or even whole episodes in which very little actually happens. In fact, it could be argued that several of those moments leave their impression well after the overtly dynamic incidents have been mentally archived. What renders such moments so tenaciously effective is not only their affective content but also their ability to wear their uneventfulness on their sleeve — to draw attention to their relative dearth of dramatic content as a worthy quality in its own right. At the same time, however, KyoAni knows full well that such a quality cannot be announced too openly as this would deprive it of its chief strength, unpretentiousness, and thus destroy its effectiveness altogether. Hence, the studio has developed strategies whereby ordinary (and potentially even boring) situations can be made absorbing and entertaining for an audience by being presented in such a way that their ordinariness itself becomes a desirable attribute, and to the point that its attractiveness increases in proportion to the growth of the audience's ability to savor the elegance with which it is conveyed.

A case in point, as jel x argues in the excellent article "KyoAni and the power of suggestion," is the ending of the 2006 version of *The Melancholy of Haruhi Suzumiya*. "Of course the thing with subtlety," the reviewer maintains, "is that it's hard to spot if you're not looking for it. I first took notice of KyoAni's machinations around the final (chronological) episode of *Haruhi* season 1. My initial reaction to the episode was 'WAIT, NOTHING HAPPENED!?' and yet I couldn't understand why I still really enjoyed it. Rather than get angry or impatient at the large gaps of 'nothing,' I felt totally in tune with the setting and how the characters felt. Even the interactions between Kyon and Haruhi felt more real to me. The few simple acts of kindness between them didn't seem like much, but they were just as effective as when they actually kissed" (jel x). Both the dynamic and the quieter moments benefit enormously from KyoAni's impeccable comic timing, delivering comedy which draws its effectiveness not only by the unquestionably amusing nature of its incidents, turns and surprises but also by its uncanny capacity always to feel just on the spot. It is also felicitous for the script to move so nimbly through the anime even though it is exceptionally reliant on narration — and indeed on a demanding type of narration when one considers its thematic richness and its tonal oscillations between skepticism and lyricism. At the same time, each scene comes across as diligently thought out, thanks to both its crystalline animation quality and its deft synthesis of a unique brand of humor with an array of fascinating philosophical ideas.

Philosophical perspectives on the concepts of fatalism, determinism and free will are repeatedly echoed by the anime as it invites us to wonder, more or less elliptically, to what extent people are able to choose and act of their own volition, and to what their every move in life is predesigned by transcendental schemata and forces — agencies of which the fictional character of Haruhi could be regarded as a parodic animated avatar. While the concepts of fate and destiny may at times seem coterminous in the logic of the show, they are in fact subtly differentiated by means of discrete implications and clues. The notion of fate tends to designate the cosmic power capable of preordaining future events and of investing them with an appearance of finality or inevitability. Fatalism, relatedly, contends that no human action can ever influence the future for good or ill regardless of its goals. On one level, *The Melancholy of Haruhi Suzumiya* appears to embrace this perspective by claiming that human lives are as preordained as the physical and biological rules which dictate the functioning of the material world. At the same time, however, the story cultivates a notion of destiny which runs counter to that rigorously fatalistic outlook. If fate is impervious to human interference, destiny, by contrast, seems to allow some leeway for an individual's voluntary involvement in its shaping. Hence, even though destiny, too, may ultimately be the product of external or metaphysical forces, human beings are entitled to take part in the realization of specific effects. The role played by Kyon in helping Haruhi come to terms with her inner emotions, and thereby preserving a state of relative stability, could be said to exemplify that position. In this respect, the anime could also be seen to allude to the concept of determinism: the notion that while the future is tied to the law of necessity, people's actions have the power to influence the way in which that future comes about. Whereas in a strictly fatalistic framework, people's vicissitudes are preordained events in which they have no critical part, in a deterministic one, they emanate from their intrinsic personalities.

In addition, the anime's philosophical spectrum encompasses allusions to the doctrine of idealism, i.e., the notion that the mind generates reality. Chaos theory is also implicitly invoked by repeated intimations that momentous and far-reaching effects can be triggered by trivial and seemingly unconnected causes. A concept to which the anime overtly accords special significance is the so-called anthropic principle. Ushered in by the theoretical physicist Brandon Carter in 1973, this idea is explicitly brought into play in a pivotal exchange between Itsuki and Kyon at a relatively early stage in the adventure. Since this idea plays a particularly interesting role within the anime's philosophical framework, the relevant dialogue deserves extensive citation in this context:

> ITSUKI: Okay, then, here goes: basically, this is the theory that the universe is the way it is right now simply because human beings could observe it and determine that it was the way it is. So did you get all that?
>
> KYON: I didn't GET any of it.
>
> ITSUKI: How about: I observe. Therefore, the universe *is*, or something along those lines. In other words, on this particular world there are sentient beings that are called humans. Now then, by discovering the laws of physics and constants, human beings can observe the fact that the universe actually exists at all. When that happens, the existence of the universe becomes apparent. Therefore, we can say that if the human beings that observed the universe hadn't actually evolved as far as they did, then there wouldn't be any observations, and the universe wouldn't have anyone to acknowledge its existence. So it wouldn't really matter if the universe existed or not. The universe *is* because humans beings *know* it is. Anyway, that's the reason from the human perspective.
>
> KYON: You're kidding, right? I mean, with or without humans, the universe is still the universe.
>
> ITSUKI: Well, that's also correct. Therefore, the Anthropic Principle isn't anything more than a speculative theory. However, this theory does bring up an interesting dilemma. Why was the universe created in such a way that human beings could survive it? It would only take a slight change in the gravitational constant or particle mass ratio for the universe to not allow a planet like the Earth to exist.

Reduced to its bare essentials, the anthropic principle simply proposes that the world is as it is because it is convenient for us that it should be so. In other words, we see in the world what we want or need to be there for us to exist. Thus, the anthropic principle could be said to supply a hypothetical explanation of the reason for which the conditions of the universe appear to be ideally suited to the existence of intelligent human life. Those conditions are assumed as fundamental to the universe's functioning because in their absence, there could be no intelligent human life — no humanity *as such*— to observe them. The existence of suitable conditions is therefore the prerequisite of humanity's own existence. In other words, if the universe were anything other than what it is, we just would not be here. The same basic idea can be seen to underpin the creation of stories insofar as every imaginary world depends on the assumption of certain axiomatic factors without which its events could not even be set in motion, let alone progress along a satisfying trajectory.

As we have seen, one of the main premises underlying the observation of Haruhi's actions by cosmic agencies is the idea that it is impossible to travel to any point in time prior to three years before the start of the story. In the light of the anthropic principle, this assumption acquires perturbing implications. It indeed becomes possible to conjecture that time did not exist prior to three years back; that time did not exist because it did not need to exist; that it did not need to exist because the life form requiring its existence for its own functioning did not exist; and that humanity itself, therefore, did not exist. This line of argument, and especially its conclusion, are only a short step from speculating that Haruhi has somehow caused the emergence of the human species singlehandedly. (After all, there are numerous suggestions, advanced by different characters in keeping with their dispatcher's beliefs, that the appearance of the universe as we know it coincides with Haruhi's advent on the scene.) If this were the case, then people's recollections of events preceding Haruhi's intervention, which they take as an inviolable guarantee of their existence before that point, would amount to false memories analogous to those implanted in *Blade Runner*'s replicants by means of snapshots. Such memories, like the conditions we perceive in the universe according to the anthropic principle, are not proof of an objective reality but are only there, in fact, in order to bolster humanity's ability to exist.

While playing with the anthropic principle, *The Melancholy of Haruhi Suzumiya* also brings into play various speculations regarding parallel universes as defined by quantum mechanics. On several occasions, the action alludes to the proposition that the universe which humans inhabit is merely one among a plausibly limitless number of universes: i.e., a multiverse. Even though humans possess no empirical knowledge of any original force which could have triggered the emergence of such universes, such a force is most likely to be random and have consequently led to the genesis of universes which vary substantially in terms of age, size, density, momentum and underlying physical principles. Concomitantly, the anime ventures into quite a different pocket of scientific speculation by obliquely invoking the so-called cosmological principle: namely, the partly scientific and partly philosophical proposition that the universe is inherently uniform. As a corollary of this supposition, the physical laws and phenomena observable on our planet are not regarded as unique but rather are illustrative of the regular modus operandi of the cosmos in its entirety. Furthermore, the cosmological principle maintains that any conceivable observer at any conceivable point in space-time will see the universe as being endowed with the same fundamental attributes as long as the scope of the observation is appropriately ample. No assessment of the conceptual subtexts underpinning *The Melancholy of Haruhi Suzumiya* would be complete without reference to an indigenous tenet of great significance for both theorists and artists. Haruhi herself could indeed be described as a true champion of the philosophical principle of *datsuzoku*: a total rejection of all notions of habit or rule resulting in the subject's endeavor to escape anything ordinary and predictable. In the case of the SOS Brigade's exuberant leader, *datsuzoku* manifests itself as a knack of transcending the conventional at every turn, and it is ultimately from this questionable, yet fascinating, gift that he anime derives much of its own dramatic flair.

The hearty appetite for unconventionality which distinguishes practically every facet of the dramatic and narrative fabric of *The Melancholy of Haruhi Suzumiya* is heightened by the non-chronological order of its original broadcast, which would inevitably add to the audience's sense of disorientation. The following table indicates the order in which the episodes contained in the 2006 series were aired against the order in which the episodes would be placed if the events they dramatize were to be presented chronologically, as well as the order in which the episodes were arranged for the purpose of the DVD release.

Broadcast	*Chronological*	*DVD*
01	11	01
02	01	02
03	02	03
05	03	04
10	04	05
13	05	06
14	06	07
04	07	08
07	08	09
06	09	10
08	10	11
12	12	12
11	13	13
09	14	14

It must also be noted that in the 2009 version of *The Melancholy of Haruhi Suzumiya*, the episodes imported from the original series are presented in a slightly different order and integrated with fourteen new installments conceived expressly for the renewed anime. The following table provides a comparative chart of the two versions.

2009		2006	2009 only
01	=	02	
02	=	03	
03	=	04	
04	=	05	
05	=	06	
06	=	07	
07	=	08	
			08
09	=	09	
10	=	10	
11	=	11	
			12–24
25	=	01	
26	=	12	
27	=	13	
28	=	14	

If the 14-episode 2006 version of *The Melancholy of Haruhi Suzumiya* gives KyoAni a splendid opportunity to challenge its experimentative stamina in the treatment of established genres and themes both within and outside the realm of SF, the 28-episode 2009 reconfiguration of the same basic story renews the challenge while also expanding the scope for structural experimentation and by deepening the first series' philosophical implications. A portion of *The Melancholy of Haruhi Suzumiya* dramatized only in the 2009 version of the show is particularly famous — or notorious as the case may be — among seasoned spectators and deserves special consideration at this juncture. This is of a loop comprising eight installments, all of which bear the title "Endless Eight" and chronicle the same basic occurrences with only a few marginal changes in each. These consist essentially of the main characters' engagement in a flurry of standard summertime activities, including a visit to the swimming pool, the celebration of the Bon Odori festival, a spot of star-gazing, a bug-catching expedition and the undertaking of assorted part-time jobs. Many viewers have deemed this dramatic gesture thrilling, keenly savoring the appreciation of each episode's variations, but no fewer, unsurprisingly, have found it downright infuriating. The explanation behind KyoAni's indulgence in this peculiar piece of animated spectacle, supplied by Yuki in the context of the second episode in the loop, is that Haruhi has caused the last two weeks in August to repeat themselves ad infinitum because she does not wish the summer vacation to finish. Kyon, Itsuki and Mikuru are most shocked to discover that the cycle has been reenacted no less than 15,498 times, even though none of them has intuited any inkling of this grotesque reiteration and it is only recently that Kyon has begun to feel troubled by a daunting sense of déjà vu. Moreover, none of them can conceive of any strategy likely to stop the loop from repeating itself again for ever and ever. The real splendor of these installments, both from a dramatic and a cinematographical point of view, lies primarily with the overwhelmingly suspenseful atmosphere which pervades the closing moments of each reiteration, where the characters sit in a restaurant commenting on various facets of the exhausting summertime routine imposed upon them by Haruhi and the heroine herself is always the first to leave the premises. Having failed many times to devise sufficiently valid excuses to stop Haruhi in her tracks as she is about to exit the restaurant, Kyon finally manages to break the cycle at the close of the 15,532nd repetition by suggesting that the club members finish their summer homework together just before Haruhi has a chance to leave the scene. Though irked by the notion that anyone other than her should dare formulate a plan, especially as she has already completed all her vacation assignments, she agrees to take part in the event — which makes it possible for the interminable summer to end and a new school term to begin at long last.

The viewers who are most likely to have found the "Endless Eight" loop unpalatable are those who automatically condemn predictability as a marker of creative sterility ineluctably conducive to tedium and blandness. There are, however, more commodious ways of understanding predictability, as well as means, through comprehension of its distinctive dynamics and raison d'être, of coming to cherish it as a dramatic strategy worthy of respect. The chief prerequisite of this stance is a willingness to approach the recurrence of foreseeable events without being blinkered by the expectation of drab repetitiveness — in other words, without assuming that a work relying on predictability as one of its dramatic ruses is doomed to reiterate known materials in a robotic fashion and, as a corollary, to deliver a stolid act devoid of any entertainment value whatsoever. If one is to appreciate the peculiar pleasures inherent in the presentation of predictable moves, it is in fact necessary to focus not on repetition per se but rather on the grains of difference — however marginal or infinitesimal these might be — which any repetitive act inevitably entails. In the domain of drama, as in real life, there can be no such thing as total and undiluted repetition insofar as an element of difference is always bound to creep into the mix whenever the ingredients of a set scene or series of actions are blended together and played out. The same principle applies to predictability: no matter how foreseeable an action may be, it is always destined to exhibit at least a trace of difference — and one can never know for certain where or how this difference will show itself. Even the tiniest change in the circumstances or mood surrounding the blending and playing out of those ingredients, and even the slightest adjustment to the composition of their receivers and perceivers, will inexorably lead to different outcomes. It is to those minute shifts that the "Endless Eight" cycle implicitly calls attention, as each of its installments challenges us to expose ourselves again and again to something we think we already know — only to show us that we can never know it conclusively, no matter how many times we experience it, for every turn of the wheel will cause its spokes to appear to form a different pattern as if they were glass shards in a kaleidoscope. It is also worth noting, in this regard, that the "Endless Eight" sequence expands the philosophical frame of reference proposed by *The Melancholy of Haruhi Suzumiya* in both its narrative and animated forms by alluding to the concept of Eternal Recurrence: an idea typically associated with Indian thought but also found, in various configurations, in the tradition of ancient Egypt, in pre–Socratic Greek philosophy and in the writings of more recent Western thinkers such as Arthur Schopenhauer and Friedrich Nietzsche. Even though this is clearly not the place to go into a detailed inspection of each available interpretation of Eternal Recurrence, it is useful to emphasize the basic principle which the "Endless Eight" loop shares with it: that is to say, the suggestion that the cosmos in its entirety has been recurring and will continue to recur in an analogous form a countless number of times across immeasurable stretches of both time and space.

The two TV series centered on the SOS Brigade's adventures are beautifully complemented by the volume *The Melancholy of Haruhi Suzumiya Official Fanbook*. Especially worthy of notice are the pages devoted to detailed assessments of the individual characters, where the book provides portraits of each persona garbed in a variety of costumes which range in style from the casual to the formal, and from the playful to the martial. Many of these outfits do not actually feature in the series themselves but work marvels in consolidating the most salient aspects of the actors' personalities and distinctive patterns of conduct. Moreover, they have the power to stimulate our imagination by implicitly inviting us to envision a character's likely behavior in situations other than those dramatized in the show itself. In other works, they emulate the principles of Method Acting with the exception that instead of requiring the actors as such to produce in themselves the thoughts and emotions associated with their roles, they encourage the audience to employ a comparable ruse on the characters' behalf. In the larger plates depicting group portraits, the actors tend to exhibit the expressions and postures one has come to associate with their typical performance in the animated mode. Accordingly, Kyon's expression gives off an aura of narky disdain in many of the pictures, while Itsuki is invariably smiling. Mikuru, whom Haruhi insistently treats as the apotheosis of sexy cuteness, emits a burning sense of mortification as her lovely body is time and again forced into sexy outfits intended to show off her assets. Undoubtedly, the viewer in search of fan service is likely to value the visual experience provided by several of the images here supplied. Yuki is almost invariably portrayed in the process of perusing a book. Haruhi, needless to say, looks incessantly — almost insanely — eager, regardless of the contingent activity in hand. The attitudes and poses displayed in such pictures further reinforce many familiar character traits. In the tableau staged on the beach, for instance, Haruhi brandishes a giant water gun as she dominates the scene astride of Kyon's shoulders. Itsuki can be seen waterboarding balletically in the background, the emblematic smile steadily carved on his mien so pronounced as to have become almost inane. Mikuru looks overwhelmingly embarrassed in the skimpy, though undeniably becoming, bikini which Haruhi is most likely to have forced on her as ideal garb for the occasion. Yuki placidly reclines on a deck chair, with a cool drink on one side and the inevitable tome in her hands. The obvious embarrassment flooding Kyon's blushing face leaves us in no doubt as to his reading of the whole situation.

As noted in Chapter 1, the school central to the anime is based on an actual building, Nishinomiya Kita High School in Hyōgo Prefecture in the Kansai region. The images of both the school's interiors and grounds presented in *The Melancholy of Haruhi Suzumiya Official Fanbook* give us a vivid sense of the sorts of photographs which KyoAni is likely to have obtained in its thorough location scouting, enabling us to intuit the processes leading from those documentary materials to the actual settings and backgrounds witnessed in the anime. The rooms, specifically, seem wonderfully alive even though they are depicted in a restrained grayscale palette and, most importantly, contain no obvious traces of animate occupation. As sites devoid of human life yet capable of radiating a vibrant sense of aliveness through their bareness, the rooms depicted in the volume remind us that empty space is neither inert nor meaningless for it actually harbors infinite potentialities for creation and growth. Thus, they could be said to exemplify in a figurative guise the preference for emptiness which has constituted an essential trait of Japanese architecture for centuries. Emptiness, in this perspective, is conceived of as a state which gives the imagination maximum leeway by allowing its processes to unfold unrestrained by the dictates of what is physically present. It is also noteworthy that the original TV series is merrily supplemented by two sets of short animations released directly on the internet, *The Melancholy of Haruhi-chan Suzumiya* and *Nyoron Churuya-san*. The former is a comedic spin-off of the original TV series originally featuring all the main characters redesigned to look like cute caricatural kids, and offering various parodies of the events dramatized by the original storyline which derive much of their humor from their attentive portrayal of each persona's defining oddities. *Nyoron Churuya-san*, for its part, is based on a *doujinshi* four-panel spoof manga which, as a result of its notable fringe popularity, was selected for adaptation to anime. This set of shorts follows the quirky adventures of the *chibi* character Churuya-san, a comical reinvention of the supporting character Tsuruya-san from the TV series, and focuses specifically on her obsessive quest for smoked cheese.

Having tested its talents with great exuberance in the execution of both the 2006 and the 2009 versions of the TV adaptation of major events from Tanigawa's light novels, KyoAni set itself a fresh challenge with the transposition of another facet of Tanigawa's series to the movie screen. The result is a cinematic jewel by the title of *The Disappearance of Haruhi Suzumiya*. Adhering intelligently to its source text, the fourth book in the series, the film stands out as one of the most proficient page-to-screen adaptations of recent years (both within and beyond the anime world) and offers an emotively charged visual experiences which meshes together all of the key elements explored in the TV series but assiduously tinges them with novel, and generally graver, nuances. Relinquishing the TV series' hectic dynamism in favor of thoughtful, unhurried and atmospheric sequences, the film yields an exquisitely muted mood of rare charm. Some spectators may find its frugal use of jokes, measured plot progression and unusually prolonged scenes somewhat perturbing. However, few would be loath to concede that *The Disappearance of Haruhi Suzumiya*, in turning a quirkily energetic series into a meditative, wistful and poignant movie, charts a remarkable metamorphosis: a feat which only KyoAni's alchemical genius at its best could have realized. The tonal divergence between both of the TV shows and the film is comparable to the shift from the flamboyant to the somber presented by the transition from *Full Metal Panic? Fumoffu* to *Full Metal Panic! The Second Raid*.

Dates are important to the movie's diegesis and these are therefore mentioned whenever necessary in the following outline. The film opens on 16 December with the ever-hyper Haruhi's announcement that the Brigade is going to hold a Christmas party in their clubroom, and that traditional Japanese *nabe* (hotpot) is going to be the dinner menu. The SOS members, habitually resilient in the face of Haruhi's eccentricities, begin to prepare everything necessary to make the party a success, costumes and decorations included, in the knowledge that their boss is never prepared to settle for anything other than the best. The action takes an unexpected turn when, on 18 December, Kyon arrives at school on a bitterly cold morning to discover that Haruhi is inexplicably absent and, which is even more alarming, that no-one seems to think that Haruhi has ever been a student at that school. To fuel Kyon's disorientation further, Mikuru claims not to be acquainted with Kyon, and has no inkling of what time travel is about. Itsuki appears to have gone missing alongside Haruhi and Yuki, now the only member of the Literature Club, is an utterly ordinary human with perfectly human emotions — including, it soon transpires, a quasi romantic interest in Kyon. The new Yuki instantly comes across as exceptionally shy, vulnerable, unworldly and easily unsettled by the slightest of mishaps. Last but not least, the humanoid interface Ryoko Asakura from the early part of the TV series, has reappeared — which compounds Kyon's confusion with sheer dread as he recalls the creature's attempts on his life and his narrow escape courtesy of the superpowered Yuki of old, an ally he no longer has in this reconfigured scenario. The only person in his entire world to be aware that a massive reality shift has occurred, Kyon longs for a means of reverting everything back to normal: the world he has hitherto taken for granted, or even dismissed with characteristic sarcasm, has now suddenly acquired unsuspected — and inimitable — value. As his psyche suffers one blow after another with each encounter, he despairs of finding any helpful clues until he discovers a bookmark left behind by the alien version of Yuki before the change, and instructing him to gather the "keys" necessary to run a program.

The clue supplied by the old Yuki triggers a quest back in time which is intimately bound up with the sci-fi storyline pursued in a particularly important segment of the 2009 TV series: the installment titled "Bamboo Leaf Rhapsody." In this episode, Mikuru takes Kyon back to the Tanabata festival (7 July) of three years before, at which point he has a chance to encounter both the time-traveler's older self and a younger Haruhi. Having already developed a bossy disposition despite her age, the latter forces Kyon to help he draw some intricate markings on her school's grounds at night. Upon returning to the present thanks to Yuki's intervention, the youth suddenly realizes that he is indeed the one who inspired Haruhi to hunt for otherworldly and superpowered entities. In the film itself, the truly decisive date is 20 December — the day when Kyon finds out that Haruhi and Itsuki are attending a different school alongside a number of other characters whom Kyon would have thought of as schoolmates until two days earlier. Having forcibly engaged her attention and disclosed his identity to her as "John Smith" — namely, the alias he adopted upon first meeting the young Haruhi three years earlier — Kyon persuades the girl of the veracity of his extraordinary tale. With her support, he gathers the SOS Brigade in the club room, thus bringing together the "keys" alluded to by Yuki's cryptic message. Wanting to return to his older life, Kyon activates the program and travels back in time to the Tanabata festival of three years earlier. After a precious encounter with the ever helpful future Mikuru, he gains an uninstall program from the past's Yuki which must be shot at the person responsible for initiating the change right after its occurrence in the early hours of 18 December. That person, alas, is Yuki herself. Drained by the demands imposed by her creators upon her circuitry, which is immensely sophisticated yet not utterly impervious, Yuki has ended up developing feelings incompatible with her functions. Consequently, as it transpires, she has borrowed Haruhi's powers to create a world in which she can be normal and take part in ordinary human relationships. Her growing attachment to Kyon would seem to have played a significant role in precipitating this character metamorphosis. While she has altered everyone else's memories to lend her new reality coherence, the rebellious Yuki has deliberately left Kyon's untouched in order to grant him the power to choose which world he wishes to live in. She has not, therefore, constructed a trap for the man at the center of her burgeoning emotions, which makes her character one of KyoAni's most fully rounded and engaging creations ever. Opting to return to his original world, Kyon attempts to insert the magic program into Yuki as told but is stabbed by Ryoko, who has not only retained the psychotic and homicidal proclivities seen in the TV series but also developed an unwholesomely protective attitude toward Yuki. Saved by future counterparts of Yuki, Mikuru and himself just as the lethal alien is about to finish him off, Kyon wakes up in a hospital a few days later, with Itsuki keeping vigil over him and Haruhi — who is said not to have left the room at all during his comatose slumber — in a sleeping bag by the side of his bed. While the world of Kyon's choice has been safely reestablished, the youth's return from his heroic quest is marked by a wonderfully bathetic assessment of his state, since everybody believes that the reason for which he has been asleep since December 18 is a prosaic fall down the stairs.

Valuable information regarding the film's conception, execution and contents is supplied by an in-house conversation involving Ishihara, its chief director and storyboard creator, Yasuhiro Takemoto, director, storyboard creator and key animator, and Touko Takao, storyboard creator, unit director and key animator. Titled "Director Roundtable," the conversation is available online in pdf format. Although the three artists harbor personal views about *The Disappearance of Haruhi Suzumiya*, and do not therefore claim to be advertising some kind of corporate line on the venture, their respective contributions to the exchange collectively indicate that in the creation of this movie, KyoAni went the extra mile to integrate its macrocosmic and microcosmic dimensions in the understanding that neither can shine unless the other achieves comparable excellence. As a result, all facets of the film's design, characterization and cinematography dovetail to the desired outcome — from seemingly secondary aspects of character portrayal, such as fleeting expressions and gestures, to key components of the shooting process, such as specific camera angles and moves. The conversation offers a paradigmatic instance of KyoAni's devotion to the collaborative ethos, emphasizing that no conclusive decisions concerning the film's central message, or concept, were made until all members of the team had had a chance to express their opinions and discuss them at length with one another.

"Before we put [a concept] into effect, we gathered ourselves," Takemoto explains, "the Chief Animation Director Nishiya, Super Chief Animation Director Ikeda, and the important animation staff and we talked about the direction of this work" (Takemoto). The gender composition of the core team is another factor worthy of consideration in this context, insofar as *The Disappearance of Haruhi Suzumiya* constitutes the first anime in the franchise to have featured a female artist as a major creative agent. Takao had actually been involved in the production of the storyboards for the 2009 version of the TV show but at the time had been somewhat dissatisfied with her input in the project, sensing, as Ishihara recalls, that she had "left things undone." With the film, Takao takes on a directorial role in contributing to its storyboards much more substantially, and hence with the wherewithal to have a greater say in its overall development. Ishihara and Takemoto alike have unreservedly expressed their gratitude both to Takao personally and, more broadly, to the idea of modifying the established gender balance. "I'm very interested in a woman's point of view," Ishihara maintains, "and also from a mental point of view when producing the work itself. I've done what I could with a man's point of view, but it's very interesting to have a woman's point of view for *Haruhi Suzumiya*. I can say that Takao-san was very helpful" (Ishihara 2011). Takemoto concurs: "I have the same opinion. I used her opinions as a reference many times" (Takemoto). Takao herself proposes that her main contribution to the project in gender terms had to do with her natural tendency to think of Yuki — the character whose abrupt transformation provides the trigger for the movie's entire diegesis — "as a 'woman'" rather than simply as "a humanoid interface" devoid of all human affects and foibles (Takao).

The creators recall with particular enthusiasm the moment when the film's essential concept was being discussed and alternate perspectives on the source novel were outlined by the team's members. These recollections show quite unequivocally that KyoAni's commitment to the cooperative approach is by no means tantamount to the deadening of individual positions, conflicting though these may sometimes be, in the name of communal conformity and an enforced consensus. Thus, Ishihara and Takemoto make it quite clear that they initially contributed two distinct — and not necessarily compatible — concepts to the planning stages of *The Disappearance of Haruhi Suzumiya*, and that even though both elements were eventually integrated into the film, they are not altogether in agreement over the manner in which the synthesis was achieved. Ishihara was inclined to focus on the drama as a "love story," whereas Takemoto was eager to concentrate on the "story of Kyon's resolution and return." The term "resolution," Takemoto explains, "is referring to the time when Kyon is alone and gives up. Up until that time he had 'resolution' by pretending not to look at the truth." With the term "return," conversely, Takemoto designates "Kyon's inner actions to return to the SOS Brigade. It's those wishes and desires that drive his 'return.' I proposed designing the movie around these two points to everyone." Reflecting on the place of Ishihara's own concept in the final product, Takemoto observes: "I get the sense that not only did we design the movie around 'resolution and return,' we also designed it around Ishihara-san's 'love story' as well" (Takemoto). Ishihara's own perception of the coalescence of the two initial concepts is somewhat different: "I disagree. My impression is that 'love story' and 'Kyon's change' were woven together. This might be a different approach" (Ishihara 2011). Ultimately, Takemoto avers that "the love portion of *Disappearance* is quite thin (*laughs*)," and that the essence of the movie is effectively "the story of Kyon seeing things in a new light" (Takemoto), while for Ishihara the love element appears to remain fairly central to the drama. Regardless of whether one embraces Takemoto or Ishihara's perspective on the film, what truly matters is that most spectators are likely to feel that the two concepts coalesce harmoniously in KyoAni's yarn to the extent that the love element is deployed as a catalyst to trigger a journey of personal evolution. This outcome attests to KyoAni's consummate ability to function collaboratively while concomitantly honoring the individual's imagination.

Commenting on the specifically technical side of the operation, both Takao and Takemoto have drawn attention to the aesthetic value of relative motionlessness as one of the most salient features of their approach to filming. "I became aware of this when working on images for the 're-airing,'" Takao maintains. "I made sure to show the feeling of the atmosphere in the work by not moving the camera, showing the surroundings, and other techniques for the viewer [to] become aware of what was going on inside Kyon." Above all, Takao was keen to expose the disabling sense of isolation befalling all of the key characters following the world's precipitous metamorphosis. "After the world changed," the artist observes, Kyon is "very lonely. Nagato, Koizumi, and Asakura too were very lonely.... Everyone on the staff conveyed 'loneliness' in images as well as techniques" (Takao). Takemoto corroborates Takao's comments regarding attenuated motion and its impact on the movie's ambience: "from the start of our drawing, we decided that we weren't going to move the camera much, especially not carelessly. In those cases, it helped make the atmosphere a very important feature" (Takemoto). The cinematographical strategies outlined by Takao and Takemoto endow *The Disappearance of Haruhi Suzumiya* with a very special ambience. From one scene to the next, the dilemma at the heart of the drama is gradually built up by means of silence no less than dialogue, as the actors perform many small actions and engage in snippets of small talk which by and by coalesce into a convincing whole. Every line is intentional, every frame of movement has a function, and every lighting move serves to throw into relief particular aspects of the story while temporarily relegating others to the shadows. At times, desaturation is efficiently deployed as a means of shrouding parts of a frame in lingering gloom while other parts are brilliantly lit with the warmest of shades. Although *The Disappearance of Haruhi Suzumiya* demonstrates that KyoAni does not demur from lavish animation when a viable opportunity arises, it does not indulge self-complacently in either cinematographical flourishes or emotive pyrotechnics unless they are rendered legitimate by their context and objectives. Relatedly, the studio shuns the overtly grand technical gestures so often found in Western movies driven (or so it seems) by the desire to let CGI and the presumed thrills of 3D run the show. On the contrary, the studio channels painstaking care into the capture of the subtlest of expressions, movements, inflections and mannerisms so as to allow the actors to emote in credible ways. This approach yields a quietly riveting and unobtrusively engrossing viewing experience which stands out as a commendable achievement not solely in the recent history of anime but also in that of cinema at large.

On the surface, many of the actions which the film methodically chronicles feel ordinary, routine or even banal. Yet, an absorbing energy courses relentlessly just below that veneer. As a silently overwhelming sense of stagnation swallows the action, mimicking the muffling effect of the snow which mantles the outdoor setting, it becomes increasingly evident that this ubiquitous power emanates from Kyon's rampant realization that a reality without Haruhi is destined to be dull and inert. Much as he might have detested the girl's despotic conduct in the days predating the change, he now acknowledges her ascendancy as an irreplaceable bonus. Thus, even though the film's pace and tone endeavor to convey an overall impression of stillness by recourse to appropriate cinematographical tactics, the movie's soul is pregnant with a longing so intense, so visceral and so sad as to appear ready to burst through its casing at a moment's notice. As argued in Chapter 1, KyoAni's philosophy is underpinned by a keen sense of irony: this contention is fully validated by *The Disappearance of Haruhi Suzumiya*. Its apparent focus on trivial motions belies a serious message, while the air of ordinariness which bathes many of its key scenes is the product of meticulous dedication, not of a lazy pandering to facile solutions. The movie therefore bears witness to the studio's power to generate a disarming impression of effortlessness from intensive application and, conversely, deeply meaningful situations from ostensible meaninglessness. A further irony, which epitomizes *in nuce* the studio's penchant for this master trope, is posited by Kyon's gradual realization that the thoroughly normal environment in which he has descended feels quite abnormal to him in comparison with the world he has grown accustomed to courtesy of Haruhi and her preternatural observers. Likewise ironical is the implicit contrast between Kyon's attitude—which is marked by a desperate effort to pull himself together emotionally as the absurd threatens to suffocate him—and Yuki's stance—which, conversely, denotes a no less acute desire to let her emotions flow unrestrained as she explores the hidden recesses of her new self.

While *The Disappearance of Haruhi Suzumiya* unquestionably evinces rare refinement in the team's handling of its thematic, dramatic and cinematographical components, its overall impact could never have been achieved without the sensitive approach to setting which distinguishes the action from start to finish. Takao has underscored the vital significance of this aspect of the film as follows: "when I read *Disappearance*, the first thing that popped into my head was a winter scene. I had been able to sense the colors until then, but now I could sense the scenery. That was an awfully good atmospheric feeling I got. It linked Nagato's loneliness and sense of helplessness to winter. I thought it would be a lovely video" (Takao). While the wintry ambience created by Takao and her colleagues is undeniably "lovely," it is also much more than that insofar as its distinctive and patiently modulated hues, its play of light and shadow, and its palpable temperature are in fact capable of evoking a wide range of both complementary and conflicting feelings from one scene to the next. The film's depiction not only of the environment pivoting on North High but also of further parts of the city not previously explored by the anime stands out as a major artistic achievement in its own right by supplying a rich tapestry of correspondences between the frigid climate in which its reality is locked and the main characters' private emotions. It is worth stressing, in this respect, that the feelings of isolation and vulnerability which Takao aptly highlights as the most distinctive attributes of the human Yuki's situation also define, though in different guises, Kyon's post-change predicament. Having no-one with whom he can genuinely share his confusion and torment, and having abruptly lost just about everything he could take for granted while Haruhi was around, Kyon can no longer be labeled as an unproblematic incarnation of the comedic cynic. In fact, his characterization emits so powerful a current of pathos as to verge on the tragic — a dramatic mode which, in its pure form, is rarely attained in anime.

In assessing the movie's setting, it is also important to acknowledge the studious care with which KyoAni researches the real-life locations behind its settings. This skill is persuasively demonstrated by the documentary charting the studio's attentive inspection of one of the key locations used in *The Disappearance of Haruhi Suzumiya*: the hospital inspiring the execution of the establishment in which Kyon recovers following the climactic confrontation — or fall down the stairs as the case may be. Officially established on 7 July 1934, as the commemorative plaque placed at the entrance informs us, the Kounan Hospital (Central Tokyo) exudes an old-fashioned atmosphere — a feature of the chosen edifice which the movie simultaneously brings out with documentary zeal and capitalizes upon for the purpose of nurturing its own distinctive mood. Minoru Shiraishi, the voice actor behind the supporting character of Taniguchi, draws attention to the hospital's affecting air in the early part of the piece: "it has a nostalgic feel ... there's a certain something about this place" (Shiraishi). Thumbnail-style screenshots from *The Disappearance of Haruhi Suzumiya* are occasionally superimposed upon the footage following chief director Ishihara and his colleagues as they explore the old building to call attention to the animated images' faithfulness to their model. In the course of its location scouting expedition, the crew were granted access to a patient's room, which supplied them with a veritable goldmine of visual cues and sparks of inspiration. The finished product is remarkably close to its source, insofar as it reproduces with flawless realism not only several individual items of furniture, aspects of the decor and props found in the original venue but also their relative positions within the overall arrangement, and their proportional relations to one another. It is through its assiduous dedication to the ensemble rather than the single elements that KyoAni manages to elevate the art of documentary research to an independent art in its own right.

A further example of this devotion to the whole is provided by the documentary as it informs us that the crew was keen to gather information regarding the hospital's facilities, infrastructure and rules (e.g., concerning the provision of gowns) as a means of imparting the anime's presentation of its world as a credible and engaging scenario. The footage displaying the building's corridors, for its part, offers evidence of KyoAni's loyal imitation of its model not solely in the handling of the hospital's general layout but also in the rendition of the lighting and color schemes: that is, those aspects of an anime which contribute most delicately, yet often most decisively, to its creation of an unmistakable mood. There is an air of understated coziness to these locations which one could never expect to experience in a spanking modern hospital. It is as though the mellow patina of age had laid an ethereal coat of fairy dust on the walls, floors and ceilings, saturating them with an aura of *wabi-sabi*: a quintessentially Japanese concept upholding the unique beauty of the aged and the unpretentious. The portion of the documentary devoted to the crew's inspection of the hospital's roof is likewise memorable. Not only does it provide a spectacular view of the surrounding metropolitan area, which would warrant its viewing unto itself: it also does an excellent job in immersing the viewer right into the ambience of the climactic exchange between Kyon and Yuki. This scene, which some spectators may choose to read as a quasi-diplomatic meeting and others as a romantic rendezvous, replicates the rooftop ambience shown in the documentary with great accuracy, down to the "retro" sign crowning the building. However, KyoAni does not confine itself to an industrious imitation of its source. In fact, the rooftop scene is also, and no less expertly, reimagined by means of lighting, chromatic and atmospheric effects intended to infuse it with emotive currents which the original setting could never have provided of its own accord.

KyoAni's creative revision of its architectural matrix was rendered necessary by the crucial importance of the rooftop scene within the movie's diegesis. If mood is a key aspect of *The Disappearance of Haruhi Suzumiya* as a whole, it is in that scene that its role becomes absolutely paramount. This is because its action and dialogue mark the culmination of the dramatic changes in the main characters which distinguish the movie from the TV series which precede it. As Takemoto observes, "outside of *Disappearance*, Haruhi is always the troublemaker in the series. But in *Disappearance*, it's Nagato who becomes the troublemaker." The director is also keen to emphasize that the change in Yuki's portrayal is paralleled by a comparably drastic redefinition of Kyon's personality and attitude. As the youth is "thrown into a world all by himself," Takemoto points out, he can no longer afford to blind himself to the truth of his feelings about the Haruhi-centered world he has lost. "Up until then Kyon had ignored the part of him that thought everything was interesting, but now he wanted to return to it. I had a hunch the readers were like 'Ah, he's finally got it now'" (Takemoto). Ishihara develops this point, maintaining that Kyon's transformation stems precisely from his finally having to acknowledge the nature of his feelings toward Haruhi. This, he argues is "something that *Disappearance* really brings out," as attested to by the fact that "he heads to her immediately and when he sees her again, it's almost like he falls in love again at first sight (*laughs*). When they first entered North High and Kyon began talking to her, he didn't have that same reaction. In fact, it was more of a refusal then. But, I like that '*tsundere*' aspect of him.... The biggest *tsundere* in *Haruhi Suzumiya* isn't Haruhi; it's Kyon." To highlight Kyon's belated acknowledgment of Haruhi's real significance in his life, the relatively "few scenes" in which the girl features in the movie were designed so as "to ensure the viewer got a 'sparkling feeling' when she appeared" (Ishihara 2011). According to Takemoto, it is in the scenes where "Kyon is surprisingly reunited with Haruhi" that she appears to radiate most palpably that "sparking feeling," leading the KyoAni team to opine that "'to Kyon, Haruhi is the sun.' If she's gone, so is that 'sunlight'" (Takemoto).

Ishihara intimates that Yuki's reality-twisting maneuvers are pivotal to the character dynamics which distinguish *The Disappearance of Haruhi Suzumiya*, and especially to Kyon's developmental curve. "At the time she changed the world," the chief director contends, "you realize that Nagato designed a world that was quite convenient for her. It was designed well to change Kyon's mind. It was very Haruhi-like for her to do that. However, she didn't change Kyon. She thought 'I want Kyon to choose.' That's the sweet side of Nagato.... This story is one where a new Nagato is born" (Ishihara 2011). Yuki's liberal approach has a considerable emotive impact on Kyon insofar as it renders his final decision much harder than would have been the case if he had been coerced into accepting (and acting out) an altogether new reality. In asking him to ponder his options carefully and to rely on his own evaluation of the situation in hand rather than on an external agent's orders, Yuki indirectly prompts a developmental curve of lasting significance for the protagonist-narrator. Ironically, the human Yuki, with her placid and introspective disposition, could be said to embody the very kind of world which the old Kyon, with characteristic cynicism, claimed to yearn for as an alternative to Haruhi's mania. In the light of this realization, it would be quite spurious to argue that either of the worlds available to Kyon is somehow more *meant* to obtain than the other. The situation faced by the male lead in fact exposes one more irony — and an unpalatable one to boot. Much as he may long for one or the other of the realities at his disposal, he cannot embrace either without effectively sentencing the other to death, and simultaneously decreeing the annihilation of the vast universe of possibilities inherent in each. Paradoxically, this state of affairs makes Kyon himself a metaphorical creation figure comparable to Haruhi as portrayed by the extraterrestrial organizations observing her behavior. In addition, Kyon is not faced with a starkly defined choice polarizing Yuki the timid school girl with her reconfigured world on one side of the equation against Haruhi the stormy force of nature with her SOS–driven whims on the opposite side. In fact, he also has to look into his own soul, and honestly admit to himself which of the two versions of Yuki associated with each reality he is more naturally drawn to — the superpowered Yuki of old or the timid Yuki created by her predecessor in her yearning for an ordinary existence. *The Disappearance of Haruhi Suzumiya* places such passionate detail into the portrayal of these affective vicissitudes as to develop an intimate connection with its audience: a bond whereby we end up authentically *caring* about both the characters themselves and the choices with which they are faced.

It would be hard to deny that Yuki's and Kyon's metamorphoses rank at the top of the character reorientations witnessed in the film. Nevertheless, the changes affecting some of the supporting actors are also effective, albeit less blatant. The character of Ryoko is a case in point. According to Takao, the alien creature is fundamentally "genuine" and should not be regarded as "a simple murderer." In fact, Ryoko has no choice but "to follow orders," and her actions therefore exemplify the idea that "we as humans can't escape our 'fate.'" This makes the humanoid's personal ordeal a perfect allegory of the fatalistic perspective outlined earlier in this chapter. Takao also maintains that Ryoko is one of a set of characters whom she views as "'people not chosen.'" This concept, which the artist associates not only with Ryoko but also Itsuki and, ultimately, Yuki herself is described as "a very important aspect in the *Disappearance* world" (Takao). Commenting on the supporting characters, Takemoto pays special attention to Itsuki's portrayal. "After the world changed," he states, "Koizumi became a Pierrot type of character. Other characters' emotions and states were overwritten, but his remained the same as ever. I felt so sad for him. At the voice studio I asked of his *seiyuu*, Daisuke Ono, 'I'd like you to express the sadness of Pierrot.'" A likewise wistful tinge colors the film's depiction of the older Mikuru. The girl's comprehensive grasp of all the events, both past and future, with which Kyon has to wrestle entails that she is obliged to observe them as an external witness without being truly able to participate in either their flow or their drama. On the surface, she is an engaged actor but at root, she is something of an isolated outsider. Takemoto comments on this aspect of the story as follows: "this time the older Mikuru knew the entire story as if she was a bystander. Conveying that feeling was very important" (Takemoto). Takao, for her part, underscores the character's emotive import, laying special emphasis on a key line she speaks: "she does say 'I know that you'll look back on these high school days nostalgically.' I was impressed by that line. Looking over the timeline, and with Nagato and Haruhi, she's only one little point. She knows what she should do, but she also knows what's inevitable. I feel sad for her" (Takao).

The psychological implications of the drastic transformation undergone specifically by Yuki in *The Disappearance of Haruhi Suzumiya* is exhaustively chronicled by the "Winter" section of the art book *Haruhi*

Suzumiya Illustrations — Autumn & Winter. This is achieved by means of pictures portraying the amazing alien as a perfectly ordinary girl in a range of human situations not dramatized by the film itself. These enable us to fathom Yuki's tormented soul, letting us penetrate the hushed seclusion of its inner sanctum, and catch precious glimpses of the sorts of visions she may conjure up as she fantasizes about her possible experiences as a regular adolescent. This is the Yuki longing to forget, albeit transiently, that she has in fact been conceived as an unimaginably complex system having to endure all manner of absurd phenomena courtesy of a capricious life force — including, for instance, thousands upon thousands of repetitions of the same trivial events. In addition, the volume showcases a series of hypothetical contexts which Yuki herself would not necessarily daydream about but in which she could plausibly find herself if both she and Haruhi were common people, and she were inveigled by her more willful counterpart into bizarre or even slightly risqué situations.

The pictures included in the "Autumn" section, for their part, consolidate our perception of the SOS Brigade's inner dynamics by focusing on a colorful variety of themes. Some of the more memorable plates resort substantially to variations on a musical theme which allows them to portray the characters as performers of different kinds of music (both traditional and trendy). These images place Haruhi and her followers in a wide variety of settings which enable the viewer to imagine some of the possible worlds stretching beyond the microcosm of their school — especially, in keeping with the passion for detail characteristic of KyoAni's art, by means of minute aspects of urban design and palettes exuding a powerful sense of the season in which these scenes are supposedly staged: a crane looming against a gold-tinged sky, a cobbled street dappled with dusky shadows, the enticing glow radiating from a set of stage spots. Concurrently, the actors are cast in musical roles intended to highlight emblematically particular aspects of their characteristic temperament, as well as to allude figuratively to their respective roles within the SOS Brigade. Haruhi, unsurprisingly, features as an extroverted conductor thrilled at the prospect of filling a monumental auditorium with her awesome notes, while Yuki is cast in the part of a pensive violin player focused entirely on the instrument and hence indifferent to either her surroundings or the likely impact of her performance on possible listeners.

Beside the music-led images, some of the book's most striking contents include a series of lavish portraits focusing on the female characters singly, in pairs or in triads. These illustrations are meant to throw into relief salient facets of the key characters' personalities in symbolic terms by means of costumes inspired by a variety of styles characteristic of indigenous street fashion. Several of the more spectacular outfits reveal the influence of various aspects of the Lolita vogue — the Gothic Lolita, where lace-trimmed frocks and blouses, ruffles, corsets and dark hues are dominant, alongside trimmings typically associated with both Victorian fashion per se and the Western Goth subculture; the Sweet Lolita, with its pastelly colors and childlike garb and accessories, such as oversized bows and cute parasols; and the Punk Lolita, the Camden-Town-market inspired style in which the Lolita style's mellow tone is boldly combined with Punk's iconoclastic preferences. The French Maid look, with it full and white lace-trimmed black miniskirt and puffed-sleeve blouse, is also alluded to in some of the frillier designs. Some of the pictures also hint at Visual Kei, a vogue distinguished by flamboyant clothes, bizarre hairstyles and elaborate makeup redolent of the Western glam rock style, and Dolly Kei, a trend inspired by European fairy tales and medieval imagery associated with that tradition. (Please note that these and other facets of contemporary Japanese street fashion will be mentioned again in the context of Chapter 4 in relation to the *K-ON!* franchise.) In addition, the costumes evince occasional (and very possibly fortuitous) echoes of Western designers such as Vivienne Westwood, John Galliano and Jean-Paul Gaultier. As a graphic ensemble of remarkable finesse, the *Autumn & Winter* collection serves to reinforce the artistic and conceptual significance of *The Disappearance of Haruhi Suzumiya* as one of KyoAni's most impressive achievements to date. Most vitally, its images intimate that the conundrums embedded in the movie carry existentialist implications of considerable gravity, even though KyoAni's tactful hand chooses to depict them in muted tones. The philosophical message inherent in the film's unsettling events emerges gradually, as Kyon comes to realize that the kind of world he most cherishes is one centered around a screwy, officious, and yet indescribably attractive Haruhi. Yet, the knowledge that returning to this world inevitably implies leaving the human version of Yuki behind undoubtedly presents him with the biggest obstacle he has to face in the entire story. *The Disappearance of Haruhi Suzumiya* is the kind of movie that can carry us away not by engulfing us in a fanfare of bouncy gags, frantic adventure rides, wrenching melodrama or epic struggles but rather by gently tugging at our sleeve and then, with equal grace, nudging us along until, to our surprise, we find that we have been walking arm in arm with it for a while, and will continue doing so until the credits have finished rolling — and very possibly *beyond*.

Homage to Kyoto Animation

"*The first big break the studio had was the chance to animate one whole season of the Mecha Anime* Full Metal Panic, *previously done by GONZO. The series they created was not a typical sequel ... it was more of a comedy/gag/ parody of the original, fans of the original* Full Metal Panic *loved it and some of them still proclaim it to be better.* Full Metal Panic? Fumoffu *was the first hit Kyoto Animation had and the producers of the show acknowledged this enough to have them animate the second season, the true second season if you will* Full Metal Panic: The Second Raid.... *With every new show and with every year KyoAni seemed to find a new market to tap into and unlike other studios they continued to service that new market by incorporating whatever it is they seemed to like in their subsequent shows.... They continue to deliver quality shows each and every year and while they may have had a hiccup here or there, they learn from that and work upon those very mistakes in their upcoming titles.*"— Kidd

3

Crossing Worlds

The sorcery and charm of imagination, and the power it gives to the individual to transform his world into a new world of order and delight, makes it one of the most treasured of all human capacities. — Frank Barron

A successful work of art is not one which resolves contradictions in a spurious harmony, but one which expresses the idea of harmony negatively by embodying the contradictions, pure and uncompromised, in its innermost structure. — Theodor Adorno

In the three anime examined in this chapter, KyoAni engages with the topos of crossing worlds on two complementary planes, simultaneously *performing* and *representing* the act of traversing disparate realities. On the one hand, the studio crosses the boundary between two distinct areas of contemporary popular culture by translating a particular type of computer game into anime (*performance dimension*). On the other hand, it experiments with the interpenetration of ostensibly incompatible dimensions at the thematic level, allowing the mundane to intersect with the mystical while also blurring all manner of temporal and spatial dividers (*representational dimension*). The specific variety of computer game on which the three anime under scrutiny are based is commonly known as "visual novel" (*bijuaru noberu*). An understanding of the chief generic and stylistic attributes of this form is necessary if one is to appreciate adequately the autonomous significance of KyoAni's anime adaptations as cinematic products. It should also be emphasized, in this respect, that the sources behind these adaptations are works produced by what is possibly the most acclaimed studio in the sector, Visual Art's/Key. However, before proceeding to delineate the essential characteristics of the visual novel itself, it is apposite, for the benefit of contextual accuracy, to acknowledge that form's status vis-à-vis the gaming universe at large as a mode of entertainment, interaction and communication underpinned by specific codes and conventions.

What first deserves attention is the visual novel's standing as a distinctive sub-category within the Adventure/RPG (Role-Playing Game) format. This kind of game is distinguished by a style of gameplay which situates the player as the story's protagonist, asking him or her to interact with disparate personae and their (real or fantastic) worlds, as well as solve various puzzles in the process. The Adventure/RPG does not necessarily incorporate intense action elements, and therefore tends to develop at an unhurried rhythm. This allows the player to pay close attention to its multilayered plot and detailed graphics, and thus enjoy both the game's textual components and its subtle artistry in a fashion not usually afforded by highly dynamic games capitalizing on rapid-fire action sequences, and subjecting the player to exacting time constraints. Its eschewal of extreme action and its methodical pace, allied to its frequent utilization of a fairly undemanding point-and-click interface, have made the Adventure/RPG typology attractive even to people who do not habitually engage in computer gaming. An embryonic version of Adventure/RPG is the Text Adventure game: an exercise in interactive fiction (IF) deploying a treasure hunt littered with puzzle-solving challenges as its narrative core, and keen to experiment with textual techniques likely to maximize the player's participation. The Text Adventure game initially depended on written language but the evolution of more and more refined technologies for the creation of digitized images paved the way to the advent of a more sophisticated format, the Graphical Adventure. At this point, visuals rapidly began not only to supplement but even to replace the written word as essential building blocks of a particular game world. Moreover, players became able to interact more directly with that world by means of hyperlink icons and buttons. Also worthy of notice, in the present context, is a later development in the field known as Dialogue game. In this instance, the player's progression through a narrative is not based on the performance of missions but rather on the deployment of verbal skills in the course of conversations with virtual characters. An even more recent development of overtly theatrical stature is the live-action role-playing game (LARP), a ludic venture in which players physically act out their chosen characters' actions.

The visual novel itself constitutes a multibranching and interactive game, greatly reliant on the written word, which requires the player's imaginative engagement in the ludic event. Insofar as the player's inventiveness is consistently expected to complement and enhance the production studio's own creativity, the visual novel can be said to transcend the limitations entailed by the type of computer game which seeks to wield tight control over the player's moves. The visual novels produced by Visual Art's/Key usually develop their narrative patterns by means of extended text conversations accompanied by delicately depicted generic backgrounds, as well as dialogue boxes with character sprites superimposed upon them intended to define the speaker at each stage in the exchange. At certain crucial points in the story, more detailed settings executed expressly to amplify the mood of those moments are included. These often incorporate cinematic camera angles and CGI, which serve further to augment their dramatic impact. The visual novel's ending changes in accordance with its players' decisions at key stages in the game, which motivates most dedicated users to replay it several times, and to choose alternative possibilities each time. In the capable hands of Visual Art's/Key, painterly opulence, lively palettes, and painstaking commitment to plot depth, character design and psychological development are requisite ingredients of the genre. These are aspects of their source texts which KyoAni's adaptations consistently follow with the greatest devotion.

Just as the visual novel constitutes an art form of independent standing within the world of computer games, as demonstrated by its contextual assessment vis-à-vis other ludic modalities, so KyoAni's adaptations of visual novels could be plausibly approached as an art form in its own right within the studio's oeuvre as a whole. In assessing the implications of KyoAni's adaptations of the visual novel form to the anime screen, it is also noteworthy that when a series is based on a type of computer game packed with graphics, the animation team is automatically in a position to draw on an large pool of images for inspiration. However, when the ludic source is a visual novel, this is patently not the case given that this form, as stressed, relies substantially on the medium of writing as its chosen vehicle. In this instance, it is therefore the responsibility of the anime's director and animators to envisage all of the numerous elements which simply do not feature on the computer screen. Tatsuya Ishihara, the director responsible for the three anime here examined, has emphasized this point while commenting specifically on his adaptation of the *Kanon* game. According to Ishihara, the first challenge which an anime production team must confront when creating a series with a visual novel as its source is precisely the obligation to visualize all sorts of elements entirely from scratch. "When the original game is graphic or onscreen," the director explains, "you have something to consult, but this original is mainly text, so there are a lot of things that don't appear on screen at all. We try to make sure that the props are appropriate to the 'Kanon' world" (cited in "A Close Look at an Anime Production House Part 1").

Character designers face a related challenge in their area, insofar as the parent game often supplies motionless figures seen only from one perspective, whereas the comprehensively animated characters must be visualized from a wide range of angles with perfect consistency, making sure that no discrepancies occur in the representation of different aspects of their look (e.g., hair length) when they are observed in profile or from the back instead of frontally. Moreover, in order to ensure consistency in character presentation, it is vital for the animators never to lose sight of an actor's distinctive features and dynamic idiosyncrasies. Ayu from *Kanon*, for example, is left-handed: without assiduous reminders from the director, it would have been easy for the key animators and in-between animators to forget that this was indeed the case, and hence deliver unpalatable incongruities in the representation of her movements. Even occasional out-of-character motions must be carefully thought out, and introduced only if there is a valid reason for doing so, not simply for the sake of spicing up a sequence. In the *Kanon* credit sequence where Ayu is seen running through snow, for instance, the director was aware that "the swinging of her arms was a little too big for Ayu" but deliberately included this kinetic peculiarity in the finished product as he deemed it necessary to convey a realistic impression of how people run through snow in real life. On the whole, one of KyoAni's chief priorities in all three of its adaptations of Visual Art's/Key's visual novels was to follow as faithfully as possible the original works. Commenting specifically on the implications of this objective for character design, Ishihara explains that in order to keep the anime actors as close as possible to their game models, it was critical to ensure that the "timing" of their "lines" was consonant with the source text. In the case of *Kanon*'s Nayuki, for example, he stressed the importance of preserving her distinctively "lazy" delivery as instrumental in the achievement of a fully rounded character portrait loyal to its visual-novel antecedent (cited in "A Close Look at an Anime Production House Part 5").

It is here also worth noting that at times, the need to reinforce a character's association with a particular habit or quirk may lead animators to play with distortion—a ruse which KyoAni does not overtly deploy in the context of a relatively realistic environment like *Kanon*'s but clearly incorporates to excellent effect in more experimental works such as *Nichijou*, as well as in the overtly comedic portions of anime as diverse as *Full Metal Panic? Fumoffu* and *Lucky☆Star*. After all, as Ellen Besen points out, the power to distort is one of the most distinctive features of the art of animation as such — as borne out by its exuberant use of "caricature," the tendency to "simplify and exaggerate"; its creative manipulation of "movement," which is also the medium's prime form of communication; its handling of "fantasy," the principle through which the medium can "achieve magic"; and its take on "reality," the principle through which it can construct "an alternate world." Indeed, the "alternative worlds" evoked by animated cinema do not, in Besen's intriguing perspective, "come from nowhere" but are in fact set up in a coherent and mindful fashion: animators "need to ultimately move from anything being possible to a logical, coherent structure in which only certain, well-defined things (some real, some not so real) are possible." That is to say, they "need to give those worlds some rules" (Besen 2003b). At the same time, by ushering in a virtually limitless range of potential scenarios, animation opens up "a whole hidden 'what if' world for the storytellers" — a web of *crossing worlds*, as it were, which "both builds the platform and provides the strategies for a meaningful, multileveled show" (Besen 2003c). KyoAni's adaptations of Visual Art's/Key's visual novels attest to the studio's ability to capitalize on anime's power to generate a limitless range of hypothetical worlds, while also exploring their intersecting potentialities with passionate commitment.

In the series here studied, KyoAni does not presume to translate the source medium's defining traits into anime-specific rules in a literal sense, for this would inevitably curtail its staff's creativity, imagination and experimental flair. Nor is it interested in merely parroting the visual novel's features. In fact, it seeks to recreate several of its model's characteristics in the context of its own medium by regarding them essentially as founts of inspiration in the conception of independent visual and structural strategies. Most prominent among those attributes is the preference for multiperspectivalism, which is conducive to the articulation of a story from diverse, and at times even contrasting, viewpoints and to the dramatization of deliberately inconclusive resolutions. (A related strategy consists of the incorporation of ramifying and intertwining yarns in which the mundane and the supernatural are ingeniously integrated.) By presenting the story as it is perceived by different characters and from variable perspectives, multiperspectivalism encourages the audience itself to engage continually in the conception of alternate and even incompatible interpretations. The anime's consistent emphasis on their characters' erratic emotions serves to intensify to memorable effect the feeling of instability conveyed by the multiperspectival approach in the first place. At the same time, the anime's preference for multifarious plot ramifications, compounded with a fascination with open-ended finales, echoes the penchant for nebulousness and uncertainty traditionally cultivated by Japanese art as supreme aesthetic values.

In examining KyoAni's translation of its models' conventions into anime-specific properties, it must also be noted that the visual novels behind its adaptations deliver potential, rather than realized, narratives. In other words, they only contain the raw materials of storytelling, such as characters, locations and events. The game's elevation to the status of an actual narrative is conditional on the player's deployment of his or her imagination, inventiveness and sheer curiosity — that is to say, on the player's desire to narrativize the game's raw materials by constellating them into a coherent structure. To secure their players' imaginative participation in the production of the story, Visual Art's/Key's works strive to absorb them into their textual fabric by means of various immersive ruses. Yet, they do not use narrative immersion as a means of turning the player into a passive receiver (or consumer) of the entertainment they provide. In fact, they consistently draw attention to their constructed status both as narratives and as games by recourse to self-reflexive and metafictional gestures. Moreover, the design principles applied to the depiction of both characters and settings are employed specifically for the purpose of urging players to approach the games as creative agents. Thus, subtly individualized character portraits and well-defined environments are capable of yielding a profusion of graphic and affective stimuli even without the assistance of dialogue. KyoAni's adaptations replicate the processes just outlined by implicating the audience into the production of the story's meaning, and by relying on a considerate use of immersion to achieve this goal. In KyoAni's adaptations, as in the visual novels behind them, the audience's immersion in the work is only ever meant to encourage its active involvement in the semiotic process. Hence, the studio's immersive techniques are never so extreme as to blind the viewer to the work's artificial status. This, in fact, is consistently upheld as one of its defining traits as a multilayered textual construct. KyoAni's adaptations consistently endeavor to integrate their graphic, dramatic and narrative components in ways which will induce their viewers to contribute to the story's emergence by formulating their personal interpretations both of individual story arcs and, more importantly, of crisscrossings between disparate textual strands. Design is instrumental in prompting the audience's participation and conscientious engagement. The vibrant realism and chromatic lavishness typically evinced by KyoAni's settings, allied to interesting character dynamics, draw us into the anime's virtual — and crossing — worlds with almost physical intensity. At the same time, the agile treatment of overlapping narrative arcs contributes vitally to the dramatic effectiveness of both the characters and the settings, creating considerable scope for the portrayal of subtly nuanced psychologies which can be seen to develop in plausible ways even within apparently clichéd contexts. Therefore, a cast of characters which might initially seem to consist entirely of formulaic types with foreseeable personality traits holds the potential to evince unexpected levels of sophistication.

The three visual novels on which the anime here examined are based utilize a structural orchestration which can be considered quite typical of the form, though significantly enriched by the uncommon creative genius of Visual Art's/Key. Let us look at each in the chronological order of their release. In the *Air* game (2000), the first scenario invites the player to assume the role of the male protagonist, Yukito Kunisaki, an itinerant puppeteer on a quest for a legendary girl with wings. The player is given choices meant to establish which of three parallel yarns he or she will subsequently enter. Each of the available arcs pivots on one of three female personae: Misuzu Kamio, Kano Kirishima and Minagi Tohno. Cheerful and highly sensitive, Misuzu is a rather immature and pathologically lonely girl with a proclivity to fantasize about flying in the sky. Kano is portrayed as a sprightly animal lover inseparable from a likewise frolicsome puppy named Potato. Minagi, a quiet girl with a passion for astronomy, is also constantly accompanied by a precious friend: in this instance, a younger girl named Michiru. These present-day characters inhabit the first scenario, titled "Dream," whereas the second scenario, "Summer," journeys back in time to ancient Japan to chronicle the ordeal of Princess Kanna and her devoted helpers Uraha and Ryuuya. Even though this scenario does not offer scope for actual choices, it does require the player's imaginative contribution to the story-building process by expecting him or her to forge metaphorical and symbolic connections between present and past events through autonomous creative effort. Furthermore, the "Summer" arc is palpably engaging, and sprinkled with sexual innuendoes congruous with the *Air* visual novel's origin in a format targeted at mature audiences. (The anime itself generally dissociates itself from the parent game's erotic contents to focus instead on the story's more dramatic components. Quite appropriately, in this regard, the version of the *Air* game chosen by KyoAni as a basis for its series is the "All Ages" edition, where the story's more explicitly amorous elements are not included.) In the third and closing scenario, "Air," the player is asked to play the role of a crow named Sora (i.e., "Sky"), a bird adopted by Misuzu as a pet who has developed a deep attachment to the unusual girl. This character is hostile to both Yukito and Misuzu's guardian, her aunt Haruko, whom he appears to perceive as enemies. The player-as-crow must decide whether or not to antagonize the opponents, which first of all requires him or her to evaluate the nature and significance of Misuzu's connections with both Yukito and Haruko. The closing scenario also explains the origin of the myth surrounding the winged maiden whom Yukito tirelessly searches in his pilgrimage.

The protagonist of the *Kanon* game (1999), whose role the player is required to assume, is Yuuichi Aizawa: a skeptical and disenchanted seventeen-year-old high-school student who enjoys making fun of the girls in his milieu with no regard for chivalric conventions, yet is capable uncommon sensitivity and selflessness when circumstances require. The plot's starting point consists of the protagonist's return to a town he has not seen in seven years with no clear memories from the time he spent there as a child. The visual novel asks the player to engage with an ample and meticulously detailed text alternating between dialogical passages involving various characters, and monological sequences focusing on the protagonist's perspective. On occasion, the player is required to take decisions which will determine the course of his or her subsequent participation in five possible storylines. The number of narrative strands uncoiling in different directions, compounded with *Kanon*'s thematic richness, encourages its players to experiment with multiple replays over time. In the depiction of its five female characters, all of whom are somehow connected with Yuuichi's past and with his current amnesia, the game delivers a richly diversified gallery at the levels of both physiognomy and psychology. While Nayuki Minase, Yuuichi's cousin, is an athletic and exuberant girl with a pathological resistance to waking up in the morning, Shiori Misaka is physically weak and reserved. The puckish Makoto Sawatari comes across as consummately unsocialized, whereas Mai Kawasumi is so earnestly formal as to seem virtually unapproachable. Ayu Tsukimiya, the central heroine, is effervescent and strong-minded, yet tormented by the imperative to look for a supposedly precious object of which she has no clear recollection, and by intimations that her time to find this treasure may be running out. Yuuichi's interactions with these characters are portrayed over several interlocked arcs which cumulatively lead to the climax of the game's main strand: namely, the evolution of Yuuichi and Ayu's relationship from a traumatic event buried in their childhood to the present day.

The original *Clannad* visual novel was released in 2004, giving rise to alternate versions of the game between 2006 and 2009. KyoAni's anime adaptations constitute a mini-galaxy unto themselves comprising the TV series *Clannad*, the one-installment OVA *Another World: Tomoyo Chapter* and the TV series *Clannad After Story*. (The franchise also includes the movie *Clannad*, released in 2007, directed by Osamu Dezaki and produced by Toei Animation.) The *Clannad* visual novel includes two arcs, "School Life" and "After Story." The latter only becomes accessible once the player has progressed successfully through the first arc's various developments and gathered eight "orbs of light"—one of which vanishes in the "School Life" segment but resurfaces again in the second arc. "School Life" concentrates on the final high-school year of the protagonist, Tomoya Okazaki: a formative phase in the youth's life which brings him into collusion with all of the principal personae in the game, and specifically its five heroines—Nagisa Furukawa, Kyou Fujibayashi, Tomoyo Sakagami, Kotomi Ichinose and Fuko Ibuki. Tomoya, the character whose role the player is asked to take on, is portrayed as a third-year student with a bad reputation bred by disrespect for authority in virtually all forms, a disappointing attendance record, and an alternately suspicious and apathetic stance to life at large. So honest as to often come across as unpardonably boorish, the youth is chiefly distinguished by a fearlessly loyal and generous personality: an asset he tends to dismiss, no less characteristically, on the grounds that he just does not have anything better to do with his by and large empty existence.

Like *Kanon*'s female personae, *Clannad*'s heroines are highly diversified. Nagisa, the visual novel's main heroine, is a placid and self-doubting girl, forced by her frail constitution to be absent from school for lengthy spells, who longs to restore the school's disbanded drama club at any price, and perform a play she has long been rehearsing in private. Funnily enough, even though Nagisa appears to be driven by a burning passion for the thespian world, she has never even entered a theater, let alone watched a performance. This factor adds a unique dimension to her characterization, distinguishing her neatly from the commonplace heroine with a love for one art or another one often finds in popular entertainment. By contrast with Nagisa, Kyou is rough-spoken and violent, though she secretly harbors a gentle and protective temperament — particularly in her feelings toward her younger sister Ryou: a shy girl with an obsession for (inaccurate) fortune-telling. An exceptionally competent fighter whom even the most infamous street gangs regard with awe and fear, Tomoyo is actually an emotionally convoluted girl whose greatest ambition in life is to become the president of the student council. With Kotomi, *Clannad* introduces the character of the lonely genius girl whose most striking traits are an aura of infantile innocence and a dismal lack of communication skills. Fuko, finally, is an energetic and highly motivated first-year student who, in fact, turns out to have been the victim of a traffic accident and to be lying unconscious in a hospital at the time when she appears to be interacting with Tomoya and his mates. All of these characters — even the ones who are accorded the most marginal functions and the ones who are deliberately caricatured for the purpose of comic relief— evince convincing personalities in which virtues and foibles interplay at all times with palpable realism. It is noteworthy, however, that the personae who inhabit the real-world component of *Clannad*'s multidimensional universe are not the visual novel's only major performers. In fact, no less pivotal to its two arcs' progression are the girl and the robot-like doll located in the fantasy domain punctuating Tomoya's dreams. The girl, it transpires, stands for Tomoya and Nagisa's daughter, Ushio, in the wake of her demise, whereas the robot is portrayed as a nameless entity constructed by the girl out of scrap metal as a surrogate for Tomoya himself. Intersecting assiduously with *Clannad*'s real world, this parallel scenario accommodates the full-fledged development of the visual novel's supernatural component, which finds its culmination in the game's true ending. This is available at the close of the second arc, "After Story," where the narrative focus is on the decade following the main actors' graduation. "After Story" prioritizes the experiences undergone by Tomoya and Nagisa as a couple, allowing the other characters from the first arc either peripheral roles or cameo appearances. In order to partake of the visual novel's true resolution, the player must obtain a total of thirteen orbs of light.

As ludic products, all three of the titles assessed above can be seen to incorporate the stylistic ingredients outlined earlier as defining traits of the visual novel as a form, specifically shining in their sensitive use of various branching points. This entails that the choices they lay out before their players yield an absorbing sense of drama even though they are generally quite uncomplicated. The employment of vivacious palettes and powerful lighting effects contributes crucially to the games' overall mood. Moreover, their undisputed visual caliber in the representation of disparate settings, their clever storylines and their intelligent characterization make them eminently replayable for users of different generations and from disparate backgrounds. The pursuit of all the possible routes opened up by particular decision points draws their players into journeys of self-exploration akin to the physical and emotive voyages undertaken by the games' protagonists. This is in a sense consonant with the reflective proclivities characteristic of the visual novel as an art form. After all, it is conceivable that heedful players will not confine themselves to making decisions in order to advance a game but will also, at some point, examine their reasons for making certain decisions instead of others, and for following particular trajectories while leaving others untracked. On these occasions, self-scrutiny is bound to come into play, albeit at a subliminal level. It could be argued, therefore, that players are not simply expected to make progress within the ludic realm. In fact, they are also encouraged to explore its intersecting dimensions as opportunities for a thought-provoking experiential process, and to regard their personal choices as communicative and expressive gestures rather than purely functional strategic moves.

KyoAni's plots can be said to draw immediate inspiration from their sources insofar as they adopt multi-arc formats, with each arc focusing closely on particular characters and relationships. In the anime format, viewers obviously cannot be expected to determine plot developments in quite the same way as players can be required to do in their dealings with a visual novel. This entails that they cannot be put in charge of giving the text a coherent and dynamic shape through their personal decisions in a direct manner. Therefore, KyoAni has had to act on the audience's behalf by taking the initiative to prioritize certain aspects of the parent stories as leading threads which are capable of imparting the dramatic content with both coherence and momentum. The analyses of the three anime's themes and events offered in the following pages bear witness to the scope of KyoAni's imaginative transformation of the borrowed materials. In the process, they throw light on the development of the two types of world-crossing outlined in the opening part of this chapter — the performative and the representational — by showing how the intersection of the visual novel and anime unfolds in parallel to the intersection of everyday and mystical dimensions.

KyoAni's anime adaptation of the *Air* visual novel capitalizes to great effect on two of the source game's most salient characteristics — namely, its multiperspectival approach and its open-endedness — in order to cultivate simultaneously two forms of world-crossing. On the one hand, it weaves its model's narrative threads into a rich tapestry in which the mundane and the unearthly meet and merge in mutual suffusion. On the other hand, it mingles romance and myth with rare subtlety in order to transcend the generic boundaries of both, and thus throw into relief the drama's more perturbing connotations. (The movie version of *Air*, released in 2005, directed by Osamu Dezaki and produced by Toei Animation, further intensifies the drama's more baleful connotations.) As ancient legends merge with the modern world, and magical lore seeps into reality, *Air*'s audience is drawn into a memorable voyage of loss, love and redemption. The realm in which this journey unfolds is an intriguing blend of reality levels in which fact and fantasy are both perceived and negotiated as mutually interpenetrating dimensions. The story's mystical tropes are accentuated by *Air*'s enchanting scenery, where azure skies and sparkling waters play a major part in abetting the poetic evocation of an excursion through time and space in which a single summer is at once as fleeting as the "twinkling of a star" and as prolonged as "eternity." Concomitantly, the anime's unique sense of realism enables its interpretation of the topos of crossing worlds to stand out as an autonomous creative effort, in spite of the series' obvious dependence on a preexisting text. *Air*'s realism is most spectacularly borne out by its treatment of the crucial temporal jump at the heart of the story, whereby the action abruptly switches from the present to medieval Japan. Though it leaves the present-day action on a cliffhanger, which some viewers might deem disconcerting, the transition is rendered effective by KyoAni's knack of drawing us immediately into Princess Kanna's parallel world by means of its splendidly detailed portrayal of Heian costume and architecture. With these visuals, *Air* captures the Heian Period's unmatched sense of elegance with palpable gusto, celebrating its commitment to an all-encompassing aesthetic of courtly refinement (*miyabi*) in an economical, yet luscious, style.

Simultaneously, the anime's thematic emphasis on supernatural motifs said to originate in that same era draws attention to the Heian Period's world picture, underscoring the ascendancy throughout its fabric of beliefs associated with preternatural phenomena. These included curses, demonic possessions, creatures such as *youkai* and *mononoke* (weird apparitions, monsters and ghouls), esoteric practices, cleansing rituals and exorcisms. In order to grasp the exact import of *Air*'s deployment of the ultramundane, it is vital to bear in mind that in the Heian Period, it was common for people to feel spiritually ruled by superstitions more than by systematized religious doctrines. As Ivan Morris explains, some beliefs, "notably those related to witchcraft, necromancy, and other occult practice, were influenced by Shintoism, and represent the shamanistic strain in the native religion" (Morris, p. 123). Others, "including many that are concerned with ghosts and demons," are likely to have originated in "ancient native folklore whose origin is still obscure." Other superstitions underlying the Heian milieu portrayed by KyoAni in *Air* emanated from Chinese culture, and principally from "omen lore based on *yin-yang* dualism and the five elements" (pp. 123–124). This prismatic body of beliefs is ubiquitous in *Air*. On the one hand, it manifests itself overtly, as demonstrated by the episodes focusing on Princess Kanna and the body of lore at the root of her ordeal. On the other hand, it operates implicitly, yet more persistently, as a shadow text: a ghostly metanarrative haunting the anime at all levels of its diegesis and symbolic fabric, and infusing it at every turn with somber pathos. In the process, we are continually reminded that the Heian world was "heavily populated with goblins, demons, spirits, and other supernatural beings" (p. 130). On a broader level, it is worth remembering that the cultural climate inhabited by Princess Kanna and her loyal associates is suffused by a fatalistic belief in the irreversibility of degeneration as a plight besetting not solely secular human affairs but also religion and its age-old structures. In exploring the enduring legacy of an ancient curse in the present-day scenario, *Air* concomitantly reminds us that the otherworldly has never quite forsaken Japanese culture but has in fact retained a powerful hold on the collective imaginary even in an age of rampant technological progress and pervasive secularization in thought and lifestyle.

The anime introduces its male lead, Yukito, as he journeys from town to town with no valuable possession other than a puppet left him by his mother upon her death, which he has the power to move without recourse to any strings or mechanical devices, and he therefore relies upon to improvise street performances and thus obtain some modest earnings. Though seemingly random, Yukito's travels are not in fact directionless, insofar as the youth is on a quest intended to find validation for a time-honored legend which he has inherited from his late mother alongside the peculiar puppet. This surrounds a winged being, lyrically portrayed as a maiden "beyond the sky," whose dreamlike existence is hinted at throughout the anime. Ascertaining the authenticity of the ancient myth, ideally by identifying the winged creature, is not Yukito's only task. Far from being presented as a detached observer or investigator, able to maintain a safe distance between his personal destiny and the object of his research, Yukito is actually required to participate intimately in the legend's legacy, as his ultimate mission consists of challenging the dictates of fate to forestall the girl's surrender to a cruel and timeless plight. Shortly after his arrival in the seaside town where the present-day drama is set, Yukito discovers that the local kinds have little respect for his skills as an entertainer, and is about to give in to dejection as he accidentally chances upon an unusual girl named Misuzu, who might well be connected with the venerable tale. Misuzu's most outstanding oddity, it transpires, is an undiagnosed illness which causes her to fall victim to serious seizures whenever she becomes too close to another human being, even though a real friend is the treasure she most yearns for in life. This sinister dimension of Misuzu's personal history is refreshingly counterbalanced by her comical gaucheness and infantile partiality to dinosaurs, which repeatedly results in her utterance of the guttural sound "*gao*" (i.e., "grrr"), often to the irritation of the people around her. As the drama develops, it is suggested that Misuzu's condition is somehow connected with a thousand-year-old curse linked with the quasi-mythical character of Princess Kanna. Though hypothetical rather than empirically demonstrable, this correlation invests the anime with timeless poignancy.

The *Air* anime replicates the parent game's structure by embracing three arcs. The first arc dramatizes Yukito's interactions with the characters of Misuzu, Kano and Minagi. As Theron Martin points out, the "cast of female characters" introduced in the anime's opening scenario "provides a broad array of looks and personalities which cover all the normal bases" of standard visual novels: "the clumsy girl, the clearly underage one, the one who always leads with physical harm, the infallibly sweet and nice one, the troubled one, the older sister who had to raise a younger sibling, the still-young-at-heart adult woman, and so on" (Martin 2007b). This marginally formulaic approach to characterization influences the show's initial appearance, so that at this early stage in the drama, *Air* might come across as a relatively lighthearted series indebted to the classic conventions of the harem anime. In fact, *Air* is anything but frivolous. The story's gravity gradually reveals itself as the series explores the three characters' hidden histories, unveiling a painful legacy of traumas, fears and fixations tinged with supernatural connotations. The anime's portrayal of Yukito's uncanny ability to animate his dolls without recourse to mechanical devices could be regarded as the first hint at a rich subtext of otherworldly motifs pervading the series from beginning to end. The supernatural dimension reaches its apotheosis in the dramatization of the arcs which pivot on Misuzu's and Princess Kanna's experiences, incrementally alluding to the existence of potent connections between the two girls' predicaments despite their temporal disparity. However, it is important to recognize that the events pivoting on Kano and Minagi, though less pivotal to the drama than those centered on Misuzu and Princess Kanna, also rely to a significant extent on supernatural elements. Thus, the world-crossing experiment conducted by KyoAni in *Air* should not be regarded as a gesture limited to the dramatization of its main segments but rather be acknowledged as a defining component of the series as a whole.

In Kano's case, as in Misuzu's, the ultramundane subplot pivots on an ancient curse. In this instance, the girl is possessed by the soul of Shiraho, an estranged mother reputed to have lived in feudal Japan, and to have committed suicide in order to prevent the immolation of her child Yakumo. This otherworldly motif is deftly intermeshed with Kano's feelings of guilt about her own mother's death in childbirth, which indeed coincided with the girl's coming into this world. In the Minagi-centered arc, the supernatural comes into play in the guise of Michiru, a spirited young girl who, though presented as a flesh-and-bone real person, is actually a fragment of a dream unfolding in Minagi's own psyche. This fantasy serves the function as a self-protective barrier: a shield unconsciously forged by Minagi in response to her mother's descent into a serious mental illness following the miscarriage responsible for her loss of a much-awaited second child. Michiru could therefore be regarded as a visible incarnation of the lost baby. The audience is drawn into the fantasy, and hence implicitly enjoined to impart it with objective veracity, by being led to believe that Michiru is no less real than any of the other girls encountered by Yukito in the new town. As we shall see, the inclusion of a character of nebulous ontological status is a ploy to which KyoAni also resorts in its two other anime based on visual novels originally created by Visual Art's/Key. *Kanon*'s Ayu Tsukiyama and *Clannad*'s Fuko Ibuki share with *Air*'s Michiru the uncertain reality of characters which the action invests with a strong presence and an intriguing personality even though, strictly speaking, they are merely physical manifestations of hidden fantasies — imagined things which have become so dominant and absorbing in their creators' minds, albeit in a subliminal fashion, as to have acquired a life of their own. Assessed in tandem vis-à-vis the main narrative, the Kano and Minagi subplots evince two levels of multi-world crisscrossing. On the one hand, their common concern with the articulation of supernatural tropes dovetails with the overarching plot surrounding the otherworldly correspondences between the present-day drama revolving around Misuzu and the ancient legend revolving around Princess Kanna. On the other hand, the two subplots crisscross in their shared thematic emphasis on tormented mother-daughter relationships pregnant with symbolic connotations.

The second arc's protagonist, Princess Kanna, is the doomed heroine in the legend passed on to Yukito by his mother: a winged being held to have lived in the Heian Period and to have been feared by ordinary people on account of her wings and superhuman abilities. First imprisoned and then exiled to the sky, the doomed creature is said to have been sealed in an interminable nightmare for time immemorial. Ryuuya, a guardsman in love with Princess Kanna, strove to rescue her against all odds but, in doing so, was beset by an unknown and terminal illness before he could achieve his noble goal. The segment of the anime devoted to the semi-mythical characters of the fated maiden and her associates tells us that winged people, though persecuted in Princess Kanna's times, are magical entities destined to inherit "the planet's dreams from previous generations," and that they "have imparted pearls of wisdom to the people since the days of old." Sadly, instead of being revered in recognition of their superior powers, they were held captive and exploited as weapons in many bloody wars. Princess Kanna's mother was herself the fatality of a curse conceived by all those "she had been forced to kill over her lifetime," part of which was inherited by her female descendant. Princess Kanna is believed to be the last creature of her ilk. While bearing the curse bequeathed upon her by her mother, the girl must endure further misery as a result of her flight from the "sacred mountain" in the company of Ryuuya and Uraha, which has engendered a recurring nightmare. Uraha states that the day Princess Kanna ceases to experience that vision, "her spirit will descend to the Earth in a reincarnated form. But putting the spirit of a winged being into a human is like pouring the water of the ocean into a small vial. The vial will overflow and eventually shatter. The spirit will not have a chance to heal and she will continue to reincarnate." The show also proposes that Ryuuya, aware that Princess Kanna's torment would be reenacted every time she was reincarnated, decided to divulge the story in the hope that one of his heirs would be able to release the girl's soul from its endless tribulation. In *Air in Summer*, a two-episode special intended to complement the primary show, some of the key events presented in the TV series' second arc are reproposed in an expanded version, and the relationship between Princess Kanna and Ryuuya developed with a greater focus on its romantic, rather than strictly platonic, dimension. In addition, the TV special offers some dramatic insights into the loyal guard's background as a parentless kid adopted by a nomadic monk, which allows the action to feature a splendid range of settings chronicling in a telescoped fashion Ryuuya's and his foster father's wanderings through the changing seasons. Though the special's finale offers a considerably cheerier message than the one delivered by the main series, it is no less inconclusive to the extent that it highlights the ongoing nature of its characters' peregrinations without pinpointing any clear destinations, outcomes or rewards.

The third arc returns to the present, chronicling Yukito's struggle to ward off a sinister destiny. The events concerning Misuzu presented earlier in the drama are here retold from the perspective of a crow, Sora, whom Misuzu has adopted, and who seems to be interchangeable with Yukito himself. This impression is succinctly communicated by a few portions of the voiceover recording the young man's interior monologue, and further reinforced by the scene where, having seemingly disappeared from Misuzu's life altogether, Yukito momentarily reappears suffused with ethereal light in Sora's place. As the series draws to a close, Misuzu's condition worsens, rendering her incapable of even recognizing her surrogate mother Haruko. At this point, *Air* lends itself to a pointedly mystical interpretation, based on the revelations provided by Uraha in the Princess Kanna-centered arc, which posits Misuzu as Princess Kanna's latest successor and Yukito as Ryuuya's heir. This reading requires the audience to suspend their disbelief most generously and unreservedly. As mentioned earlier in the discussion of the *Air* visual novel, the game engages its players in self-exploratory experiences comparable to its protagonists' learning curves to the extent that it invites them to examine their reasons for embracing particular courses of action at given decision points. There is a sense in which the KyoAni adaptation emulates this procedure. When its viewers are prompted, albeit implicitly, to decide whether or not the mystical construal of the anime's finale is an option they are prepared to countenance, they must also ask themselves what this decision says about the capacity of their preparedness to willingly suspend their disbelief. Relatedly, the anime's spectators are enjoined to take full cognizance of the boundaries which delimit their purview of both realism and reality.

If the *Full Metal Panic* and *Haruhi Suzumiya* franchises demonstrate KyoAni's knack of reinventing a number of established genres, especially science fiction, *Air* leaves us in no doubt about the studio's ability to penetrate emotions with visceral immediacy. It could hardly be denied that *Air* stands out as a dispassionate anatomy of grief, disillusionment and thwarted dreams. These are affects which, in the hands of a studio given to prioritize spectacle over reflection, could easily have led to slushy melodrama but, in KyoAni-land, in fact convey a maturely refined vision of humanity's laborious and anguished struggle to negotiate reality. The undercurrents of melancholy introspection which accompany the action throughout abet the accomplishment of this dramatic effect, imparting the series with a quietly meditative tone which never deteriorates into morbid self-indulgence. In this perspective, the "curse" so axial to the drama's figurative infrastructure does not merely constitute a convenient mythical trope but can actually be seen as a metaphor for an eminently human predicament of almost universal relevance. The drama yielded by *Air* throughout its main arcs and, though to a less manifest degree, its summer special, is consummately distressing. Martin has underlined this point with uncompromising terseness, maintaining that "the underlying sadness is ever-present; sometimes overt, sometimes not, but never far way from the events at hand ... that sadness will work on you, slowly but relentlessly. Most viewers will find it hard to resist the tragic appeal of Misuzu, a character who seems doomed to solitude and suffering by circumstance and Fate, or Haruko, who realizes almost too late that Misuzu has grown on her too much for her to deny any longer that she really does want to be Misuzu's mother and not just her guardian." However, this does not prevent the show's ending from communicating a potentially promising message. Indeed, "watching the finale of *Air* can be a powerfully cathartic experience, one which dims not at all on repeat viewings. It is not perfect and will not work for everyone, but those who do get wrapped up in the emotions portrayed here will find themselves periodically rewatching this volume over time" (Martin 2007c). It seems plausible to surmise that these are precisely the emotions which KyoAni would have sought to distill from its ludic precedent, and bring to life on the screen in the guise of an intelligent drama capable of encouraging not only philosophical reflection but also a modicum of self-introspection.

Whereas *Air* immediately announces its environmental specificity with the image of a sun-drenched seashore, *Kanon* ushers in its distinctive atmosphere by introducing us to a snow-blanketed provincial town. As the analysis of the series offered in the context of *Anime and the Visual Novel* points out, "the glistening snowy look readily associated with *Kanon* enables it to gather fresh resonance through the inclusion of smooth dynamic effects and dexterous lighting. The ubiquitous snow is not only instrumental to the definition of the anime's atmosphere. In fact, it also operates as an elegant metaphor for the characters' frozen emotions: as the candid mantle gradually thaws, so the actors' defence mechanisms accordingly melt, allowing hitherto repressed affects to surface" (Cavallaro 2010, p. 84). Location hunting and attendant fieldwork played a major part in the construction of this ambience. As Ishihara has observed, these tasks were carried out at the time of the year in which *Kanon* is actually set — i.e., mid-January — in suitably snowy areas of Japan. Moreover, the fact that both the director himself and scenarist Fumihiko Shimo grew up in icy regions assisted them greatly in their venture. The team's main goal was to imbue *Kanon*'s world with climatically and culturally accurate attributes by communicating not only the superficial features of snowy places but also the "lifestyle of the townspeople" (cited in "A Close Look at an Anime Production House Part 1"). As noted in Chapter 1, the anime draws inspiration from a number of actual towns, including Moriguchi (Osaka Prefecture), Yokohama (Kanagawa Prefecture), and Tachikawa (Western Tokyo). However, Sapporo, the capital of Hokkaido, is undoubtedly the key model behind *Kanon*'s snow-clad sceneries. The anime's environment captures most palpably the ambience of the proverbially snowy world associated with Japan's northernmost island. In fact, the region's mood does not only affect *Kanon*'s natural setting: it also impacts on its character portrayals insofar as in this series, as indeed in several of KyoAni's most memorable achievements, the human actors are intimately influenced, even molded, by their habitat — its colors, shapes, rhythms and scents. To heighten the importance of snow, and hence reinforce the idea of *Kanon*'s world itself as synonymous with "snow country," the series' director asked the background artists both to make the snow more prominent in the anime than it had been in the visual novel behind it, and to concentrate closely on each of its manifestations, the least glamorous ones included, such as "shoveled snow piled up on the sides" of streets and pavements (cited in "A Close Look at an Anime Production House Part 6"). Trivial though it may seem, this detail speaks volumes in documenting with candid conciseness KyoAni's commitment to everyday life in all its expressions. In assessing the scope of the studio's adaptive task, it is also worth pointing out that the realization of *Kanon*'s wintry ambience posed major challenges in the areas of coloring and lighting. With *Air*, as Ishihara notes, the summer feel pervading the action made it possible to make the "skies" a "clear blue" and the "shadows" quite "clear-cut." *Kanon* precluded such a straightforward approach insofar as its predominantly snowy settings required the use of "much less vivid" colors which were not realistically compatible with the evocation of strong contrasts. Yet, the director was also well aware that "to the human eye," it is "pictures with sharp contrasts" that "look wonderful on screen," and hence that the visuals could not be toned down excessively without sacrificing their effectiveness. It was therefore necessary to establish an ideal "balance" between brightness and dullness, which often presented technical challenges for both the director and the art team (cited in "A Close Look at an Anime Production House Part 7").

The *Kanon* anime plays with the theme of crossing worlds at three levels. On the structural plane, it capitalizes on a number of intersecting arcs. In the realm of characterization, it consistently points to thematic and symbolic interconnections between the world associated with its main heroine and the worlds surrounding the other female characters pivotal to its diegesis. In generic terms, it fosters the continual interpenetration of the ordinary and the supernatural, whereby the drama's slice-of-life component and its inexplicable occurrences repeatedly traverse each other with both pathos and flair. The ensuing paragraphs address each of these three areas of world-crossing exploration in some detail. Like the parent text, the *Kanon* anime dramatizes a series of variously overlapping arcs. Yuuichi, having relocated to the frozen North to live with his aunt Akiko and his cousin Nayuki, struggles to come to terms with his lacunary memory. Though determined to fit into his new world, once familiar but now inexplicably alien, Yuuichi is time and again tested by the resurgence of fragments of the past which tenaciously resist rational explanation. Time and again, he is challenged by uncanny images and objects which strike him as potentially meaningful clues to the solution of a vital mystery, yet stubbornly defy his understanding—as though he could instinctively feel that they must mean something very important but were powerless to identify either their intrinsic import or their relevance to his own life. Yuuichi's ongoing interactions with the narcoleptic Nayuki, the demon-fighting Mai, the unsocialized Makoto, the ailing Shiori and the mysterious Ayu fill up his days but cannot quite quell his bewilderment in the face of the scrappy memories which periodically flood his senses with no regard for logic. In the process, all of the female characters with whom Yuuichi interacts appear not only to know him from the past but also to know something about him of which he himself has no conscious grasp. As the action progresses, it becomes increasingly evident that at the heart of Yuuichi's jumbled memory lie tragic secrets which he has self-defensively repressed, and that his recovery of those submerged truths is pivotal to his protection of all the people he cherishes most, and especially Ayu, *Kanon*'s key heroine. The sense of uncertainty besetting Yuuichi impacts on the viewer's own experience insofar as the anime resolutely refrains from doling out any cut-and-dry answers. We are therefore implicitly invited to channel our own imagination into the solution of various riddles, relying on the sporadic assistance of a scattering of subtly camouflaged clues.

Of the various items triggering the protagonist's mnemonic confusion, the most significant, from a narrative standpoint, is the red hairband he inexplicably finds among his belongings. An apparently marginal accessory, the hairband in fact turns out to hold crucial symbolic significance in the drama as a whole by functioning as something of an objective correlative for both Ayu as an individual persona and the time-defying bond between Ayu and Yuuichi. Its employment bears witness to KyoAni's competent grasp of the value of analogy as a versatile dramatic tool. As Besen explains, the effectiveness of analogy resides with its capacity to establish a powerful "correspondence" between a "theme" expressing "certain characteristics" of a work "abstractly or figuratively," and a "vehicle" conveying those same traits "physically or literally." In other words, the vehicle "translates the theme into a physical form" (Besen 2003a). In investing its abstract concerns with visible (if not always tangible) shapes, *Kanon* relies consistently on oneiric language. Dreams play a particularly important part in Yuuichi's and Ayu's experiences, supplying the coded messages which allow the two characters' respective worlds to intersect in symbolic terms even while they inhabit irreconcilable reality levels. In Yuuichi's case, dreams constitute a major component of a painful journey toward memory-retrieval and hence self-discovery. This aspect of the youth's experience finds a direct parallel in Ayu's own trial to the extent that the heroine herself is time and again presented as the prisoner of a putatively everlasting dream. It is through her dream, exasperatingly monotonous though it is, that Ayu is able to prevent her memories from "fading away in the eternity of time." It can also be surmised, in fact, that the whole drama consists of a visual projection of the girl's dream, and that the Ayu we see for most of the series is a chimerical apparition — though it is also feasible that the character emanates from Yuuichi's repressed knowledge of past events which are simply too painful for him to bear. A riveting hint at Ayu's illusory status is the sequence in which she and Yuuichi return to the clearing in the forest where her tragic accident took place and she begins to wonder whether she actually has a right to be there at all or is in fact living a lie. Doubt deteriorates into sheer panic when Ayu discovers that the winged backpack, which she seems to take as evidence for her reality as a real schoolgirl, turns out to be uncompromisingly empty. In a last frantic effort to locate the treasure she has been hunting in vain since the start of the story, she starts digging holes in the ground — again to no avail. Her fantasy shattered, Ayu tells Yuuichi that they are unlikely ever to meet again and disappears. The haunting reverberation of her words in the youth's mind lingers behind as the only vestige of her having ever existed.

Moving on to the second level of world-crossing effected by the anime, what now deserves attention is *Kanon*'s orchestration of subtle intersections between Ayu's and the other characters' worlds. In its closing episodes, the anime exploits this ruse most memorably. Even though at this climactic point one could expect Yuuichi to be wholly absorbed in his quest for the elusive Ayu, the drama shows him capable of transcending his immediate concern, and thus engaging in meaningful interactions with various other characters and their own efforts to achieve a modicum of emotional closure, if not exactly fulfillment. At the same time, the youth's openness to others entails that he remains amenable to their influence instead of being overpowered by his potentially paralyzing grief. An especially decisive chapter is the sequence in which Yuuichi, physically and psychologically depleted by his fruitless search for the key to Ayu's revival, is rescued by the real-life model behind the temporary human form willed by the fox spirit Makoto out of sheer love. The human Makoto Sawatari is an older girl whom Yuuichi is said to have cherished in his childhood, and who turns out to share the supernatural Makoto's passion for bells and meat buns. Sprightly, resourceful and inexhaustibly optimistic, the real Makoto plays the part of a rather unusual *dea ex machina*, not only by sheltering Yuuichi and restoring his failing strength but also by providing him with an affective context in which he can finally express the anxieties he has been suppressing for years, and buried in the pit of his crippling amnesia. In so doing, Makoto encourages Yuuichi to honor the promises he has made as the key to his personal maturation. While dramatizing Yuuichi's experiences, *Kanon*'s closing segments also reinforce the anime's world-crossing preferences by enabling several supporting characters to come to the fore. Yuuichi's interaction with Makoto, for example, is deftly intercut with no less critical events in Nayuki's developmental curve. This hinges on the epiphanic realization, which she reaches with the help of her friend Kaori, that by responding to her mother's seemingly lethal accident through self-imprisonment in a solitary cocoon of grief and silence, she is contravening Akiko's most treasured moral precepts — just as Kaori's resolve to pretend that her sister Shiori did not exist as a means of protecting herself from the reality of her younger sister's terminal condition showed no regard for Shiori's brave acceptance of her own fate. As she surfaces from her taxing rite of passage, Nayuki finally finds the strength not only to confront her current predicament but also to let go of the past, and come to terms with the reality and implications of Yuuichi's steadfast commitment to Ayu without recrimination or spite. As these examples indicate, *Kanon* firmly refrains from presenting any of its characters, protagonists included, as its exclusive preoccupation, laying emphasis instead on the collective network of intertwining worlds in which all the characters are more or less intimately embedded.

As anticipated, *Kanon* also experiments with world-crossing in the generic domain. This proclivity is borne out by several events in which the ordinary and the supernatural freely intersect: from Akiko's unexpected recovery from a seemingly fatal traffic accident and Shiori's recuperation from a terminal illness, from Mai's overcoming of a tangle of demon-infested delusions to the fox spirit Makoto's assumption of human form. However, the most sensational — and dramatically protracted — evidence of the everyday world's infiltration by the ultramundane indubitably lies with the mystery of Ayu's "existence." Regardless of whether we view the character of Ayu as a persona contrived by the girl's own dream, or else as a projection of Yuuichi's dormant memories, her participation in the action as a major player is clearly a portent. No less prodigious is her physical reinsertion into the real world at the close of the anime. This climax is beautifully accomplished by means of a series of deftly choreographed sequences which allow the drama's momentum to build up gradually, yet relentlessly, toward a satisfying finale. Initially, Yuiichi presumes that Ayu has conclusively relinquished this world, and that he is therefore left with no option but to resign himself to fate and lay the past's demons to rest. This pragmatic attitude is reinforced by his eventual realization of the nature of the tragedy which caused his amnesia: Ayu's ostensibly fatal fall from a tree seven years earlier, before he could give her the iconic hairband as a parting present. The revelation only serves to strengthen his belief that Ayu is no longer of this world. Reality appears to have triumphed unequivocally over the fantasy realm which could admit Ayu's existence despite its illogicality. However, the discovery that his prized friend is in fact alive, though trapped in a seven-year slumber, shakes Yuuichi out of his resigned pragmatism and rekindles his faith in the possibility of a world with Ayu in it after all. At this stage in the drama, it becomes possible not merely to revive the fantasy realm which could accommodate Ayu in visionary terms, but also to translate it into a tangible reality. Intriguingly, given the anime's debt to an eminently narrative source, the vehicle through with this extraordinary transformation is effected is precisely the art of storytelling. With the stories told by Yuuichi to the sleeping Ayu, KyoAni delivers a gorgeous cinematographical flourish, offering a telescoped recap of the series' most significant moments, and culminating with Yuuichi's crepuscular reunion with a precious childhood friend. Ironically, it is when the protagonist becomes able to *tell himself* a story, figuratively speaking, and thus force himself to confront his self-blinding tendencies, that he is able to move ahead. He finally realizes that he never had a chance to give Ayu the hairband with which he had meant to seal their special friendship, but convinced himself that he had performed this symbolic gesture to protect his aggrieved soul from memory's deadly weight. With these realizations comes Yuuichi's strength both to put an end to Ayu's interminable dream and to heal his own fractured self.

One of the most intriguing aspects of *Kanon*'s take on the otherworldly, and specifically of its portrayal of the pivotal character of Ayu, consists of its ingenious adaptation of the traditional figure of the ghost. In fact, all three of the anime here studied incorporate the topos of spectrality in various guises as an important narrative thread. Like *Kanon*'s Ayu, *Air*'s Princess Kanna and Michiru, as well as *Clannad*'s Fuko and the figure of the girl stranded in an empty world, are characters whose unearthly connotations and dramatic functions within the three plots are redolent of ghosts or ghostlike figures. In their characterization of those personae, the anime could be said to pay homage to Japanese culture's inveterate fascination with specters and haunting: a preference which stems directly from the ascendancy of the subject of death in Japanese folklore and mythology. In the West, ghosts are commonly conceived of as residual vestiges of the departed. In Japanese culture, by contrast, the realm of spectrality is enhanced to accommodate some tantalizing incarnations of the principles of death-in-life and life-in-death. It is also noteworthy, as Patrick Drazen emphasizes, that "in an atmosphere such as Japan's, in which natural spirits can even be found amid the skyscrapers of downtown Tokyo, and where many homes have their own Buddhist altar or Shintō 'god-shelf,' it should be no surprise that spirits are presumed to visit the human world" (Drazen). Michiko Iwasaka and Barre Toelken pursue a related argument, averring that death represents "the *principal* topic in

Japanese tradition," and that this is attested to by the fact that "nearly every festival, every ritual, every custom is bound up in some way with the relationship between the living and the dead, the present family and its ancestors" (Iwasaka and Toelken, p. 6). Moreover, Japan's approach to ghostliness bears witness to a cultural mentality wherein "the realms of the living and the dead interpenetrate in a system of mutual responsibility" and "the world of the dead," accordingly, "remains 'alive'" among the living" (p. 8). This ethos is confirmed to by the fact that "the performative media — theatre, Kabuki, film and storytelling (such as the *kaidan banashi* [ghost or horror story] recitals) — are well stocked with stories which feature death, ghosts, *oni* [demons] and other monsters" (p. 13).

KyoAni's vision as articulated in the three works under scrutiny corroborates this contention to the extent that its representation of ontologically ambiguous characters such as Ayu is sustained by those very principles. The studio's key achievement, in this regard, is an imaginative and thought-provoking appropriation of motifs which have been passed down from generation to generation by both textual and oral means. Most vitally, KyoAni's unique juggling of pathos and verve ensures that his quasi-ghostly characters are not portrayed as undilutedly baleful phenomena, and are therefore spared the fate of compartmentalization as straightforward spooks to which many Western phantoms have been consigned by convention and complacency. In the specific context of *Kanon*, KyoAni's representation of the main heroine's haunting presence underscores at every turn the character's liveliness, colorfulness and self-motivation; Ayu is clearly not envisaged as a pale ghost skulking sullenly amid gathering shadows. This reminds us that Japan's spectral lore often presents the world of the inanimate as vibrantly alive by virtue of its incessant participation in the beliefs and practices of the world of the living, which entails that the two dimensions are forever enmeshed in patterns of mutual correspondence and responsibility. Thus, the ghost figure could be said to have given KyoAni a perfect opportunity to stretch its world-crossing audacity so far as to challenge the ultimate, supposedly most impenetrable, of all barriers: the one between life and death.

KyoAni's treatment of spectrality is also redolent of Avery F. Gordon's approach to this phenomenon as expounded in the seminal volume *Ghostly Matters*. For Gordon, "the term *haunting*" designates "those singular yet repetitive instances when home becomes unfamiliar, when your bearings on the world lose direction, when the over-and-done-with comes alive, when what's been your blind spot comes into view. Haunting raises specters, and it alters the experience of being in time, the way we separate the past, the present, and the future. The specters ... appear when the trouble they represent and symptomize is no longer being contained or repressed or blocked from view" (Gordon, "Introduction to the New Edition"). Though relevant to all three of the anime here explored, this theoretical perspective is most pointedly pertinent to *Kanon*. The placement of the inert Ayu's phantasm among healthy and active people in the guise of an effervescent presence, which allows her inner world to cross over into their everyday reality, radically destabilizes the ordinary world's common assumptions. All those who seem to come into contact with Ayu's haunting company are to some extent affected by this redefinition of their reality's coordinates. The character most deeply affected by Ayu's "ghostly matters," so to speak, is clearly Yuuichi himself—which is entirely logical when one considers that he is also the person who has suffered most acutely as a result of the girl's tragic accident, and still bears the burden of that trauma in the form of his amnesia. In fact, in one viable interpretation of *Kanon*'s intentionally ambiguous story, Yuuichi is the *only* character who actually perceives Ayu as a flesh-and-blood creature even though the real girl is actually lying inert in a hospital bed. The other characters may simply be humoring him along in appearing also to interact with Ayu's presence— possibly in the hope that, given Yuuichi's crucial importance in Ayu's life prior to the tragedy, his spectral fantasy may ultimately be conducive to Ayu's recovery. Like the ghosts described by Gordon, Ayu appears when the painful reality with which she is associated in Yuuichi's psyche can no longer be suppressed or kept at bay: namely, when the youth's return to the cold North compels him to confront his selective memory loss and to address its possible causes.

A crucial aspect of *Kanon*'s world picture which brings together all three levels of world-crossing examined above is its use of Johann Pachelbel's *Canon in D major*—also more formally known as *Canon and Gigue in D major for three Violins and Basso Continuo* (*Kanon und Gigue in D-Dur für drei Violinen und Basso Continuo*)—as the accompaniment for particularly affecting moments, such as the dialogue between Ayu and Yuuichi in the coffee-shop where they take refuge in the first episode. The conceptual significance of the canon as a musical composition is voiced by the supporting character of Sayuri Kurata (Mai's sole friend up to Yuuichi's arrival) in the scene where she visits the same location with Yuuichi, and Pachelbel's *Canon* can again be heard playing in the background. In this context, Sayuri explains that a canon reiterates the same melody several times to enable the charm of its harmony to manifest itself incrementally. The canon indeed utilizes a contrapuntal structure in which a principal melody (*dux*) leads to one or more replications of that melody (*followers*) played in different voices. Sayuri's words provide a metaphorical assessment of the experiences and interactions on which *Kanon* itself depends as both a dramatic and a narrative construct. By charting the gradual, often barely noticeable, development of several parallel lives over time, *Kanon* yields a heartfelt and lucid analysis of humanity's painful quest for concord. Just as each repetition in a canon echoes the initial melody as its root, so the anime's actors insistently return to the past as an inevitable stepping stone to fruitful growth. Hirito Kawasumi has persuasively emphasized the symbolic significance of Pachelbel's *Canon* in the series' affective makeup. "One thing I derived from the usage of *Canon*," the critic avers, "could be that in order for a perfect harmony between different people," to obtain, "there must be a certain level of synchronization between them," enabling them "to understand each other" and "lend a helping hand when needed, which brings to the point of '*One can never walk alone*' or basically, Unity through Friendship" (Kawasumi). Therefore, Sayuri's remarks cannot be dismissed as simply an instance of the kind of conversational digression often used by slice-of-life anime to lend a naturalistic feel to the action. This would be to do them an unpardonable disservice. In fact, the message they convey underlies the series in its entirety, while also supplying a terse illustration of what therik, in his review of the anime for *Anime-Planet*, beautifully describes as *Kanon*'s "philosophical poetry" (therik).

The canon's cumulative effect and consistency pivot on the pursuit of gradual change through the repetition of a central motif, and hence on the accretion of impressions in a fashion redolent of a coral reef's growth. In this regard, it could be argued that the formal constitution of the canon as a piece of music finds a close correlative in the processes entailed in the production of an anime. Just as the reiterated melodic elements coalesce in the climax of the composition, so the visual elements generated in the various phases of production collude in the photography/CG stage. At this point, the "animation data created in the finishing process and the backgrounds created in art design are combined" to produce the complete picture through the deployment of "various camerawork" ("A Close Look at an Anime Production House Part 8"). The principle of harmony, posited by both the musical organization of the canon and KyoAni's approach to production as the supreme ideal, can also be seen to underpin *Kanon*'s attitude to its characters and plot. Distinguished throughout by uncommon maturity, restraint and sensitivity, the series is able to accommodate even the most eccentric of characters within a credible mesh of human relationships, which makes it possible for the audience to empathize with their flaws and foibles as though they were real people. Concurrently, even the most preposterous actions appear justifiable thanks to their judicious situation in a convincing dramatic framework. Consequently, even the episodes in which the everyday and the supernatural coalesce to potentially bizarre extremes do not come across as facile concessions to a standard spiritualist mentality. In addition, *Kanon*'s careful avoidance of glamour and excess impacts positively on its handling of humor. As therik points out, the anime's preference for "moderation" entails that "although the show is funny, it's not too funny. In fact, the humour in *Kanon* is masterful in knowing its role. It doesn't elbow you in the ribs and laugh raucously at its own jokes; instead it lightly strokes your shoulder, reminding you that it's always there and giving you the choice of whether to laugh or not" (therik).

In formal terms, the *Clannad* anime follows closely the visual novel on which it is based in developing two interrelated arcs, the source text's initial arc corresponding to the first TV series, and the second to its sequel. Like *Kanon* before it, *Clannad* provides a triangular exploration of the topos of crossing worlds, capitalizing simultaneously on the intersection of distinct storylines; of the experiences of its main heroine and those of supporting female figures; and of everyday and preternatural occurrences. Initially, *Clannad* seems to prioritize the former two of these categories to the extent that its plot comes across as substantially more down-to-earth than anything we have witnessed in either *Air* or *Kanon*. However, things change radically, as we shall see, with the sequel and particularly its finale, where the supernatural is reinstalled as a primary player. The narrative principle of multiperspectivalism, no less vital to *Clannad* than it was to *Kanon*, relies on the orchestration of a carefully crafted ensemble of interconnected plots and attendant experiential trajectories. *Clannad* is so eager to maximize the visual novel's penchant for plural points of view as to carefully avoid singling out any one individual persona as an unequivocally dominant presence at any one point in the action. Even its female lead, Nagisa, is time and again made to take a back seat in order to allow other actors to gain center stage. The cardinal role to be played by Nagisa in the final portion of the series is presaged by her initial presentation as the story's principal heroine, and by the action's emphasis on her efforts to resuscitate the school's drama club. However, before Nagisa can rise to the status of undisputed female lead, the drama focuses on Tomoya's interactions with the other female personae: namely, Fuko, Kotomi, Kyou, Ryou and Tomoyo. As these interactions evolve, Tomoya and Nagisa's developing relationship comes to provide an unobtrusive dramatic leading thread, capable of lending coherence and continuity to the overall story in spite of its multi-arc structure.

The various relationships around which *Clannad*'s arcs revolve are held together by the concept intrinsic in its title. The Irish word "*clannad*" translates as "family" or "clan," and serves to highlight the importance throughout the story of the web of feelings, responsibilities and goals which emanate from an individual's situation within both literal and metaphorical families. Parents and siblings feature prominently in all of the anime's arcs. At the same time, the clan motif is consistently reinforced by Nagisa's endearing obsession with the fictional Dango Family, whose colorful shapes punctuate the series as a memorable visual refrain despite their seeming crudeness. In the arc hinging on Fuko, the importance of the family topos manifests itself in the form of the young girl's manic resolve to arrange a wedding ceremony for her sister Kouko at which all of the school's staff and students will be present. The degree of Fuko's obsessiveness is borne out by the dedication with which she untiringly carves wooden starfish, which she doles out throughout the school as invitations. These actions would come across as simply amusing (or perhaps slightly irritating) were it not for the fact that Fuko is not a flesh-and-bone human but actually a projection created by her comatose self as she dreams. What renders Fuko temporarily visible to others is the sheer strength of her love for her elder sister. The most touching aspect of this arc is the uncompromising generosity with which Nagisa and her parents, aware that Fuko's dream is only a transient illusion, endeavor to nurture it while it lasts by devoting whole nights to the manufacture of the iconic starfish.

The arc devoted to Kotomi, whose story is intercut with several forays into the parallel experiences of the sisters Kyou and Ryou Fujibayashi, relies no less conspicuously on the family motif. In this instance, the heroine is a genius student who must learn to negotiate some profoundly traumatic childhood experiences through a painful journey of self-exploration: a task she embraces, unsuspectingly at first, with Tomoya's encouragement. If the *Kanon* scene in which Sayuri describes the formal characteristics of the canon for Yuuichi's benefit encapsulates the series' philosophy with lyrical poignancy, then the *Clannad* sequence which most faithfully captures the entire anime's vision is the one chronicling a teddy bear's journey across the continents. The toy, purchased by Kotomi's parents prior to the plane crash in which they lose their lives, is here seen to voyage from country to country, as kindly strangers unquestioningly agree to take care of it, and hand it over to the next person likely to help it reach its intended destination. This sequence stands out not only as one of the most outstanding segments of the entire *Clannad* franchise but also as one of the rarest gems in KyoAni's output at large. The individual atmosphere of each of the lands touched by the teddy bear in the course of its odyssey is economically conveyed by means of immediately recognizable aspects of its climatic, architectural and vestimentary identity. The journey itself can effectively be regarded as a figurative correlative for Kotomi's own tortuous pilgrimage toward self-understanding. The sequence can also be said to epitomize *Clannad*'s distinctive world picture to the extent that it celebrates in a telescoped fashion the feelings of generosity, altruism and solidarity which punctuate the action throughout, and invariably underlie both the more decisive and the more moving moments in its development. However, the teddy-bear sequence is also true to the unsentimentally pragmatic facets of *Clannad*'s sensibility in its emphasis on the importance of acknowledging—and coming to terms with—the inevitability of loss, loneliness and displacement. Thus, even though the toy does eventually reach the intended destination, this happy ending (so to speak) does not cancel out either the reality of Kotomi's abysmal loss or the immensity of the haunting loneliness and sense of displacement she has had to endure in its wake.

When the action turns to Tomoyo, we learn that this seemingly indomitable heroine is in fact tormented, like Kotomi, by an unhappy family background. Tomoyo's emotional turmoil is specifically connected with painful memories of her younger brother, Takafumi: a boy prepared to forgo his very life for the sake of familial harmony. When the action finally focuses on Nagisa's story, we learn that *Clannad*'s main heroine, too, is tormented by family-related issues. What troubles Nagisa is the belief, potent though inchoate, that at some point in her childhood she has behaved harmfully toward her parents. Sanae and Akio insistently maintain that Nagisa's fears are unfounded but it soon transpires that they have in fact relinquished their aspirations and careers for their daughter's sake, and embraced their humble existence as bakers to provide a safe haven for Nagisa and her own dreams. Although the eventual discovery has devastating effects on the oversensitive girl, family values win the day as her parents' unflinching support give her the motivation to perform at last the play she has been writing and rehearsing for a long time. As Nagisa's thespian ambitions thus reach fruition, *Clannad* regales us with some unforgettable sequences pregnant with delicately layered symbolism. The play chronicles the ordeal of a lonely girl stranded in "a world that has ended," and whiling away the time by constructing a doll out of "pieces of junk" in a desperate effort to alleviate her solitude. This performance closely echoes a recurrent dream experienced by Tomoya, and its content is destined to acquire thematic centrality in *Clannad After Story*.

While dramatizing the crossing of coexistent worlds by means of its multi-arc structure, *Clannad* concurrently fosters the intersection of different generic domains with its amalgamation of drama, romance and humor. In fact, it would not be an exaggeration to argue that *Clannad* offers an outstanding experiment with multigeneric anime, transitioning even in the context of individual episodes between slice-of-life naturalism and complex symbolism; between ominous premonitions, which occasionally verge on tragedy, and madcap farce. Some of the most amusing comic moments coincide with the sequences in which Nagisa's parents indulge in downright absurd demonstrations of either gastronomic pride or addictive uxoriousness. Likewise hilarious is the scene where they go out of their way to give Tomoya a more distinctive name and suggest, as possible options, words such as "Galaxy," "Cosmos" and "Eternal"—which unaccountably manages to morph into "Ethanol" from one line to the next. No less entertaining than the set pieces revolving around Nagisa's parents is the portion of the story focusing on the antics between Tomoyo and the supporting character of Sunohara. These scenes are particularly notable for their use of self-reflexive gestures which bring the language of computer games squarely into play. Thus, whenever Sunohara claims that Tomoyo is not really a girl and challenges her to a duel, invariably to be defeated by the formidable female fighter, a combo counter of the kind typically found in fighting computer games appears at the bottom of the screen, adding up from one confrontation to the next as the series progresses. It should also be noted, on this point, that the anime as a whole features numerous RPG-based spoofs and intertextual allusions to the gaming world. In these instances, KyoAni's penchant for world-crossing manifests itself in the form of a parodic intersection of the medium of anime and the ludic construct at its root. The Sunohara-Tomoyo larks are rendered even more entertaining by Tomoya's tongue-in-cheek advice, which repeatedly urges Sunohara to give up fighting with Tomoyo, and to ingratiate himself with the girl instead by addressing her chivalrically while enacting absurdly inapposite moves — such as "naturally stretching," "pretending to bowl" or, most outrageously, "naturally doing a Hindu squat." Needless to say, Tomoya is well aware that these ridiculous gestures will only serve to intensify Tomoyo's vexation to explosive extremes. Most importantly, the comical moments never detract from the anime's more serious dimension but actually enhance its import by providing a challenging ironical contrast. As a corollary, even when the anime gives the zany spirit free reign, the characters involved in the wacky scenes are not unequivocally depicted as formulaic conduits for comic relief. The characters in fact evince carefully nuanced psychological traits which preclude monolithic categorization. Sunohara, for instance, shows a sensitive temperament when he begins to forget Fuko, and his initial perplexity turns into genuine grief as he struggles to recover the recollections which stubbornly escape his grasp. In the sequel, as we shall see, the overall action's reorientation in the direction of greater somberness is matched by a diminution in its comedic content. In this instance, humor would not have highlighted the anime's drama by means of contrast but either diluted it or trivialized it by causing it to come across as maudlin sentiment.

The *Clannad* visual novel requires the player to interact with extensive and meticulously detailed textual passages, and, at designated decision points, to select one particular route out of a set of five primary plot strands, each of which corresponds to one of the principal female personae. It is, of course, possible to play the game several times and to choose a different route each time in order to sample all the available narrative and dramatic developments of which the game is capable. Were one to engage in such multiple replays, a total of thirteen mutable endings could, in principle, be experienced. The *Clannad* anime endeavors to translate the parent text's passion for variations into an axial aspect not only of its own approach to storytelling and action but also of its release history as a composite work. Both of the TV series capitalize on the principle of permutation in their dramatization of alternate scenarios which involve consistent shifts of focus from one character to another, one life story to another, and one journey of self-discovery to another. A further instance of KyoAni's experimentation with transformational cinematic syntax is provided by the Tomoyo-centered OVA, where the drama offers a variation on the first series' conclusion. (The OVA is commonly referred to as episode 24 in the first *Clannad* season.) The OVA can be regarded as a unique achievement in the genus of visual-novel adaptations to the extent that its alternate finale enables a secondary heroine to play a vital part in the story's resolution by portraying Tomoyo as the male protagonist's chosen partner in the laborious voyage to maturity. The second TV series presents us with an even more radical reorientation, insofar as its play with the permutational principle is not merely conducive to a spotlight adjustment but actually alters the story's generic identity by displacing the first series' focus on the adolescent perspective. It thus enthrones as its pivotal concerns first the trials of a largely unfriendly adult domain, and then the mysteries of a world which appears to transcend intelligible human reality altogether.

KyoAni's *Clannad After Story*, like the segment of the Visual Art's/Key visual novel behind it, tends to push the supporting actors to its action's periphery, minimizing their impact or even leaving them out totally if they are not integral to the action's development. This allows Tomoya and Nagisa's affective evolution to gain unequivocal centrality, and hence to evolve in a more realistic manner. However, this does mean that the anime's secondary personae are rendered altogether irrelevant to the sequel's unfolding. In fact, despite their relative marginalization, they are accorded an important part in the overall diegesis to the extent that the drama makes it incontrovertibly clear that their active presence in the protagonists' lives has contributed critically to both Tomoya's and Nagisa's personal growth. The clan motif can thus be seen to remain pivotal to the story throughout. One of *Clannad After Story*'s chief dramatic strengths consists of its depiction of the protagonists' mutual influence, whereby Tomoya and Nagisa, having already grown as a result of getting to know each other in the course of the first series, can now be seen to go on maturing convincingly just by virtue of being together, and of being able to learn from each other's weaknesses no less than from each other's moral assets. This is especially true of the male lead, whose day-to-day interactions not only with Nagisa and his closest friends but also with distant or new acquaintances is so credibly and maturely portrayed as to place him among the most fully rounded male characters in the history of modern anime. At the same time, while the sequel retains its antecedent's passion for a smooth synthesis of drama, romance and humor, it clearly prioritizes the former two modes. Even when comic elements from the first series reappear — e.g., the clownish set pieces centered on Akio and Sanae — their tone is more nostalgic than unproblematically humorous.

In thematic terms, the first series' developments can be seen to pave the way to the sequel's own plot insofar as they introduce all the emotional and psychological ingredients destined to play a key part in the evocation of *Clannad After Story*'s finely tuned drama. As Ascaloth points out in comparing the sequel's tone to that of the first series, "it is noteworthy that the exceptional pathos utilized within the story would not have worked as perfectly as it did if the first season had not focused on the relatively halcyon days of the schooling life of the cast, especially the main couple; put both seasons into the context of each other, and it becomes apparent that the time spent on the happier days of Tomoya and Nagisa is but an invitation for the viewers to make heavy emotional investments in the two, which is crucial for the execution of the high drama later on" (Ascaloth). This drama, as one has come to expect of KyoAni's series, is persistently abetted by top-notch animation capable of capturing with disarming pathos all the essential visual details on which the story's emotive impact depends — from a wide vista of nighttime sublimity to a wistful smile, from an expansive sky coursed by racing clouds to a timid glance. As *Clannad After Story* develops, the action is increasingly plagued by malevolent harbingers of separation and loss, while unearthly motifs simultaneously gain ground on the domestic dimension. Like *Kanon*, *Clannad After Story* averts a potentially tragic conclusion by invoking a supernatural agency. It is at this climactic juncture that the exact significance of Tomoya's recurrent dream is finally revealed, and the actual identities of the girl and robot seen to inhabit the anime's parallel world are thereby unveiled. The finale's otherworldly thrust reaches its apotheosis as Tomoya, now able to reverse the course of his family history, is miraculously granted the opportunity to create an alternate existence in which Nagisa miraculously survives Ushio's delivery, and the couple have a chance to raise their child together unhaunted by either sickness or loss. As Nagisa and Tomoya give Ushio her first bath, we are presented with a truly magical view of the light orbs punctuating the dream world which intersects with the real world throughout the anime.

As noted earlier in this discussion, a major stylistic trait typical of the visual novel as a ludic and narrative form consists of its dedication to gorgeously rendered backgrounds and settings. This is the feature of the parent medium which KyoAni honors most devotedly and with the most stunning results throughout its entire output. Pictorial opulence and a flair for exquisite shading and graceful chromatic nuances are essential to

KyoAni's anime, and therefore play a key role in the evocation of the environmental, atmospheric and seasonal characteristics of both individual frames and recurring scenes. As a result, they contribute crucially to the elaboration of an anime's affective drift, maintaining the audience's focus even as the story glides from one arc to another. As components of the studio's cachet which pervade its modus operandi, philosophy and mission, those visual properties deserve extensive examination at this stage in the discussion. It is worth remembering, in this context, that the term "backgrounds" strictly designates the "painted pictures used in each scene," while the term used to describe the "pictures that are to be the samples for standardizing the backgrounds" are generally referred to as "art boards." The process of background creation first requires the studio's artists to execute "line drawings" of the "art designs." With background art as with character design, multiperspectivalism is paramount. Thus, "various places and buildings are drawn from many different angles. Once the art designs have been determined, a meeting is held to determine the colors to be used. The same place will change in color depending on the time of day" ("A Close Look at an Anime Production House Part 6"). By observing even a fraction of such a meeting, one gets a clear sense of the kind of meticulous attention which KyoAni devotes to virtually each frame in assessing the colors and lighting effects most appropriate to each. Deciding which palettes are most suited to the depiction of a certain ambience at specific points in the day is not the only task in hand: establishing where the light is supposed to come from and where shadows, accordingly, should gather is no less crucial an aspect of the studio's mission.

Much of the time, KyoAni's uniqueness lies less with its introduction of original themes and techniques than with its ability to take established concepts to entirely new levels. This is bountifully demonstrated by the studio's approach to the depiction of its anime's backgrounds and settings. It is feasible that many viewers, if asked to mention the most distinctive aspects of KyoAni's cachet in the art department, would immediately cite the painstaking attention to details and chromatic sumptuousness evinced by their backgrounds and settings. It could, of course, be argued that any conscientious studio knows full well that characters simply cannot exist without contexts in relation to which they can be situated and appreciated as both individual presences and interacting personalities. In fact, even competent manga artists in both the professional and amateur arenas are likely to have learned that lesson at an early stage in their careers, well before anybody even dreamed of adapting their works to the animated format. However, the degree of sensitivity to the minutest facets of a scenery's mood and tonal gradations consistently demonstrated by KyoAni's works sets them apart not only from the average creator in the field but also from several of the most accomplished and internationally renowned names in the anime world. This confirms the proposition that it is by striving to excel where others have been content merely to succeed that KyoAni leaves a singular and indelible mark on its audience's collective memory. While these crucial components of KyoAni's signature pervade its entire output to date, they appear to acquire special prominence in the three anime studied in this chapter. This is probably a corollary of their status as adaptations of games issuing from a company whose works have themselves been repeatedly commended for the unparalleled brilliance of their own backgrounds and settings, and could therefore be seen to have fueled KyoAni's passion for those specific aspects of visual creation.

Even though its sensitivity to ambience is axial to KyoAni's achievement in the art department, it is important to recognize that this quality does not exhaust the spectrum of the studio's prismatic skills in the field. In fact, the geometrical precision of its backgrounds and settings is also pivotal to its productions, to the point that it is absurd to presume that their worth can be adequately gauged solely on the basis of affective factors, decisive though these indubitably are. The varied compositional harmonies and contrasts communicated by KyoAni's stage sets can only be properly grasped with reference to the studio's punctilious take on the technical side of the operation. Most vitally, KyoAni's sceneries handle point of view (POV) very imaginatively, often switching the angles of view and introducing new potential vanishing points to complicate and add drama to the perspective as the action progresses. At times, items such as mountains, buildings and trees seem to stretch and recede upward as the POV gets nearer to them. While their shapes show little distortion when viewed from a distance, since each point is allowed to converge on the eye with equal intensity, as the POV draws closer, they incur distortion insofar as the points nearer to the POV appear larger. This ostensibly simple principle is capable of evoking a wide range of effects in the hands of an inspired animation team, and hence facilitate the stimulation of diverse emotive responses in an audience.

KyoAni is not, it must be emphasized, interested in exploiting the ruses of perspective as a means of parading its technical virtuosity as an end in itself. In fact, it consistently capitalizes on the multifarious resources of perspective as fundamentally dramatic devices. Even a familiar strategy like the worm's-eye view can be deployed in tantalizingly unexpected ways by KyoAni's artists to communicate a sense of scale or even menace by allowing a portion of the image to tower over the spectator's point of view. A bird's-eye view may be introduced in a likewise original fashion either in order to induce a disorientating sense of vertigo by allowing viewers to see all the way down into a frightening scenario, or for the purpose of immersing viewers into a scenery by allowing them to look down into it. This type of perspectival arrangement is one of KyoAni's favorites — even though it is notoriously time-consuming in artistic circles — insofar as it enables the creator to include a stupendous amount of detail in the area surrounding the focus of the image, and is therefore a uniquely valuable means of establishing a specific spot as an important location. Furthermore, KyoAni's sets often invest a scene with a sense of realism by deploying a spatial layout in which the vanishing point falls outside the boundary of the picture. This kind of framing imparts a realistic feel on the scene because in real life, one does not necessarily perceive the finishing point of a perspective line. Thus, KyoAni's treatment of space can be seen to possess a rare form of magic: the ability to show even perfectly ordinary everyday situations in a fresh and intriguing light.

In the execution of both present-day places and quasi-historical sites, KyoAni's artists follow the premise that no locale can ever be dismissed a priori as uninteresting, and therefore approach all available localities as potential wells of inspiration. This applies to both the extant places on which they base many of their edifices, which they are actually in a position to visit in person, and the ancient venues speculatively extrapolated from historical and archaeological reconstruction. Valuable sources of reference, in KyoAni's philosophy, can be found virtually anywhere around us — and beyond. It is therefore vital to be prepared to study any locale as closely as possible, and to record one's observations systematically by taking photographs of its various aspects from many different angles. What ultimately distinguishes KyoAni's backgrounds and settings, however, is not merely their documentary accuracy. This quality is sufficient to explain the technical flawlessness of their visuals. Yet, the ultimate magic of those artworks lies in a far less definable and quantifiable power: a capacity which it is up to each individual spectator to sense and interpret in accordance with both his or her proclivities and the contextual requirements of a specific anime. This is nothing less than the ability to bring those images to life — to *animate* them through and through even though they often consists of fundamentally immobile masses. Unsurprisingly perhaps, it is in the representation of natural settings that this enlivening energy often manifests itself most vibrantly. Meticulous research into disparate facets of an area's climate, flora and distinctive color schemes appears to underpin KyoAni's habitats at every turn, regardless of the story's geographical and temporal setting. Many of KyoAni's natural locations portray sweeping vistas of sublime beauty which might at first seem to focus the eye on the setting's overall effect and away from its individual details. Nonetheless, even in these cases, the studio's passion for minutiae soon announces itself— for example, by means of an unobtrusive close-up of a bird surveying the scene. Subtle techniques are concurrently deployed in order to evoke a stirring variety of textures. Thus, a tree trunk whose shape is filled with denser shades and clearly bounded by an outline will instantly appear more concrete than one painted in soft unbound colors. The effect of bright sunlight onto a copse may be economically, yet effectively, conveyed by the presentation of its foliage as a solid mass of color with the merest sprinkle of highlights, in conjunction with radial lines cutting into the treeline. Traditionally more charged with narrative potential than any other setting, sunsets provide KyoAni with some of the best opportunities for marrying characters and settings with quiet pathos. Communicating the emotional power of its sunsets through color rather than line work, KyoAni endeavors to work the chosen hues thoroughly into its sceneries by recourse to both traditional and digital means, time and again regaling the eye with exquisite interpretations of the scattering of light particles through the atmosphere as the sun plunges below the horizon, and everything becomes briefly saturated with a coruscating glow.

KyoAni devotes no less attention to the planning of the furniture, décor and props for use in interior scenes than it channels into the design of full townscapes and landscapes. Elements of an outdoor setting can certainly be used to great effect in conjunction with particular characters to evoke symbolic associations which no amount of words could venture to record. A lonely tree stump in an ancient forest, a bench amid the hustle and bustle of a contemporary town, a traditional shopping mall or an avenue lined with cherry trees in full bloom, for example, may be employed as visual refrains throughout a series as emblematic markers of a character's disposition, and hence to capture emotions and states of mind distinctive of that persona in a trenchantly concise manner. However, it is often by means of small-scale objects or even trinkets, such as common household items, that personal attributes can be most effectively denoted and embodied. In this respect, interiors play a vital role in establishing both individual characters and their interplay within an intimate grouping. To capitalize on this aspect of stage set, KyoAni focuses closely on the specifically narrative significance of every interior. Therefore, it uses the setting to tell parts of the story in accordance with the old adage, "show, don't tell." A well-constructed indoor scene viewed from many different angles, in the studio's compositional discourse, can carry a great deal more weight than a long action sequence or a performance replete with dialogue. In order to bring out its actors' individual traits by recourse to the private spaces they inhabit, KyoAni assiduously concentrates on the representation of personal details which are capable of instantly communicating particular proclivities, tastes or idiosyncrasies typical of a specific character — and, most importantly, of impressing themselves on the audience's mind so that they will continue being associated with specific personae as the action develops. When such details are introduced into a room which features on a regular basis, the audience is discreetly invited to recognize them, and to make deductions about their possible significance at that particular point in the story. In these contexts, it becomes possible for us to sense a character's presence even if this persona is not physically included into that scene. The details themselves operate as unconscious clues to a character's *implied* presence by standing in as ghostly vestiges of the character as such.

In all three of its adaptations of Visual Art's/Key's popular games, KyoAni reveals itself capable of delivering richly varied character ensembles which audiences can go on cherishing over repeat viewings thanks to their knack of coming across as deeply familiar, and yet uncanny enough to discourage total identification. These personae remain observable as separate entities from an independent critical angle even when their experiences strike well-known chords. In this respect, the three anime closely echo the visual novels at their roots. Indeed, the kind of enjoyment which the source games provide depends vitally on the employment of characters whom players can identify with, on the one hand, and distance themselves from on the other. In this way, it is possible for players to view even unpleasant developments, such as a character's moral or physical failure, as potential sources of entertainment. Players would be unlikely to entertain any positive impressions in the face of blatant personality limitations if they identified with the game's actors so unequivocally as to experience those characters' flaws as their own. However, this does not altogether negate the possibility of character immersion coming into play in a conscientiously measured manner. Visual Art's/Key is an undisputable genius when it comes to striking the perfect balance between identification and distance. No less importantly, it is by replicating this very balance in the context of its anime adaptations that KyoAni is able to give us characters which combine elements of familiarity and elements of uncanniness in their makeup, and accordingly invite identification one moment, and critical self-separation the next. On this point, the studio's perspective on its source materials is strongly redolent of Petri Lankoski's contention that the ways in which players experience role-playing games and interact with their characters and plots result from the establishment of "goals" and the related emergence of "emotions" which fuel the desire to achieve them. "Goals," argues the critic, "are the very basis of character immersion and emotional experience. As a player evaluates the character's goals meaningfully and takes them as hers in the game, she is able to experience 'shared emotions'—to feel what the character would feel in the situation." While emphasizing that clear objectives are "important," Lankoski also maintains that "habitus" holds no less crucial a function as the "framework for understanding events and decision-making" (Lankoski, p. 140).

KyoAni reflects these positions in its distinctive modus operandi. It defines the adapted characters' aims as key aspects of their overall personalities and actions, thereby prompting its audience to embrace those objectives and hence participate in the affects which the characters themselves channel into their attainment. In so doing, it relies on the concept of "habitus" as defined by the philosopher Pierre Bourdieu, who describes this social phenomenon as the product of specific "conditions of existence" which lead to the conception of "different definitions of impossible" or "probable," and thus "cause one group to experience as natural or reasonable practices or aspirations which another group finds unthinkable or scandalous, and vice versa" (Bourdieu, p. 78). Therefore, habitus could be seen as the agency which shapes the audience's grasp of the characters' aims, and enables it temporarily to embrace those aims as its own, in accordance with its contingent cultural context. At the same time, KyoAni's self-reflexive proclivities ensure that the audience does not lose sight of the constructed narrative/dramatic status of those objectives as ruses conceived by directors and animators in order to sustain a specific viewing process. Thus, we are able to enjoy the drama at the visceral level by relating intimately to its personae, and even immersing ourselves in its complications, and yet be aware of its artifice — which is in itself a fount of entertainment — and preserve the aesthetic distance which permits our imaginative involvement in the story's creation.

Homage to Kyoto Animation

"Love them or hate them, few studios have a had a bigger impact on the anime industry in the past five years than Kyoto Animation. Haruhi, Clannad, Lucky☆Star, K-ON!— their lineup reads like an Anime Greatest Hits list covering 2005 to the present. While their choice in Slice-of-Life adaptations may not be everyone's cup of green tea, they've become the best at what they do by mastering one particular skill: subtlety.

Subtlety, along with her twin sister Nuance, is not often associated with televised anime. They tend to hang out with respected film directors and shy away from the gaudy colors, loud exclamations, and gratuitous fan service found on TV.... So personally I find a well made Slice-of-Life show refreshing every now and then. A good show in the genre is all about appreciating those details in life and KyoAni has honed that skill to perfection over the years."— jel x

4

Art and Play

Play is intrinsic to human nature, a way of understanding ourselves, each other, the world we live in, so it's no surprise that several social scientists and philosophers have highlighted its importance to our cognitive and physical development, emotional growth, and social interaction. Play manifests itself most obviously in the form of games, which have their own structures and rules, but it's also vital to our sense of freedom, reminding us that we're not entirely bound to society's rigid regulations, the often obstinate, unyielding codes of community. Free play provides an escape (or to be more precise, an excursion) from these rules, allowing us to frolic mentally and physically in the margins of necessity — and find pleasure in doing so. We can't imagine a world without play because imagination is play in its purest, most personal form. It follows that art, as the product of imagination, is a form of play, and that creative artists of all kinds are, in essence, players. — Paul Benedict Grant

Play is the exultation of the possible. — Martin Buber

The anime examined in this chapter epitomize KyoAni's knack of communicating the wonders of the quotidian in the most unequivocal terms imaginable. As argued in the foregoing chapters, the two *Munto* OVAs, *Full Metal Panic? Fumoffu*, *Full Metal Panic! The Second Raid*, *The Melancholy of Haruhi Suzumiya* and *The Disappearance of Haruhi Suzumiya* all attest to this ability in their loving consideration of the most prosaic occurrences in their protagonists' lives even though their narrative and dramatic premises draw quite heavily on sci fi motifs. *Air*, *Kanon*, *Clannad* and *Clannad After Story* evince no less hearty an appetite for the ordinary as the repository of unparalleled, albeit often neglected, marvels even though extraordinary phenomena ultimately sustain their development and resolution. Thus, the desire to throw into relief the unique power of the everyday is never far from KyoAni's sensibility. However, in their assessment of anime with sci fi or otherworldly underpinnings, viewers may be inclined to attribute the impression of wonder which their stories evoke to those explicitly exceptional aspects of their makeup. *Lucky☆Star*, *K-ON!* and *Nichijou* do not afford this option. The events they dramatize are consummately and incontrovertibly ordinary. They feature no miracles, portents, prodigies or superpowers, and make no concessions to the classic formulae of the epic, the fairy tale or the action adventure blockbuster. Nevertheless, they gradually reveal themselves capable of conveying a palpable sense of the marvelous as their — largely uneventful — events accrue over time. With *Hyouka*, its latest creation to date, KyoAni gives us a first-time hybrid in which the everyday plays no less substantial a role than it does in *Lucky☆Star*, *K-ON!* and *Nichijou* but discloses its power in a different fashion. That is to say, it does not assert itself as an uninterrupted, monolithic reality but actually incorporates various hints at the extraordinary. However, these are not couched in incontrovertibly fantastic terms as they are in the two *Full Metal Panic* series, the *Haruhi Suzumiya* franchise or the visual novel adaptations. In fact, they are ironically presented *as though* they were perfectly commonplace, which imparts their presentation with uncanny overtones of a power not seen before in KyoAni's output. This strategy bears witness to the studio's attraction to the immense potentialities inherent in the "*as though*" as the springboard of all stories, all entertainment and ultimately all creativity — in other words, as the soul of art and play as a composite entity.

The analyses offered in this chapter endeavor to bring out the peculiar sense of the extraordinary exuding from KyoAni's ostensibly most *unextraordinary* shows by focusing on their themes, characters and settings, alongside distinctive facets of their formal orchestration. The discussion proposes that the ingredient on which all of the anime under scrutiny capitalize, to various degrees, as a means of evoking their vision of the marvelous is their conviction that both the practice and the reception of art in all its guises should always accommodate a ludic component. In this matter, their visions could be said to echo one of the pivotal lessons promulgated by Zen, here understood as a way of life more than as a doctrine. In the words, in themselves both artful and playful, of an anonymous Zen poet, this message proposes that "the person who is a master in the art of living makes little distinction between their work and their play, their labor and their leisure, their mind and their body, their education and their recreation, their love and their religion. They hardly know which is which. They simply pursue their vision of excellence and grace in whatever they do, leaving others to decide whether they are working or playing. To them, they are always doing both" ("Zen Buddhism"). No less relevant to KyoAni's approach to the interaction of art and play is Octavio Paz's tantalizing contention that "art is an invention of aesthetics, which in turn is an invention of philosophers.... What we call art is a game" (Paz). The four anime concentrate on different arts. *Lucky☆Star* prioritizes the arts of anime and manga (and other related forms) with its otaku protagonist, while *K-ON!* pivots on light music as the art through which its heroines evolve as both individuals and members of a community. With *Nichijou*, it is the art of living itself that gives shape to an otherwise fragmentary story through a focus on the joys and trials of day-to-day human intercourse. *Hyouka*, finally, deploys the art of literature, specifically as embodied in time-honored classics, as the fulcrum around which its protagonists' experiences unfold with paradoxically ordinary eeriness — or eerie ordinariness as the case may be.

KyoAni's treatment of the art-play pair frequently invokes, with varying degrees of explicitness, the concept of *moe*: an aesthetic term designating innocent childlike charm as embodied by cute characters (often but not necessarily female) likely to inspire protective and nurturing attitudes in the viewer. These characters' physical appearance is typically matched by the use of cute speech patterns and lexicon, while their personalities tend to be lively, enthusiastic and spontaneous without, however, coming across as downright strong or independent. A certain lack of maturity, therefore, is instrumental in the achievement of a successful *moe* portrait. The most popular character categories in the area include the *meganekko-moe* (cute character with glasses), the *meido-moe* and *shitsuji-moe* (stereotypical cute maid or butler), the *tsundere-moe* (the adorably tough and innerly caring character), the *imouto-moe* (the younger sister cutie). KyoAni's anime have featured elements of *moe* right from the beginning of the studio's career. *Lucky☆Star* is arguably the first of its titles in which the *moe* aesthetic asserts itself as a major player, while *K-ON!*, *Nichijou* and *Hyouka* can be seen to offer subsequent variations on, and enhancements of, the initial formula. In the specific context of anime, the word *moe* is normally expressed by means of the kanji signifying "to bud" or "to sprout," 萌え. This term could be said to describe both succinctly and poetically the type of young character in which the qualities of *moe* find a natural host. However, the word *moe* is also a homonym for 燃え, which means "to burn." This term can be invoked to allude to the consuming passion experienced by viewers who are so strongly drawn to the *moe* type as to nourish a somewhat obsessive fascination with its on-screen incarnations. *Moe*'s detractors draw attention to this proclivity to argue that the graphic trend which idealizes the image of the adorable young girl serves the dubious purpose of pandering to the erotic fantasies of a typically male viewer. This negative interpretation of *moe* has been fueled by the emergence and rapid spread of the so-called "Lolita complex" (*lolicon*), a fetish-oriented syndrome with the *moe* character at its affective fulcrum. In fact, it is worth noting that the "Lolita" type often linked up with *moe* on both the broadly stylistic and the specifically sartorial levels is essentially a charming female character characteristically clad in clothes of Victorian, Rococo, Regency or Gothic derivation who may radiate erotic appeal but appears to do so in an essentially unselfconscious fashion. This is clearly borne out, for instance, by KyoAni's portrayal of *K-ON!*'s heroines in costumes inspired by that style in the sequence used for the ending theme of the anime's first season. (Both this sequence and the Lolita vogue will be returned to later in the discussion.)

It is necessary, in the present context, not to assess *moe* monolithically in sexual terms, even though its underlying sexiness is what many people tend to associate with the graphic conventions followed in the depiction of certain types of anime characters. Firstly, *moe* should be recognized as being, at least at root, an offshoot of a genuine desire to give visible form to valuable human qualities and to the corresponding affects which such qualities can be expected to elicit — above all, artless attractiveness resulting from an unscheming heart and mind. Secondly, and more importantly, *moe* echoes the Zen world view and the value accorded therein to childlike innocence and spontaneity. At the same time, it is fruitful to evaluate the concept in relation to another long-standing aspect of Japanese art: the consistent valorization of the principle of simplicity in tandem with a contrasting passion for colorful exuberance. The aura of unpretentious charm exuded by many of KyoAni's *moe* characters is especially redolent of the concept of *kanso* as a form of simplicity distinguished by the preference for freshness, neatness and spontaneity. Personae as diverse as Tessa from *Full Metal Panic? Fumoffu* and *Full Metal Panic! The Second Raid*, Mikuru from *The Melancholy of Haruhi Suzumiya*, Ayu from *Kanon* and Konata from *Lucky☆Star*, to cite but a few popular instances, clearly confirm that contention. *Kanso* entails the "elimination of clutter" and a positive invitation "to think not in terms of decoration but in terms of clarity, a kind of clarity that may be achieved through omission or exclusion of the non-essential" ("7 Japanese aesthetic principles to change your thinking"). Furthermore, while *moe* attributes seem to flow spontaneously from the characters who possess them, they are carefully cultivated by their creators as elements of an aesthetic with a specific code of its own. Ironically, therefore, they are neither impulsive nor fortuitous. On this point, KyoAni's handling of *moe* brings to mind the aesthetic tenet known as *shizen*— the pursuit of "true naturalness as distinct from raw nature." *Shizen* is motivated by "a sense of creativity and purpose distinct from the naive or accidental." Even though "nothing involving *shizen* should be forced or self-conscious," the impression of "true naturalness" it seeks to foster is "a negation of the naive and the accidental. *Shizen* has about it a sense of artlessness and an absence of pretense or artificiality, but it involves full creative intent and should never be forced" (Tierney).

It should also be noted, in this context, that *moe* represents a paradigmatic illustration of the peculiar processes whereby words meant to describe abstract concepts shift and morph over time. As Martin points out in the article "Marcel Theroux goes in search of *wabi-sabi*," "'moe,' when first introduced, meant one thing. Now that the word has been absorbed into popular culture," it has become "a 'brand' and it is something completely different.... When *moe* first emerged as a concept it was used to describe the undescribable, a form of eroticism and aesthetic (erotic) appreciation that couldn't be categorised or compartmentalised. *Moe* was not fetishism, nor could it be faked. *Moe* was innocent, non aggressive and, perhaps above all, unintentional.... With *moe* being absorbed into popular culture it is no longer what it was, *moe* is now categorised and compartamentalised, it is even regarded as cute by society" (Martin). Even when KyoAni's treatment of *moe* brings into the equation the specifically erotic import of the concept, this is by no means automatically tantamount to either fetishism or perversity. In actuality, it is elliptically redolent of the longstanding philosophical legacy of the principle of *nikukanteki*. As De Mente explains, this term designates "sexual attractiveness" and the power to arouse "sensual feelings" in a spontaneous fashion, in accordance with the ancient teachings of Shintō: "Japanese culture," the critic continues, "owes its unabashed sensuality, which is both stated and unstated, to Shintō, which is based on sexual reproduction and growth. Unlike religions based on suppressing and limiting human sexuality, Shintō celebrates it ... with gusto" (De Mente). In this perspective, it becomes possible to view the incorporation of a sensuous element into the concept of *moe* as a totally inoffensive gesture meant neither to reify the cute characters into fetishistic props nor to ignite nasty drives in their viewers.

Moreover, it is crucial to acknowledge that KyoAni's presentation of *moe* cannot be dismissed as a facile exercise in eroticized cuteness insofar as it consistently entails, albeit in an often understated fashion, an undercurrent of wistfulness which captures the quintessentially Japanese aesthetic concept of *mono no aware* (物の哀れ) — a melancholy sensitivity to the inexorable passing of beauty, pleasure and, ultimately, life itself. In the *K-ON!* franchise, for example, this feeling is encapsulated by increasingly unavoidable intimations that the Light Music Club as conceived by Ritsu, Mio, Yui and Mugi is bound to come to an end when their days as junior high-school students come to an end — an inevitability which the protagonists do not fully seem to recognize until the aftermath of their performance at what is bound to be their last school festival prior to each band member's progression to a different academic establishment. Up until this point, the girls' awareness of the ineluctable ephemerality of their venture has been discreetly hinted at on numerous occasions but generally prevented from holding center stage as though to suggest that they have been unwittingly endeavoring to disavow and anesthetize its force. Nevertheless, the audience has been made sensitive to their underlying predicament by the character of Azusa who, as the only second-year member of the *Hokago Tea Time* ("After School Tea Time") ensemble, has known all along that the club she has come to love is not to last forever — at least not in the form given it by its idiosyncratic founders. Azusa, in this respect, operates as a lens through which the viewer is able to evaluate the action's deeper conceptual import, and hence savor the ubiquitous influence of *mono no aware* over a substantial portion of the drama's unfolding.

There are many viewers among audiences of all ages, genders and backgrounds who enjoy a certain element of *moe* in their anime as a pure source of visual pleasure, particularly in the depiction of young female characters, but deem its use in shows with pointedly sexual contents rather unsavory and bound to deaden its spirit in the service of robotic titillation. From these viewers' perspective, it is crucial for *moe* to retain an aura of playful candor if it is not to lose its essential aesthetic grace. KyoAni's approach to *moe* evinces precisely the kind of balance which such spectators desire by encapsulating an ideal of artless female charm which conforms with the fundamental philosophical import of that concept without straying into the territory of gratuitously salacious or risqué imagery. Triple_R enthusiastically promulgates this contention, arguing that by situating its depictions of *moe* "within the confines of anatomically correct character designs, Kyoto Animation reaches a certain idealized form of *moe*. A *moe* that feels real and sincere. A *moe with integrity*.... In Kyoto Animation titles, the presence of *moe* feels more like an honest and respectable artstyle and/or character design choice, and not like simple lowbrow pandering to the fans" (Triple_R). Writing specifically about *K-ON!*, The Captain pursues a related argument, proposing that although some may argue that the anime's "biggest selling point is the *moe* factor," it steers clear of all the strategies stereotypically deployed by many studios to exploit the allure of *moe*. Thus, the reviewer invites us to "compare it to most other *moe*-oriented shows ... and ask: Is it a harem? Does it bounce boobs every episode? Does it show cleavage every episode? Does it show upskirts every episode? Does it feature private parts? Does it use sexual innuendoes?" In response to these questions, the critic concludes: "the answer to all of the above is, of course, a rock-solid No. Yet, without resorting to these kind of cheap tactics, it has captured the hearts of millions all over the world, proving that you don't need any sexual elements to gain a rabid fandom" (The Captain).

In the construction of *Lucky☆Star*, which is based on a four-panel comic strip manga by Kagami Yoshimizu, one of KyoAni's priorities was clearly to maximize the show's slice-of-life dimension by conveying the impression that the occurrences it records could really be unfolding from one day to the next in a casual and largely unplanned fashion rather than in accordance with some grand teleological scheme. To this effect, the anime adopts a realistically loose storyline charting the everyday interactions of an appropriately diversified cast within a likewise convincing setting. *Lucky☆Star*'s realism is reinforced by the utterly prosaic and enthusiastically inconsequential nature of the subject matter dealt with in many of its dialogues. Admittedly, this is an aspect of the series which not all audiences automatically enjoy. There are viewers, even among KyoAni's most devoted aficionados, who harbor reservations about the dramatic or comical value of a relatively lengthy conversation on the topic of which end of a chocolate cornet constitutes the top and which the bottom. Even the more impatient spectators, however, will be likely to concede that such potential flaws are more than adequately compensated for by the richness of the personalities animating *Lucky☆Star*'s sitcom-type milieu, and by the quality of the animation deployed by KyoAni throughout to abet character dynamics. Although the graphic style used in the depiction of the anime's personae is generally more cartoonishly colorful and less detailed than one would normally expect of KyoAni, this does not detract from the show's overall realism insofar as it is consistently counterbalanced by fluid motion and by subtle artistic touches capable of matching perfectly the thoughts and feelings coursing through a scene — regardless of the depth of its verbal content. Even though the show deliberately sacrifices action to dialogue, when dynamism is required, it is beautifully rendered, meticulously detailed, and sensitive to the significance of body language as an invaluable character marker.

Since the story's characters — allied to the anime's penchant for capturing the weird minutiae of ordinary life with disarming frankness — play a crucial part in imparting it with its instantly recognizable identity, the major players deserve some attention in this context. Bradley Meek's portrayal of *Lucky☆Star*'s protagonist is particularly worthy of notice in assessing the anime's take on the art-play dyad: "Konata Izumi is a high school otaku hardcore enough to know trivia about seventies giant robot and *tokusatsu* shows," the critic proposes, "but not hardcore enough to own a bodypillow of her *waifu* [a 2D significant other]. Or at least, not yet.... But despite her weird habit of throwing out obscure gaming references, she's not socially dysfunctional" (Meek). This last comment constitutes a crucial qualifier because Konata's retention of normal interactive skills sets her story apart from several other anime centered on the mock trials and tribulations of obsessive fandom, such as *Otaku no Video* (dir. Takeshi Mori, 1991) and *Genshiken* (dirs. Takashi Ikehata, 2004; Kinji Yoshimoto, 2007). In both of these titles, emphasis is squarely laid on social dysfunctionality even though comedy plays an important part in both. Konata, for her part, never becomes alienated from her friends. As a result, the show exudes a genuine sense of comradeship redolent of KyoAni's treatment of the same theme in works as diverse as *Munto*, the *Full Metal Panic* series and *K-ON!* Accordingly, *Lucky☆Star*'s characters are honestly portrayed as friends and not merely clustered together for plot convenience. This is eloquently evinced by KyoAni's depiction of the protagonist's interaction with her non-otaku friends, and particularly Miyuki Takara, and the sisters Tsukasa and Kagami Hiiragi. Airheaded and delectably gauche, Miyuki stands out as a classic incarnation of the *meganekko* — namely, as noted, the *moe* type whose charm derives largely from the wearing of glasses — while also appearing to have a soothing effect on those around her by virtue of her sheer presence. The adorable and frivolous Tsukasa conforms to the dramatic role of the little sister in both her actual age and her behavior. Kagami, conversely, does her best to use her natural intelligence and conscientiousness to come across as a responsible adult, at times exhibiting the traits of a typical *tsundere* (the apparently tough girl who gradually reveals a softer underside). Despite their differences, the two girls share a generous disposition toward the protagonist. Thus, while neither Tsukasa nor Kagami seem inclined to acquire Konata's passion to addictive extremes, they respond to her idiosyncrasies in an accommodating fashion. Meek corroborates this point: "Konata will try to drag her friends to Comicon (twice), will often throw out references that go over her friends' heads, and will single-handedly stimulate the Japanese economy by feeding her otaku habit.... When she buys fanzines and *doujinshii*, she always buys three copies: one to read, and two to keep in the wrapper as collectibles. She gets a job at a cosplay café just to make sure can collect a full set of some new trading cards. Her friends are usually mystified by her behavior, but go along for the ride anyway" (Meek).

Through the character of Konata, *Lucky☆Star* asserts triumphantly its status as a metacomedy by dealing self-reflexively with the arts of anime, manga, videogaming (and other otaku-related activities) as thematic leading threads. KyoAni's treatment of Konata's otaku proclivities bears witness to the studio's fascination with irony: a trope, as noted, which can be seen to course through the studio's output as a major trait of both its philosophy and its modus operandi. In the case of *Lucky☆Star*, the irony consists of the anime's double perspective on otakuism. On the one hand, the series evinces a propensity to play up to many of the character stereotypes and narrative formulae found in various kinds of anime, manga and computer games in a self-conscious and deliberate fashion. This side of *Lucky☆Star* underscores its dispassionately metafictional thrust, and ability to observe its materials with a modicum of analytical distance. On the other hand, the show portrays its own protagonist as a fan so addicted to those formulae and stereotypes as to have lost the sense of distance necessary to see them for what they are. Thus, Konata persistently assesses the situations she witnesses in the real world with reference to how anime, manga or games would deal with analogous circumstances. In so doing, she strives to establish whether her world manages to match up to the worlds depicted in the products she avidly consumes — or else fails to do so. Through these ruses, the anime throws into relief the extent to which the fetishistic addictions which develop around certain media have the noxious capacity to warp a person's entire take on reality. One of the series' most memorable components lies precisely with KyoAni's handling of the ironical tension between its critical appropriation of the arts cherished by otaku, and its protagonist's generally uncritical take on those same arts.

Insofar as the arts treasured by Konata are persistently presented as the nub of the show's comic dimension, *Lucky☆Star* can be said to celebrate the marriage of art and play quite explicitly as a major component of its diegesis. Simultaneously, the anime's loving depiction of the everyday by means of exchanges which, though by and large funny, also offer occasions for thoughtful responses, allow its appeal to extend well beyond the boundaries of otakudom. The distinctive simplicity of *Lucky☆Star*'s character design, described earlier in this discussion, brings those two aspects of the show together. It does so by showcasing the graphic codes and conventions which many viewers would instantly associate with anime (and its sister arts) in an eminently uncomplicated fashion. At the same time, it emphasizes the show's philosophical message regarding the unique value of the quotidian in tersely symbolic terms. Most importantly, insofar as the show reveals itself capable of identifying and dramatizing the funny, quirky or touching details of ordinary life down to their tiniest component, its comedy is grounded in narrative and dramatic elements which both established anime fans and newcomers to the art could identify with and cherish — or at the very least smile at knowingly. Even a seemingly marginal comment can at times cut to the quick as we recognize how neatly it describes a trait of our own or our friends' behavior. Concomitantly, the story gains substance through KyoAni's inclusion of an eddy of serious emotions revolving around the protagonist's private experience of loss: in spite of her cheerfulness and felinely enticing smile, Konata lost her mother when she was only a kid, which has clearly left indelible marks on her personality.

In their involvement, through zeal or merely tolerance, with the products of the otaku-favored arts, the daily experiences of Konata and her friends conflate art and play in more ways than one. Not only is the art material repeatedly employed as the trigger of their jocular conversations and exploits: it also functions as the substance of their play in the sense of play as performance, or staged action. As a matter of fact, it could be argued that without that art-related matter, the anime would lack its most precious opportunities for entertainment and movement. Concomitantly, the art stuff also enables the characters to enact their play specifically as a form of role-play — i.e., the assumption of dramatic parts through which the characters can give visible and animate shape to inimitable facets of the personalities, and allow both their strengths and their foibles to come into the open. These interrelated aspects of the concept of play — and of its multifarious coalescence with the notion of art — pervades *Lucky☆Star* from beginning to end, informing both the main series and the vignette-style OVA with equal fervor.

—⁂—

An extensive franchise based on the four-panel comic strip manga by Kakifly, *K-ON!* encompasses two TV series, *K-ON!* and *K-ON!!* (a.k.a. *K-ON! Season 2*), as well as two OVAs (episode 14 in the first season and episode 27 in the second season), and a movie. Its title is an abbreviation of *kei ongaku* ("light music"): the phrase designating the name of the after-school club (*kei ongaku bukatsu* or *keionbu* for short) which brings the anime's protagonists together in the first place, and leads to the foundation of the *Ho-kago Tea Time* band (HTT), while also providing an invaluable arena for their personal and collective development. Before embarking into a detailed analysis of *K-ON!*'s handling of the art-play duet, a panoramic look at its key personae appears desirable. What the following portraits will hopefully show is that none of the anime's main characters could be unequivocally compartmentalized as a stereotype insofar as they all exhibit prismatic constitutions in which contrasting affects and proclivities alternately clash and collude to give rise to tantalizingly original personalities. Yui Hirasawa is scatty, immature and overly dependent on an almost embarrassingly responsible younger sister, Ui, who in fact seems to worship the very ground Yui walks on and hence to be totally blind to her weaknesses. As the HTT's main vocalist and lead guitarist, Yui is undoubtedly the soul of the band even though when she first joins it she has never even touched a musical instrument before. Though Yui's attention span is almost abnormally minimal, her likewise exceptional determination endows her with an impressive degree of concentration when she has a clear aim in sight. Yui's passionate commitment to her guitar, which she anthropomorphizes to deliciously absurd extremes, her absolute pitch, and her natural flair as an entertainer make her quite a competent performer despite her undeniable technical failings. In addition, Yui is uncommonly generous and exhibits unexpected sensitivity and ingenuity on numerous occasions.

The most sophisticated, classically attractive and academically accomplished member of the HTT, Mio Akiyama is the band's bass player and second vocalist. Despite her awe-inspiring gifts, Mio is endearingly humanized by her childish dread of anything even remotely spooky and by her shyness, which results in a pathological fear of being in the spotlight, and also explains her choice of the bass guitar as an instrument which allows her to avoid the agony of center stage. The girl's depiction as the very incarnation of modesty and propriety in both appearance and body language also allows her charismatic *moe* assets to shine through. This is epitomized by the installment in which the other girls, in an attempt to help Mio overcome her timidity, join her as temporary waitresses at an exclusive café, and she is accordingly encouraged to don the most fetching maid costume imaginable. A sassy tomboy with an imaginative sense of humor, drummer Ritsu Tainaka (a.k.a. Ricchan) is the most pragmatic of the band's members, her heartily down-to-earth approach to both music and life at large occasionally bordering on hard-nosedness. So resolutely unsentimental as to sometimes seem totally impervious to emotions, Ritsu nonetheless evinces a weak spot when it comes to her relationship with Mio, her best mate since early childhood. Ritsu's attachment to her cherished friend is so powerful that the slightest indication that Mio might be bonding with other school friends beyond a certain limit is enough to kindle Ritsu's jealousy and fear of abandonment.

Easy-going, dreamy and quite unfamiliar with many practical facets of everyday life which have hitherto never featured in her immensely privileged lifestyle, Tsumugi Kotobuki (a.k.a. Mugi) is the club's keyboard player — as well as the provider of hugely valuable tea sets and magnificent gourmet cakes to abet the club's favorite pursuit. Mugi's aristocratic otherness is touchingly highlighted by the episodes where she engages in perfectly mundane activities which to her have the feel of extraordinary adventures. A case in point is the sequence in which she visits a bargain candy store with Ritsu, experiencing even the most commonplace sweets as sources of infinite delight. Another memorable instance is the installment where a visit to a hardware store discloses what to Mugi's eyes constitutes a veritable treasurehouse of fascinating mysteries. Azusa Nakano (a.k.a. Azu-nyan) is a younger student who joins the club in the hope of perfecting her already remarkable abilities as a guitarist. Azusa is at first bitterly disappointed to discover that her seniors hardly ever practice at all, and in fact spend most of their after-school time ... well, *having tea* indeed as the name of their group intimates — alongside gorgeous pastries, tarts, rolls and related dainties issuing from Mugi's family pantry, which typically abounds with top-quality specialties from all over the world. In spite of her initial disapproval, which is sometimes conducive to Azusa's assumption of a censorious attitude befitting a conservative grown-up, the young girl comes to appreciate the value of the club as a space in which both she and her new mates may embark in precious voyages of self-discovery — though not necessarily ascend to the heights of musical excellence, let alone make it to the Budokan: the band's self-appointed goal. There are viewers who initially find Azusa's introduction into the light music club somewhat upsetting, fearing that it may disrupt the dramatic balance and affective harmony intrinsic in the character dynamics already established among the group's members prior to the younger girl's advent on the scene. However, these misgivings tend to evaporate once Azusa begins to transcend the role of disciplinarian in residence suggested by her excessively stringent outlook. As the girl's mentality evolves over time, she learns what it means to have fun. She concurrently realizes that there is nothing wrong about *wanting* to have fun, and even begins to develop a taste for laziness, frivolous pursuits and blissfully inconsequential fooling around. In other words, Azusa gradually discovers that without an element of play, art remains lifeless — that it may still deliver technically remarkable outcomes but is bound to lack the spirit which renders it animate and hence appealing. In witnessing these developments, even the most reticent spectators are likely to welcome Azusa's advent into the HTT's midst as a catalyst enabling the real strengths of the other girls — both as individuals and as an ensemble — to shine through in their full glory. At the same time, the younger girl's intervention can help us appreciate properly the existential significance of play as the indispensable substratum of all human-made arts, in this case music, and also, ultimately, of the intricate art of growing up. In this regard, *K-ON!* could be described as a bildungsroman woven on the magic duo of art and play.

One last character deserving of mention at this stage is the light music club's adviser, Sawako Yamanaka (a.k.a. Sawa-chan): a gentle, industrious and sociable teacher with a lazy underside and an enthusiastic appetite for tea-time delicacies. She also harbors a somewhat fetishistic passion for cosplay costumes of questionable appeal, which persistently results in attempts to dress up the five members of the light music club in all manner of fanciful outfits. Sawako is said to have been a key member of the school's light music club in her days there as a student, at which point she enjoyed a rather dubious reputation as a fierce member of a death metal band. While Sawako strives to keep this background secret in order to cultivate the image of a caring and dependable teacher, she has clearly retained a visceral attraction to the hardcore end of the music scene, and the sight of a stage and spotlights is enough to reawaken her wildest death-metal drives.

K-ON! is close in tone to *Lucky☆Star* but keener to bring out the slice-of-life component of its heroines' daily experiences and gentler in its deployment of humor. These attributes impart the anime with stylistic individuality while also enabling it to surpass codes and conventions associated with the regular cute-girl show. Cuteness is undoubtedly prominent throughout on the stylistic level but instead of being exploited as a rigid point of reference meant to govern the whole viewing experience, it is by and large used as a mobile narrative tool which always allows for the possibility of imaginative reorientations as the anime progresses. Hence, *K-ON!*'s brand of cuteness serves to instill the drama with energy and pace even in the segments where the action element is minimal, thereby exuding an uplifting sense of freshness, vivaciousness and spontaneity. While these traits are already evident in the first season of the TV show, it is in the second season and movie that KyoAni develops them specifically for the purpose of ensuring greater character development, which unleashes opportunities for the articulation of both deeper emotive moments and a sharper humor (occasionally redolent in mood of *The Melancholy of Haruhi Suzumiya*). Throughout the franchise, *K-ON!*'s harmonious character chemistry — so magical as to feel more akin to alchemy than to chemistry proper — undoubtedly plays a key role in guaranteeing its dramatic effectiveness, positing the girls' play drives as its elements ,and the art of music as the catalyst capable of bringing those elements into fruitful collusion. Art provides the syntax able to organize and sustain the anime's expressive acts, as music and musical instruments supply the vital punctuation marks for the play the girls perform from day to day. Left to its own resources, the play alone would no doubt be fun but would remain somewhat inchoate insofar as it would lack the means of channeling its energy into truly enjoyable events. It would be akin to a mass of words devoid of any structural underpinnings.

As the story develops, one aspect of the *K-ON!* universe remains constantly amazing throughout: its candid exposure of just how much an inspired director can achieve, and an audience experience, by focusing exclusively on a bunch of school girls sitting around a club room having tea and cakes — and occasionally, but only *occasionally*, playing music. It is at times hard to believe that *K-ON!* has been able to attain the caliber for which it is internationally credited with so little happening. Its distinctive tempo contributes vitally to the anime's overall impact. No scenes are wasted or gratuitously inserted and the action, accordingly, never appears to drag inexcusably. Moreover, when it does crawl along, is quite clear that its sluggish pace has been deliberately adopted as an integral aspect of its performative identity. This is paradigmatically exemplified by the episode charting the activities which fill a relentlessly rainy day, where the rhythm almost imperceptibly slackens from one scene to the next until one senses that the characters' increasing inertia is fueling their habitat's watery stillness no less than the environment itself is contributing to their apathetic state. Most crucially, as the day unfolds, the girls' languorous idleness does not simply evoke a negative atmosphere of torpor but gradually morphs into a state of utter calm capable of transmitting a soothing sense of repose. This installment epitomizes one of *K-ON!*'s most pervasive and most intriguing qualities: an honest acknowledgment of its objectives whereby it never tries to exceed its means and scope. Both honest and modest in its aims and methods, the anime knows how to be exceptionally unexceptional. From this perspective, the gold nugget at the heart of its charm could be said to consist of its unobtrusive promotion of a philosophy of simplicity which is utterly congruous with KyoAni's overarching vision as delineated in this book's opening chapter. Such a philosophy is borne out by the characters' progressive recognition of the incomparable value of the people and things that surround them on a daily basis. This message is thrown into relief with special pathos in second-season installment where Ui catches a cold and is temporarily incapacitated: the incident enables Yui to appreciate the sheer magnitude of her dependence on the loyal sibling, which in turn results in her composition of one of the series' most touching songs, "U&I."

To emphasize further its sustaining philosophy, in some scenes, *K-ON!* relies on a technical strategy somewhat unusual in KyoAni's output: namely, a relative avoidance of details. Not only is this ploy perfectly consonant with the anime's penchant for refined simplicity: it also serves as a visual metaphor capable of evoking a slight sense of vagueness. This, in turn, enables the drama to conjure up the element of mystery at the heart of the everyday in tersely poetic terms. Thus, KyoAni's deliberate use of haziness in *K-ON!* can be seen as a means of encapsulating the wonder of ordinary experience gently and economically rather than in an overtly didactic form, which would have been totally incongruous with the anime's overall tone. It would be preposterous, after all, to attribute *K-ON!*'s occasional eschewal of details to laziness on the studio's part since the anime is technically impeccable in all respects. For one thing, in the majority of scenes, *K-ON!* actually lingers on the tiniest nuances of its settings and of its characters' facial expressions and body language with undisputable brilliance. The movements of their fingers as they interact with strings, keys and drum sticks augment the overall sense of dynamic authenticity to unique effect. Furthermore, the meticulousness of KyoAni's creative effort is patently demonstrated by its consistently crisp motion and frame rates, which contribute vitally to imparting the action with a refreshing impression of raw energy. Enhanced throughout by catchy music, this contrasts perfectly with the mellowness conveyed by the intentionally less detailed scenes.

As argued in Chapter 1, KyoAni's graphics exude a philosophical message of critical significance to Japanese aesthetics at large: the imperative to adopt a deeply respectful attitude toward one's materials and tools. *K-ON!* in all its configurations (but increasingly as the franchise develops) bears eloquent witness to this contention. This lesson is most tersely conveyed by the sequences in which the characters either practice their songs or else engage in conversations concerning their instruments and their personal attitudes to these objects, which show that they acknowledge them as major identity definers, endowed with autonomous life and hence deserving of proper names. As noted in the article "This is why *K-ON* is worth your time," "*K-ON* doesn't show much of the girls actually PLAYING the instruments, but whenever they appear on screen, they almost always drawn very close to the real thing" (The Captain). The same reverential stance to materials and tools is also perceptible in scenes which do not concern themselves with the art of music — or indeed any other "art" in the academic sense of the term — but rather focus on daily activities such as cooking to show that these constitute no less honorable a category of human endeavor than the so-called high arts. The value of these activities is presented as inseparable from the energy which they derive from the materials and tools at their core. *K-ON!*'s emphasis on the physical side of creativity contributes vitally to its character dynamics, and this is what makes it a major aspect of the franchise in its entirety. At the same time, its culturally specific significance should not be overlooked insofar as it bears witness to a proclivity which pervades the whole of KyoAni's oeuvre: a penchant for more or less explicit allusions to indigenous customs and lore. *K-ON!* offers an especially imaginative approach to this recurring part of the studio's signature by intersecting with various facets of both traditional and contemporary Japanese culture. Its dialogue features some amusing (and quite unexpected) references to time-honored local stories, such as *The Tale of the Bamboo Cutter* and *The Grateful Crane*, which are normally voiced by Yui and hence hint at this character's tendency to view the world through fictional lenses.

Traditional Japan comes to the fore in its full glory, albeit in a touristicized guise, in the episode chronicling the four older heroines' school trip to Kyoto. The majority of the places seen by the girls on their ramblings, which invariably fall in the category of iconic sites, include Kyoto Tower, the Kinkakuji (a.k.a. the Temple of the Golden Pavilion), and Kitano Tenmangu Shrine. The latter is particularly worthy of notice, in the context of a school-centered anime, as a popular destination for students, especially on the eve of exams, due to the venue's reputation as a holy site built in 947 and devoted to the poet and scholar Sugawara no Michizane. The shrine's *kami* are cows, of which a great number can be seen along the path leading to the main prayer hall and gate. In the anime, both the wonderful animals and the edifices are very faithfully depicted. The itinerary traced by the girls also takes them to the picturesque world of Arashiyama, a district on the western outskirts of Kyoto, where they visit the Iwatayama Monkey Park — home to a large community of supposedly wild but in fact quite sociable Japanese macaque monkeys — and the Moon Crossing Bridge: a romantic landmark of arresting beauty, especially when framed by either cherry blossom or autumnal palettes. Yui and her mates, perhaps unsurprisingly given their scarce common sense, end up getting lost in the winding streets of a quiet residential district as they try to rejoin their group after s spell of unscheduled sightseeing, at which point they probably get to sample, quite accidentally, a more genuine Kyoto atmosphere than the one bathing the tourist-infested attractions visited earlier in their excursions. In the course of their brief sojourn in Japan's ancient capital, the protagonists stay at the Hanazono Kaikan Hotel: a location in itself pregnant with cultural associations in virtue of its long-standing connection with a Zen Buddhist temple and high school. The Japanese-style quarters which feature in *K-ON!* reflect faithfully the hotel's actual guestrooms. Most of the settings deployed by *K-ON!* are based directly on real-life sites and, in keeping with KyoAni's legendary reputation in the field of background art, are astonishingly accurate in their rendition not only of material details but also defining ingredients of a particular venue's ambience. This is blatantly obvious to most viewers in the case of the places depicted in the Kyoto-trip episode to the extent that even those who have not visited the city and its environs in person will have probably sampled some of its cultural landmarks in electronic or paper form.

It is worth pointing out, however, that even the school — which constitutes the anime's principal setting throughout its unfolding — is meticulously modeled on a real-life location: the Toyosato Public Elementary School. The real-life Toyosato is situated in the Inukami District in Shiga Prefecture, near Kyoto Prefecture. In the anime, however, the school is part of the protagonists' unnamed city, which may well be situated in the Tokyo area judging from the itinerary of their train journey to Kyoto. According to *Anime News Network*, the visuals used in the anime's depiction of the school are virtually "identical to the old campus of the Toyosato Public Elementary School, particularly the music rooms (one of them re-styled as the 'music prep room' where the band practices and has tea) and the auditorium; many unique elements from the actual school (the Aesop hare and tortoise on the banister, for example) are faithfully recreated in the fictional school.... The elementary school itself has a notable history, as the local residents' resistance of the government's decision to demolish the old school buildings made national news." Furthermore, while KyoAni's artists have undoubtedly found an invaluable source of inspiration in the venerable academic establishment, the old campus itself has been given a new lease of life by its fresh image as the prime setting of a well loved anime—an image, it must be stressed, which felicitously complements the traditional one as an instance of playful artistry. Indeed, "with the popularity of the anime, the old campus has become something of a 'mecca' for fans of the show—the music room upon which the band's club room is based has been carefully arranged by fans into a very close replica of what's seen in the anime, and a 'K-On! Cafe' has started in the building facing the old auditorium (though operating only on certain days of the month as the staff is mostly volunteer)" (*"K-ON!* [TV]"). Additional information regarding the anime's use of cultural materials grounded in real-life locations can be obtained on the website *Moé Passion*, and specifically from the articles headed "*K-ON!* School Anime Pilgrimage" posted therein.

With the Kyoto-based installment, the anime brings into play the cultural and historical realities of its creators' geographical location, thereby elliptically inviting reflection on the significance of the "Kyoto" component in the designation "Kyoto Animation." In addition, the *K-ON!* universe also offers a notable example of KyoAni's interaction with the cultural and social reality of the city in which its studios are situated, specifically in the form of an initiative which was launched in September 2011 as part of a campaign promoting the movie's forthcoming release, and scheduled to run until the end of December. This was masterminded by "Eizan Electric Railway Co. (Eiden), a local railway company that operates two lines cutting through Kyoto," and pivoted on the operation of "special trains featuring the main characters of *K-ON*." As explained in an article published by *The Asahi Shimbun* in conjunction with this publicity stunt, the scheme involved "two types of train cars," one of which featured "the five main characters from the anime series—Yui Hirasawa, Mio Akiyama, Ritsu Tainaka, Tsumugi Kotobuki and Azusa Nakano—in the center, along with the bandmates" while the other displayed the single character of "Yui Hirasawa at the two entrances." In both cases, the pictures were taken from the film portion of the franchise. "The special offer looks certain to attract much local attention," the article maintains, "with the anime produced by Kyoto-based studio Kyoto Animation Co. For the anime's legions of fans, Eiden will also provide up-to-the-minute information on the location of the trains using a real-time positioning system installed on the trains. The trains will be indicated in real time on Google Maps. Fans can also track their positions on personal computers and smartphones" (*The Asahi Shimbun*). *K-ON!* charts the happy collusion of two manifestations of creativity: the art fostered by KyoAni as a production studio, and the arts practiced by the anime's heroines as both musicians and masters of a secularized and jocular version of the tea ceremony of old. These arts have joined forces in allowing the conception of a playful urban venture such as the one initiated by the Eizan Electric Railway Company. In a sense, the *K-ON!*-themed carriages could be said to encapsulate KyoAni's commitment to the integration of art and play with lively—indeed literally kinetic—immediacy. Although the initiative launched by the Eizan Electric Railway Company is interesting, and unquestionably original as a promotional gambit, more remarkable still is *K-ON!*'s adaptability as a civic tool in the advancement of a serious sociopolitical cause. This is borne out by the Kyoto prefectural government's employment of the anime and its iconic heroines in September 2010 as a means of publicizing the forthcoming census and urging people to be counted ("Explanation of the Heisei 22 National Census").

A further instance of *K-ON!*'s coalescence with an important portion of indigenous culture—one imbricated with global trends, in this case—consists of it experimental take on fashion. In the context of this chapter, this aspect of *K-ON!* is particularly important to the extent that fashion can be regarded as a complementary art invoked by the show alongside the art of music as a means of articulating its vision of creativity as a pointedly playful human capacity, and hence of reinforcing KyoAni's commitment to the marriage of art and play. Even though the main characters are garbed in their school uniforms for a significant percentage of the anime's overall screen time, all aspects of the franchise abound with tactful hints at a variety of vestimentary styles. As Yi aptly points out specifically in relation to the second season, "besides wearing different gimmicky costumes, such as the lovely punk rock gears and swimsuits, the girls also sport some really nice casual clothes. It is very refreshing to see that they do not just have two sets of clothes (school and home) for the whole 26 episodes" (Yi). *K-ON!*'s attentiveness to fashion is attested to not only by its TV series but also by their direct-to-video supplements and by the movie. An additional reservoir of style-related visual information can be found in the illustrations of the anime's characters contained in the various art books accompanying its release. The volume *Keionbu Colorful Memories!!*, in particular, showcases most of the styles found in the anime themselves, allowing the viewer to sample in detail the outfits donned by the five heroines at different stages in their coming-of-age parable, and thus helping them appreciate to the full the painstaking care channeled into their conception by the proverbially punctilious KyoAni artists.

The show's sartorial acuity is embodied primarily by the various outfits which the girls wear at home, in their spare time or on stage. The (often ridiculous and invariably inappropriate) costumes created by Sawako contribute vitally to the amplification of *K-ON!*'s vestimentary frame of reference in an economical fashion. Their appearance is limited to a relatively modest proportion of frames (which is unavoidable, considering their frequent unwearability). However, in this cameo capacity, the costumes manage to enhance the attire-oriented dimension of the *K-ON!* world to great effect by throwing into relief the phenomenon of cosplay. It is here worth recalling that cosplay pivots on its adherents' adoption of outfits and accessories which faithfully reproduce the clothes worn by their favorite anime, manga and computer-game characters. However, the social manifestations of cosplay are not confined to the world of hardened fans and their manias since the trend has actually risen to the status of a substantial presence in Japan's contemporary popular culture — and has in fact extended to the West to punctuate the urban sceneries of cities as diverse as London, Paris, New York and Rome (among others). As Pat Lyttle explains in the both informative and colorfully entertaining volume *Japanese Street Style*, "on the street the look is watered down somewhat, but the white overalls of a medic or a blue jacket and black trousers [i.e., regular school-uniform elements] are common looks, while brightly-coloured wigs are always popular" (Lyttle, p. 13).

In its treatment of the fashion galaxy, the *K-ON!* franchise reminds us that "Japanese teenagers," as Lyttle maintains, harbor a "uniquely fertile sense of style." This quality, which incessantly results in creative gestures on unforeseeable vibrance, is best described with reference to contrasting attitudes to conventional notions of taste and decorum. Whereas "in the West," as Lyttle observes, "there is a fashion rule book" decreeing what is sartorially acceptable, Japanese culture often operates according to quite different parameters, particularly where teenagers are concerned. Therefore, much as they might pay heed to "what's hot and what's not," they will not by and large let accepted standards stifle their imagination, but will actually exploit the existing codes and conventions to their own advantage "to fertilise and cultivate their very own style" (p. 8). Furthermore, Japanese teenagers often seem to approach dress as a primary conduit for unfettered creativity — a means of giving shape and voice to their personal visions without having to feel inordinately constrained by the dicta of dominant designers, ateliers and brands. "In Japanese teenagers from Tokyo to Osaka," Lyttle avers, "you'll find possibly the largest concentration of individual style on the planet, a unique teenage culture of individual self-expression that seeks neither understanding nor approval, but just to be itself" (p. 9). *K-ON!* honors this marked sense of individuality by means of alternately stark and delicate differentiations among its heroines' preferred styles. It could in fact be argued that even the ways in which the girls wear their uniforms denote personal preferences consonant with their temperaments and ambitions. Ritsu's insistence on wearing her school blouse hanging over her skirt, for example, captures most economically her tomboy-ish attitude, whereas Mio's ingrained sense of decorum makes her look worthy of inclusion in a handbook itemizing the ideal school girl's appearance. While Mugi's look is likewise neat, her more tranquil disposition is conducive to an overall impression of greater ease. A miniature version of Mio, Azusa strives to equal her senior's impeccable appearance, though subtle touches such as a tie hanging slightly askew are sometimes included to hint at her latent inexperience in the gentlest way conceivable. Yui, for her part, seems to have a passion for black stockings, which she keeps donning as part of her academic garb even when everyone else wears socks. This is a typically *moe* accessory (sometimes dubiously invested with fetishistic undertones) and could be taken as a means of enhancing the *moe* dimension of her personality as a whole.

The *K-ON!* world alludes, at least obliquely, to all of the verstimentary trends described in Chapter 2 in conjunction with *The Melancholy of Haruhi Suzumiya*: namely, the Gothic Lolita, the Sweet Lolita, the Punk

Lolita, Visual Kei and Dolly Kei. In the representation of casual garb, *K-ON!* is sometimes also reminiscent of the Fruits mode, a style distinguished by a flamboyant disregard for conventions which often manifests itself in the ostentatious adoption of clashing hues — though in this instance, as elsewhere, KyoAni lets us sample its restrained sense of taste by toning down the style's most extreme features. *K-ON!*'s references to specific trends exhibit variable degrees of explicitness depending on the circumstances in which they manifest themselves. By and large, when they occur in the context of a fairly realistic slice-of-life situation, they tend to be muted rather than overt: they serve to evoke a particular style, or blend of styles, in a subtly allusive manner instead of associating it incontrovertibly with particular cultures, subcultures or designers. In the case of the costumes concocted by Sawako, the sartorial references are so overt as to verge on the crude or even the risqué — especially when her passion for cosplay with inflated *moe* connotations is conducive to the creation of potentially seductive clothes. The outfits donned by the protagonists in the context of their onstage exploits are generally more theatrical than the casual clothes they choose to wear outside school but, with the exception of the costumes they occasionally have to wear to comply with contingent performative requirements and the expectations of specific patrons or audiences, they evince a general preference for simplicity. The closing themes of the two TV series point more directly to identifiable vogues: a synthesis of the Gothic Lolita, Punk Lolita, Fruits and Retro in the case of the sequence used for the ending of the first season, *Don't Say Lazy*, and a blend of various Retro motifs in the case of the two sequences used for the endings of the second season, *Listen!!* and *No, Thank you!* In *Don't Say Lazy*, the predominantly monochrome palettes and sophisticated cuts favored by the Elegant Gothic Lolita (a subcategory in the Gothic Lolita mode) coexist with exaggerated make-up of the kind one encounters in both Gothic and Punk varieties of the Lolita style, while the preference for bright colors evinced by various accessories (e.g., Mio's and Tsumugi's tights) bring to mind Fruits. The stripy patterns used for part of Tsumugi's dress, Mio's gloves, Ritsu's floral headpiece and Yui's tights function as an unobtrusive visual leading thread which lends the musical ensemble both aesthetic and dramatic coherence. However, the sequence's deployment of striped fabrics, as well as its partiality for flowers and elaborate hemlines, is also redolent of Retro. The use of this term in the Japanese fashion milieu is quite complex, and hence requires specific qualification. As an article on this subject posted on *Country facts* explains, "there are certain elements that define

Japanese retro fashion. The collection of clothing classified under this heading often incorporates large details with an excessive use of buttons, ribbons, and belts, fluffed and flamed hemlines. The emphasis of Japanese retro fashion is on elegance more than anything else. The prints on the Japanese retro wear are quite old school and distinct. The use of geometric patterns and a highly vibrant colour palette with floral prints is clearly identifiable of Japanese retro fashion. Although these design elements have been taken from the fashion of the days gone by they have not been incorporated as they were. Rather what takes form is a neo version of the classic style as it is spiced up with certain futuristic elements" ("Japanese Retro Fashion").

It is with the second season's ending sequences that the outfits worn by the *K-ON!* heroines echo Retro most profusely, specifically indulging in what Yi has described as "the vintage glamour of 1980s (and late 70s/early 90s)." In *Listen!!*, the use of the "characteristic loose tops coupled with tighter pants or flare skirts," combined with accessories such as the "belts on Mio and Ritsu," the "leggings on Azusa and Mio," the "simple print designs" and Yui's "printed lips," are so recognizably iconic as to hark back to the 1980s with almost documentary accuracy. In this respect, the sequence provides concise corroboration for KyoAni's commitment to photographic precision. In addition, the palettes employed in *Listen!!* make explicit reference to Retro's chromatic preferences, and particularly its penchant for "a faded vintage palette" juxtaposed with "contrasting bright bold colors." Classic examples of this trend are provided by the "light purple boat neck top and bright red leggings" donned by Mio, and the "bold red polka dots on her white top and very blue leggings under a pale black skirt" which constitute Azusa's costume. With *No, Thank you!*, the most distinctive attributes of Retro's vestimentary cachet repropose themselves with additional verve and most prominently in "the color schemes, simple large prints, and the dead giveaway, colorful leggings." It is also worth noting, however, that clothes and accessories are not the only aspects of the heroines' outfits to be regaled with Retro features. Hairdos also echo the 1980s, as evinced most overtly by Azusa and Mugi's scrunchy-tied ponytails. In addition, as Yi emphasizes, "the wrist bands and sleeveless tops on Yui and dolphin shorts over leggings on Ritsu" allude to the 1980s' passion for clothes inspired by the fitness industry as the most desirable form of casual garb. "Mugi's layered skirt shorts, Mio's gloves and beaded bracelet, and the white loose dress with a black belt under Mio's hoodie," alongside the hooded top, itself can all be ranked as emblematic specimens of the "chic clothes of the fabulous 80s" (Yi). (These, of course, will not necessarily carry incontrovertibly "chic" connotations for readers who happened to wear them in their teens or twenties, who might actually now consider them rather naff or even something to feel vaguely ashamed of—but then, such movable feasts are part and parcel of the endless pageant of fashion as both an industry and a code.) One last trend deserves mention: Azusa's tendency to tan easily and deeply, thereby assuming an exotic look, could be interpreted as a tangential hint at one of the most extreme of Japan's contemporary vogues, "Ganguro." When it originally made its appearance in the mid-1990s, this style was intended to provoke shock by disrupting common aesthetic standards through a radical subversion of accepted notions of chromatic harmony and formal balance. A dark tan is one of Ganguro's most striking attributes (alongside outrageous make-up and bleached hair, which clearly do not feature as part of Azusa's image at any point).

In deciding to take the *K-ON!* franchise to new levels by venturing into the domain of feature-length anime, KyoAni had to face a two-pronged challenge. One aspect of the test was a direct corollary of the show's storytelling and structural patterns, whereas the other component pertained specifically to the studio's production history. Firstly, KyoAni had to devise ways of conjuring up a drama which could be deemed sufficiently engrossing to stand the test of the big screen out of the raw materials supplied by a series which, though already established as a major anime favorite, was in the main quite intentionally undramatic. It is undeniable, after all, that *K-ON!*'s distinctive narrative style is mellow, relaxed, and blatantly devoid of coups de théâtre, sensational incident or shocking surprises. Secondly, KyoAni had to take into account, upon embarking on the planning and execution of a *K-ON!* movie, that its most recent creation destined for theatrical release, *The Disappearance of Haruhi Suzumiya*, has proved a sensational hit, and met with accolades the world over. This meant that the studio, in approaching the prospect of the *K-ON!* film, was at least partly laboring under the awesome shadow of a previous silver-screen success which might prove difficult to rival or even equal. It is therefore plausible that its staff, though confident that the new project could carry autonomous appeal and that it would not, therefore, inevitably incur comparison with the earlier movie, was nonetheless conscious that a story of gentler dramatic impact, which the *K-ON!* film was bound to be, could be regarded by some fans as a bit of an anticlimax in the aftermath of the extraordinary plaudits received by *The Disappearance of Haruhi Suzumiya*.

As things stand, KyoAni would soon discover that it had nothing to fear: if it is the case that the *Haruhi* movie ranked in the top ten for Japanese box office sales in its first weekend ("Japanese Box Office, February 6–7"), and went on to earn an estimated 200 million yen in its first week ("Kadokawa: *Haruhi* Film Earns 200 Million Yen in 1st Week"), it is also the case that its *K-ON!* counterpart "was the No. 3 top-grossing film at the Japanese box office during the New Year's period. As of January 9, it has earned 1,455,230,000 yen (about US$ 18,909,000). Only two films earned more money during the last month of 2011 and the first week of 2012: Brad Bird's *Mission: Impossible — Ghost Protocol* (4,055,300,000 yen or US$ 52,680,000) and Yoshihiro Nakamura's live-action film adaptation of the *Kaibutsu-kun manga* (2,955,860,000 yen or US$ 38,398,000)" ("*K-ON!* Is #3 in December/January Box Office in Japan"). As Cytrus emphasizes, it is also worth noting that by comparison with the *Haruhi Suzumiya* movie, the *K-ON!* film held (and still holds) one clear advantage in terms of its potential for attracting viewers to the silver screen: while the former is virtually impenetrable to audiences who are not already familiar with the TV anime, "the storytelling style of *K-ON*, on the other hand, offers it an incredible opportunity to broaden the ranks of its fans. The simple premise of the show allows anyone to dive right into it without preparation. Few people are willing to watch midnight anime shows, but taking a stroll to the nearest cinema might be a different matter altogether. This would mean nothing if the movie were to be dismissed as just another 'otaku movie,' of course, but this is *K-ON*, the series featured on children's news programs and the originator of the '*tehe-pero*' buzzword spreading among female middle school students" (Cytrus).

With the *K-ON!* movie, KyoAni's unique sensitivity to the distinctive atmosphere of its settings announces itself with arguably unprecedented vigor. Whereas in the depiction of the school and of the protagonists' private residences, the film could rely on an existing substratum of imagery and symbolic points of reference, the hitherto unexplored London context posed a slew of new challenges and as many opportunities for experimentation: a pursuit, as consistently proposed in the course of this study, which KyoAni has been wont to embrace with uncommon enthusiasm since its debut. In the representation of both famous landmarks and less known or even totally obscure metropolitan spots, KyoAni's art does not only evince extraordinary attentiveness to their atmosphere and cultural associations, which one might have come to expect of the studio's inspired brushes. In fact, it also reveals a capacity to deploy them as stages for actions which are themselves imbued with local color and with hints at indigenous dramatic traditions. A case in point is the sequence, set in the hotel where the girls reside during their "magical tour," in which doors are strategically deployed in a fashion reminiscent of the classic kind of English-style stage farce where multiple doors allow for the simultaneous entrances and exits of two characters without them seeing each other. KyoAni's choice of places intended to epitomize the London scene is in itself worthy of notice due to its imaginative alternation of iconic venues such as Big Ben, and locations associated with contemporary subcultures whose adherents, like *K-ON*'s heroines, are predominantly adolescent. The introduction of Camden Town as one of the first places visited by the girls on their first day in London is especially felicitous, in this respect, and the purpose of the visit, the purchase of a pair of stylishly comfortable boots for the sore-footed Azusa, is flawlessly congruous with the type of merchandise with which Camden Town Market and its immediate environs are connected.

As emphasized in the preceding chapters, KyoAni is famous for its meticulous representation of settings based on detailed fieldwork and attendant photographic documentation, which results in breathtakingly accurate reproductions of real-life locales in all of their minutiae and, more crucially, their atmospheric nuances. Hence, it cannot quite come as a surprise, in watching the *K-ON!* movie, to find that its London scenes reflect faithfully all of the salient features of places as diverse as Camden Town itself, alongside Heathrow Airport, Chelsea, Parliament Square, the South Bank and the London Eye (among others). The cinematographical style in which these places are shown is worthy of notice as a subtle critique of the false glamour of international tourism. As Ko Ransom observes, on this point, "much of the stereotypical sightseeing the girls do is summarized fairly quickly in a montage of short moments at famous locations. The speed at which this all goes by may be a letdown to some, but on the converse, this approach does an excellent job of capturing how a highly-planned overseas vacation in an unfamiliar land might feel, as rather than actively engaging in their sightseeing, the girls' experience seems to passively happen to them as they whisk themselves off from one spot to the next. This otherworldly and disconnected feeling also manifests itself in the film's choice to put viewers in the girls' shoes by keeping the English spoken in the film unsubtitled, leaving any viewers without a solid grasp of English just as confused and at a loss as the girls" (Ransom). Although the validity of this critique is irrefutable, it would be hard to deny that there is something both uncanny and elating, for someone who has actually lived in Camden Town for some decades and happens to be intimately familiar with its Tube station, its both traditional and faddish shops, its subcultural icons and clubs, its multicultural eateries and kaleidoscopic stalls, suddenly to see those places spring to life on the silver screen in the context of an anime made six thousand miles away. The experience is exponentially more tantalizing, for that matter, when those images are met by a first-time visitor to Japan in the context of a Kyoto cinema shortly after the film's domestic release, at which point the viewer in question would hold a position analogous to the one held by KyoAni's heroines in the UK, with an ironical inversion of cultural and geographical coordinates. Among the many valuable memories associated with this experience, one of the most abiding recollection concerns the nature of the audience: a motley assortment of people including small groups of teenage girls attending the screening just after their lessons, and therefore still garbed in their school uniforms; nicely turned out middle-aged women, either solo or in pairs; heterosexual couples in their twenties; males in their twenties and thirties, normally in pairs or triads. In the context of the specific screening here cited for the purpose of exemplary illustration, spectators in the latter category formed the majority of the audience.

The presence of a substantial number of young (and youngish) male viewers at a regular performance of an anime movie chronicling the everyday experiences of a bunch of female adolescents would feasibly strike many Westerners as weird. Whether this reality is explained with reference to the otaku subculture or in terms of broader cultural factors, its peculiarity as an anime-specific phenomenon can hardly be disputed. However, what anybody would be quick to realize regardless of geographical provenance is the sheer diversity of the typical audience likely to be drawn to a show like *K-ON!*—which, in turn, throws light on the pervasiveness of KyoAni's popularity throughout virtually all strata of society. In this respect, there can be little doubt that both audience diversity and its content-related implications are cross-culturally graspable data. Naoko Yamada, the movie's director, was clearly eager to devise visual strategies which could enable her contribution to the *K-ON!* franchise to broaden its fandom base. The protagonists' features, for instance, were marginally modified for the purpose of toning down their more overt *moe* connotations, and hence lessen their latent erotic appeal, so as to render them attractive to all members of a prospective audience regardless of gender and sexual orientation. The size of the heroines' eyes, specifically, was reduced in accordance with Yamada's preference for "characters that female viewers could easily identify with, not ones focused on appealing to a male audience." At the same time, Yamada endeavored to honor the formal and graphic premises which had guaranteed the anime's popularity as a TV series, being "careful not to make HTT's performances too successful" in the knowledge that *K-ON!*'s protagonists' were never meant to be either superheroines or conventional incarnation of the Cinderella archetype. In reality, Yamada is keen to emphasize that *K-ON!* is a "complete coming of age story" and not a quasi epic quest with stardom as its ultimate grail, as evinced by the fact that "the girls never played for a nameless crowd but always for somebody important to them" (cited in Cytrus).

KyoAni's commitment to the ordinary is resonantly demonstrated by the emphasis placed within the *K-ON!* movie to the everyday events preceding the trip to London. As Cytrus points out, "anyone expecting the usual Hollywood structure out of this movie is in for a surprise. It seems not even London can win against the 'my pace' spirit of the HTT girls. If the travel preparations would normally be considered no more than cinematic 'necessary evil,' *K-ON* finds delight in showing the process" (Cytrus). Among the most entertaining sequences preceding the journey to the UK are those in which Yui, having overheard the girls from the Volleyball Club chat about a graduation trip, comes up with the idea that the Light Music Club should follow suit, and strives to talk her friends into the plan. The decision is laboriously reached, but all club members — including Azusa, though she is not yet about to graduate — eventually agree to embark on the project proposed by Yui, and soon find themselves contemplating what turns out to be the most arduous of choices: that of a suitable destination. Unable to come to an agreement, they finally resolve to resort to their pet turtle Ton as a random selector. Ritsu fancies Hawaii while Mugi, being already well-acquainted with international travel thanks to her background, would rather settle for a hot-spring resort. Mio, for her part, has her heart set on London. Yui, whose geographical competence is dismal in keeping with her paltry academic assets, is determined to go to Europe, oblivious to the existence of any connection between Mio's and her own favored destinations. Moreover, some of the most economically affecting scenes coincide with the girls' outbound flight across the continents — which is later matched, in tonal terms, by the cab journey back to Heathrow following their climactic performance at an open-air festival near the Thames. In these scenes, KyoAni relies neither on words nor on action to communicate *K-ON!*'s unique emotions but rather on the silent glory of sleeping faces — and specifically of Azusa's disarmingly beautiful mien. Ransom has also drawn attention to the relative marginality of the London-based adventures, noting that while "much of the hype" initially surrounding the film concerns the protagonists' graduation holiday in London, this actually constitutes merely "one of three acts, sandwiched in between two other segments of roughly equal length that take place back in Japan." By devoting such a substantial portion of the overall action to school-based and domestic occurrences, the movie could have easily alienated newcomers to the franchise — and possibly even disappointed some established aficionados in search of novel variations on the familiar *K-ON!* formula. However, as the critic aptly emphasizes, Yamada and her colleagues were able to secure the story's dramatic momentum by recourse to "their strong sense of comic timing," while concurrently invigorating its affective import by imparting "a surprising amount of individuality and depth to each of the five protagonists through finely crafted performances and overall presentation" (Ransom).

In truth, even the adventures set in the context of London, much as they throw into relief the heroines' often hilarious efforts to negotiate an unfamiliar reality, are generally subdued, and draw much of their cumulative import from the candidly unspectacular moments devoted to their interplay within intimate indoor spaces, such as their hotel rooms, and recording conversations and activities which could equally well have been staged in the familiar ambience of their *Keionbu* hangout back in Japan. It could therefore be argued that London simply provides a supplementary set for the protagonists' familiar interactions, and for the consolidation of personality traits with which fans of the original series would be fondly familiar. Yet, this is not tantamount to claiming that the girls learn nothing from their graduation trip: in actual fact, the London experience plays a key role in their collective bildungsroman by sharpening their awareness of both their virtues and their shortcomings, while teaching them the importance of being true to themselves irrespective of their contingent surroundings and of the challenges which unfamiliar environments might unleash. A sequence which encapsulates perfectly the *K-ON!* movie's tone and message is undoubtedly the one in which, famished at the end of a long day culminating in a most unexpected opportunity for public performance in a fashionable *sushi* joint (of all places!), the protagonists improvise a picnic dinner in one of their hotel rooms. In the process, they consume with alacrity the lavish amounts of Japanese food thoughtfully packed by Ui on her scatty sister's behalf, lest her treasured sibling and her mates should starve in an alien climate. Scenes of this nature confirm the proposition that London simply offers an ancillary stage for an established dramatic drift. Indeed, they could be positioned practically anywhere at all, and still exude the greatest affective and performative meaning.

In this regard, the *K-ON!* film could be described as a perfect example of KyoAni's sensitivity to the understated marvels of common life. The film consistently reinforces this thematic priority by means of artistic and technical choices which capitalize on a paradoxical notion of simplicity, whereby what appears most simple is actually the product of the most diligent effort. The *K-ON!* film would not succeed in conveying the sense of wonder pervading the quotidian were it not for its knack of evoking a seemingly unadorned day-to-day reality through great technical skill and artistic inventiveness. As a result, argues Ransom, "while it may seem like a light message delivered in a sugar-coated package, *K-ON!* does a brilliant job of reminding us that sometimes who you choose to spend your time with is more important than what you do with that time" (Ransom). All in all, therefore, *K-ON!* delivers a veritable paean to ordinariness, rendered memorable by KyoAni's unsurpassed ability to lend the mundane an extraordinary twist through the combination of a keen eye for the absurd and the grotesque and a painstaking devotion to the depiction of everyday backgrounds and props — a skill which makes even the most prosaic setting or object appear magically alive. Consequently, the franchise as a whole has the power to inspire an unusual sense of awe, to leave one wondering how exactly such magic has been accomplished when the anime itself, strictly speaking, is an unexceptional story about unexceptional things. If there is any answer to this question, it is bound to lie with the exquisite beauty and pure passion with which that story has been made.

Based on the popular comedy manga by Keiichi Arawi, the series *Nichijou* (a.k.a. *My Ordinary Life*) appears to lack any overarching plot, its substance consisting of a conglomerate of stories and ministories which tend to last between ten seconds and five minutes on average. "At its best," as Carl Kimlinger points out in his notable review of the series for *Anime News Network*, "the series dances with playful abandon between the real and unreal, unearthing punchlines of purest insanity and incongruous mundanity. The result is authentically strange" (Kimlinger). In the absence of any provider of formal coherence in the classic sense of the term, *Nichijou* does not, however, dispense with consistency altogether. In actual fact, it does put forward its own idiosyncratic notion of aesthetic uniformity in the guise of a distinctive kind of humor, which is channeled into virtually all of the snippets of action of which the anime cumulatively consists. This brand of comedy capitalizes on a candid exposure of the intractably ridiculous goals motivating people's actions and interactions from day to day. *Nichijou* communicates this message with almost manic insistence, to the point that its reiteration could easily become monotonous were it not for KyoAni's ability to diversify its manifestations with such sensitivity and inventiveness as to enable each incident to stand out as a dramatic occurrence of autonomous worth. In the process, the challenging art of ordinary living is rendered synonymous to a form of play insofar as in *Nichijou*'s logic, living is in effect inseparable from fooling around. At the same time, the orchestration of the show's dramatic fragments appears to be governed by a pervasive sense of randomness whose ultimate objective is to throw into relief—in a jovial yet uncompromising fashion—the fundamental absurdity of human life. The show's randomness underpins its belief in the ubiquity of the absurd in concurrently thematic and formal terms, contributing significantly to *Nichijou*'s assumption of its inimitable flavor and utterly unprecedented take on the classic slice-of-life formula. Unpredictability is built into each and every installment, though KyoAni's appetite for variety ensures that we can never be quite sure at what point in its development the crucial shift might take place. Relatedly, viewers are time and again unanchored from the situation they think they are following and thrown into unfamiliar waters at the most unexpected junctures: the screen's focus may be a character engaged in some farcical tirade, a high-octane action sequence, a surrealistically dreamlike cluster of images, or an entertaining but entirely esoteric flash of bustle. The flow of events is made to appear especially unsystematic by the fact that the anime's two main strands—the events centered on Mai, Mio, and Yuuko and those revolving around Nano, Hakase, and Sakamoto—do not intermesh until the series has moved past its half-way mark (even though hints at their eventual crisscrossing have graced the earlier installments).

While it is crucial to appreciate *Nichijou*'s gloriously arbitrary texture as a defining trait of its unique dramatic cachet, it is also important to recognize that like chaos theory, the series' sense of randomness harbors an eccentric conception of order. Indeed, in spite of its ostensibly disjointed and haphazard take on ordinary life, *Nichijou* still succeeds in conveying a sense of proportion and poise. It does so, primarily, by providing a good graphic balance whereby the disparate styles it deploys in each installment, while delivering some tantalizing contrasts, never clash more than is strictly desirable in the service of dramatic momentum. As a corollary of this balanced approach, the constellation of disparate vignettes within an episode evokes an overall sense of pattern: an underlying design which does not find any obvious correlatives within either the dramatic or the literary arts but rather brings to mind the art of music by recalling the arrangement of musical sections or movements of shifting tempo within a composition. Another relevant parallel would be the use of complementing and contrasting elements of a palette in a visual artifact. The impressionistic scenes of which the show's individual segments consist typically focus on different members of *Nichijou*'s cast, sometimes telling a ministory and at others just conveying a rapid impression of a particular character trait, a setting or an ambience. These are deftly varied, modulated and gradated with each successive installment.

If the exposure of the ultimate ludicrousness of the art of living is key to the series, no less axial to its anomalous diegesis is an existential paradox: i.e., the intimation that people's lives can be perfectly ordinary and yet downright weird at once. In positing this peculiar contradiction as the essence of its characters' quotidian routines, *Nichijou* ultimately makes one wonder whether this may in fact be the case with human existence as a whole. However, it is important to emphasize that with *Nichijou*, KyoAni is not proposing that the universe in its entirety is weird, and that all of its inhabitant simply accept it for what it is — which might have been amusing at first as a proposition but could barely have sustained twenty-six episodes of largely fragmentary events. At best, it would have allowed the studio to dish out a string of comic-strip-type snaps to be consumed for their immediate entertainment value, but would have afforded no scope for reflection, feeling and psychological depth. The characters' unquestioning acceptance of life's inanity would inevitably have precluded those options. In truth, there would have been no reason or excuse for KyoAni to delve into its characters' hearts had it been established a priori that they did not expect — and never could expect — the universe to be anything other than weird. As things stand, while intimating that practically everything in life is totally and tenaciously absurd, KyoAni refrains from proposing that the characters unthinkingly accept that this is the case. On the contrary, though by and large distinguished by astounding levels of resilience, which is one of their most endearing attributes, they fervidly insist on living *as if* things were normal. They therefore remain indomitably intent on carrying on at any price in the conviction that reality, albeit senseless, might still be handled as though it were not. The stone-sucking eponymous character in Samuel Beckett's *Molloy* springs to mind as an apposite predecessor for *Nichijou*'s resilient cast.

It is as a result of its affective subtlety that *Nichijou*, despite its undoubtedly peculiar approach to both drama and narrative, is able to yield one of the most imaginative coming-of-age comedies of recent decades. While the anime's relatively plotless arrangement may suggest a lack of emotional and psychological development, this is far from true. Both its main characters and the relationships in which they are quotidianly embroiled actually evince a marked potential for growth even though this is not charted in a systematic or logically incremental fashion. It could therefore be argued that if the fundamental art at the heart of the series is the art of living from day to day, the art of evolving through the experiences which each day brings about is ultimately no less vital to its overall message. Accordingly, its play — as comical interaction and as performance — resides both with its characters' engagement in their everyday tasks as these contingently arise from one moment to the next, and with the capacity to embark on such tasks as potential opportunities for personal and intersubjective development. The actors' potential for growth is slowly, almost imperceptibly, brought to light, and signaled not by momentous reorientations or epiphanic discoveries but rather by gentle hints at the possibility that they may actually be learning from past experiences and endeavoring to alter their customary conduct in accordance with this lesson. Therefore, unlike many slice-of-life series concerned merely with delivering snapshots of everyday existence, *Nichijou* gradually comes to feel as if it is effectively advancing toward some new objective as each installment gives way to the next.

The weirdest and most wonderful thing about *Nichijou* is that just as you are about to give up watching it for the sake of the story, and to resolve to watch it for its technique instead, something magical happens. At this point, you unexpectedly discover that much as you are prepared to watch it for its technique alone, which grows progressively stunning as the series unfold, you have also — unconsciously perhaps — already become absorbed into something which might not be an actual story, yet feels *like* a story. What must be emphasized, in this context, is the concept of "something *like* a story" because what *Nichijou* offers is not a narrative progression in the orthodox acceptation of the term, but rather a coral reef of incrementally accruing situations rendered irresistibly appealing by its amazing character chemistry. The series' characters will be examined in some detail later in this chapter. At this stage in the discussion, a further aspect of *Nichijou*'s approach to the storytelling dimension requires consideration. This pertains to the show's handling of its finale. It is indeed crucial to recognize that any desire for storyness (as both narrative substance and plotting dexterity) left unsatisfied in some viewers is more than copiously fulfilled by the last two installments. Both of these are in effect replete with thoughtfully modulated emotions and food for thought — especially regarding the true meanings of friendship and identity, and of the beguiling relationship between the two. The key image around which these reflections revolve is the giant screw on Nano's back: a burden which could be seen to symbolize, in a grotesquely material guise, those facets of our inner selves which we most fear or despise. What the reactions evinced by Nano's human friends intimate is that much as the robotic girl may resent the aspects of her being she deems abnormal, to them they are integral parts of her identity — they are what makes her the person she really is, and their removal would therefore deprive Nano of her genuine value as both a person and a friend. Despite these serious overtones, however, *Nichijou*'s ending does not relinquish totally the show's facetious disposition. In other words, the series never loses touch with the playfulness at the core of its artfulness — the play on which its art is woven. Accordingly, it mellows down the drama's more poignant connotations by deploying some refreshingly debunking strategies redolent in tone of the atmosphere characteristic of *Full Metal Panic? Fumoffu* at its zaniest. This is exemplified by the antics involving the school's Principal and Vice-Principal alongside their supposedly emblematic statues; Mio, Yuuko and Mai's exploits in the face of an ostensibly unsmashable pumpkin; and Hakase's disastrous handling of a party cake in what could be regarded as an anime correlative of the custard-pie farce quips of old. Commenting specifically on *Nichijou*'s closing segment, Takaii has trenchantly captured its mood as follows: "it takes something special to give a series a good ending episode — especially for series longer than one-cour and this last episode of *Nichijou* didn't just push the envelope. It stared at that envelope, ripped it in half, ate the pieces, and then lit itself on fire in order to make sure that there was no trace of an envelope" (Takaii 2011b).

It is by consistently honoring this unreservedly ludic premise that the series succeeds in proclaiming, in its characteristic off-the-wall style, the philosophical lesson regarding the unmatched value of the quotidian dimension which is so crucial to KyoAni's whole output. This message is at one point economically communicated through the character of Koujirou Sasahara as he mysteriously declares: "our everyday lives might in fact be a series of miracles." The boy's words sound entirely incongruous in the circumstances in which they are uttered, given that at this point, he is supposed to be answering his homeroom teacher's question concerning the meaning of the jabot he insists on wearing with his school uniform. However, the absurdity of the context in which those vital words emerge is in itself important insofar as it serves to throw them into relief in a defamiliarized fashion, and hence to make them more significant than they would seem if they had been spoken in the context of a serious conversation about metaphysical issues. *Nichijou* could therefore be said to represent the apotheosis, at least to date, of KyoAni's penchant for artistic gestures which concurrently highlight the wondrous richness of the everyday, and radiate a sense of spontaneous simplicity through their meticulous execution and thoroughly planned construction. In this regard, *Nichijou* could be said to epitomize a major component of Japanese aesthetics which finds paradigmatic formulation in the time-honored principle of *shibui* (渋い). This term (which originally means "bitter") refers to the balance of simplicity and complexity within the overall form of an object. While the object as a whole should appear simple, its composition ought to encompass refined details (e.g., in the use of color and texture). As a result of this unique aesthetic equilibrium, an object imbued with beauty of the *shibui* variety has the power to retain timeless appeal insofar as its beauty is bound to be enhanced by its incremental acquisition of new layers of meaning. Given the technological underpinnings of contemporary anime, it is here worth noting that the "elegant simplicity" and "articulate brevity" with which *shibui* is traditionally associated has led to its current use not only in the original sense of the term but also "to describe something cool but beautifully minimalist, including technology and some consumer products" ("7 Japanese aesthetic principles to change your thinking").

It is by means of its unique character gallery that *Nichijou* brings this philosophical lesson to life, enabling the audience to absorb its import over the series' duration instead of enforcing it from the start in a peremptorily didactic manner. Even spectators who find the series disconcerting from a structural viewpoint, harbor doubts as to the quality of its comedy, or deem its numerous allusions to indigenous traditions somewhat cryptic, stand to derive pleasure from getting to know *Nichijou*'s cast over time. As any viewer, including the most casual, will readily concede, in anime, character types are often identifiable straight away. This is certainly not the case in *Nichijou*, where the character ensemble forces us to think before arriving at any decisions regarding dramatic typologies and conventions. There can be little doubt that in the character area, the show is far more mature than appearances might at first indicate. *Nichijou* comprises two main sets of actors whose interactions and daily adventures form the most substantial and narratively cohesive aspect of the show as a whole. These key figures are surrounded by a stunningly diversified assortment of supporting and peripheral personae, most of whom make regular appearances within discrete vignette threads. The principal sets of characters have been vividly described as follows in one of the series' most astute reviews: "*Nichijou* features three friends in high school (the quiet genius who likes to mentally torture others, Mai; the normalish blue-haired girl who likes to draw the boys in her class in her personal and detailed *yaoi* manga, Mio; and the stupid, but fun-loving daydreamer, Yuuko), but added to its main cast are a cute robot girl with a giant turn-key on her back named Nano, and Nano's creator, Hakase ('Professor'), who happens to be an adorable 8 year-old girl. Oh, and Nano and Hakase's talking cat, Sakamoto-san" ("*Nichijou—My Ordinary Life*"). Mai Inakami Mai is incredibly good at everything she tries her hand to but this does not automatically make her a stereotype. By intimating that she is by and large unable to put her achievements to any practical advantage, the show indicates that her Renaissance-girl genius is just *irrelevant* to the real world. Her outlandish sense of humor, which she shares with two pet dogs but her friends tend to find thoroughly frustrating, reinforces Mai's detachment from practical reality. Mio Naganohara is the seemingly most normal of *Nichijou*'s principal personae. However, her relationship with her older sister Yoshino—comical but also bordering on bullying and familial abuse on occasion — adds complexity to Mio's portrayal. So does her talent as an exceptionally accomplished author of *yaoi* ("Boy's Love") manga: a skill which often intersects with her unrequited love for her school mate Koujirou.

Yuuko Aioi is very possibly *Nichijou*'s most intriguing character from a psychological perspective insofar as she exhibits personality traits which many viewers would instantly recognize as familiar (however grudgingly), yet epitomize *Nichijou*'s appetite for the absurd to such extremes that it is at times tempting to dismiss them as just a pretext for preposterous humor. This aspect of the girl's characterization is not only important in defining her distinctive personality; it also provides us with valuable insights into the special sensitivity animating KyoAni's approach to character portrayal. It would have been relatively easy to depict Yuuko as *either* a realistic persona meant to function as the audience's intradiegetic avatar *or* a cardboard comic type whose sole function is that of an automatic joke trigger. KyoAni, dissatisfied with such simplistic binary options, has chosen to bring *both* of those alternatives into the equation, thereby yielding one of the most unexpectedly challenging anime characters in its whole opus. The first impression elicited by Yuuko is that she is neither very smart nor very funny and going out of her way to do and say things which other people — and especially Mio and Mai — will consider clever or amusing. Yet, we soon discover that there is nothing truly scheming about her: she is just outrageously naive. This renders Yuuko disarmingly helpless on countless occasions, and even downright pathetic at times, while making her the vehicle for the elaboration of an authentically unique brand of humor. This contention is exemplified by sequences like the one in which the girl literally bends over backwards to find reasons for which people might not think that her drawings are the very best; the one in which she likewise goes out of her way to fathom why on earth Mio and Mai do not consider her so-called jokes amusing; or the one where she cannot quite accept in her own head that she simply has no hope of winning an iron arm contest against the formidable Mai no matter how hard and how often she tries. There is a sense in which Yuuko's all-too-human failings make her the most lifelike presence in *Nichijou*'s entire cast. As Takaii intimates, it is the combination of vulnerability and endurance evinced by Yuuko throughout that turns her not merely into "the unluckiest character in this series," which would have made her actions funny but not necessarily interesting, but also a model of everyday mettle: "with life pelting her with things falling from the sky, witnessing live Super Deer Fighter, and objects lodging themselves into her best friend's hair, it's amazing that she hasn't gone crazy yet. Then again, you have to love that resilient personality of hers [which] is probably what keeps her bouncing back" (Takaii 2011a).

Hakase, a name which translates simply as Professor, is a child prodigy whose intellectual assets contrast sharply with her infantile tastes, weak spots and pursuits. Not needing to go to school for the simple reason that she already possesses some enviable qualifications, she spends her time playing and drawing sharks — not even her scientific interests distract her for long from these occupations, since the amount of time she spends in her lab whenever the need for a new invention crops up is invariably negligible. One of the show's recurrent sources of humor lies with Hakase's efforts to look mature even though she is obviously a cute and somewhat spoilt kid at heart, as epitomized by her total addiction to snacks. In addition, she also behaves rather selfishly toward both Nano and Sakamoto on numerous occasions but hers is the selfishness of a growing child who, in a sense, *must* be allowed to be marginally egotistical as part of a healthy developmental trajectory. The Professor's major creation to date is Nano Shinonome, a robot who has taken on the roles of caretaker and guardian within the kid's household. Nano vainly strives to keep her artificial nature hidden from other people even though the presence of an enormous wind-up key on her back makes it patently clear to even the most careless passerby that she is hardly a regular school girl. We see Nano's quest for normality repeatedly frustrated in the course of gags which throw into relief her peculiar nature: particularly those in which one of her body parts unexpectedly opens up either to unleash peculiar superpowers (generally of scarce practical use or necessity), or to disclose bizarre items installed therein by Nano's maker unbeknownst to the robot — which may be practically anything from jelly rolls to cutting-edge weapons. Like virtually everything else in *Nichijou*, Nano's longing for normality becomes absurd, as evinced by her longing for "cavities" when her maker informs her that whether or not she brushes her teeth before going to bed, Nano will not run the risk of this unpleasant orthodontical affliction for the simple reason that it is not encoded into her robotic structure. Sakamoto, a black cat endowed with the power of speech by a red scarf created by the multi-talented Hakase, perceives his role at the Shinonome Laboratory less as that of a pet than that of an authoritative elder (he is, after all, twenty years older than its human and android inhabitants). However, in spite of the condescending tone he typically adopts toward both Nano and the Professor in order to assert his senior position within the pseudo-family, and his determination to behave and sound like a dependable adult, Sakamoto harbors a secret weakness: he is, like most members of his species regardless of age, instinctively inclined to play in the presence of the vaguest stimulation to do so. Hence, he looks deeply embarrassed whenever Nano and the Professor surprise him in the process of behaving frivolously (by accident or unaware of being observed). The tension between Sakamoto's idealized self-image as a responsible father figure and the reality of Sakamoto the oversized kitten battling against inner temptation and instinctive drives provides the series with some of its most memorable comedic gems. There is clearly a sense in which the cat's natural conduct, in emphasizing the sheer irresistibility of play, captures in nuce this chapter's central theme.

As RYHZUO maintains, "the best thing about *Nichijou*'s characters ... isn't their individuality, but how they interact with each other" (RYHZUO). It could be argued, for instance, that Mai and Yuuko could often seem just irritating, and Hakase and Sakamoto just stereotypical, if taken individually, yet deliver hilarious situations as pairs of sparring voices. Throughout the series, "the personalities of various character groups clash, contrast and complement each other in extremely interesting ways." This is most notable in the depiction of the dialogues and incidents involving the Yuuko/Mio/Mai and Hakase/Nano/Sakamoto triangles, which effectively constitute the series' more substantial components. It could be argued that the interactive dynamics involving just these personae are in themselves so powerful that they could feasibly have carried the whole series even in the absence of the ancillary narrative strands articulated through briefer vignettes. Nevertheless, *Nichijou* could never be what it is without the myriad character satellites following the two principal sets from start to finish. This is because in the absence of a comprehensive and many-sided cast, the series would have been powerless to convey to the fullest its philosophical message concerning the absurdity of existence. It is crucial to appreciate, on this point, that even though Yuuko's experiences encapsulate the series' appetite for the bizarre to the highest degree, all members of *Nichijou*'s dramatic ensemble ultimately have to endure the ascendancy of the absurd in human life to the best of their ability. The ludicrously outsized difficulties which they encounter in the process are attested to most vibrantly by the moments in which things just refuse to *fit*—when circumstances and interactions just elude all of their noblest efforts at any kind of control (self-control included).

Relatedly, all of *Nichijou*'s actors sooner or later reveal latent weaknesses. A case in point is the flamboyantly wealthy Koujirou Sasahara, a student who insists on acting like an aristocrat even though he is actually a farmer's son, and complements his self-styled role by riding a goat (Kojirou Sasahara) to school, and ensuring his personal butler is always at his beck and call. Despite his apparent power, the boy behaves with uncharacteristic meekness toward the formidable *tsundere* Misato Tachibana, whose grotesquely distorted romantic feelings for Koujirou almost invariably result in her shooting him all over the school with heavy weaponry (which seems to spring out of nowhere). Another recurring character riddled with secret frailties is Izumi Sakurai: a young, incessantly anxious and easily scared teacher who endeavors in vain to enforce the school's regulations, and thus honor its ruling body's commitment to discipline in the face of what it perceives as rampant moral degeneration, but proves invariably incapable of accomplishing her goals. One of *Nichijou*'s most hilarious, yet sensitively handled, character portraits is the one devoted to one of Izumi's colleagues, Manabu Takasaki. Torn between the belief that his romantic interest in Izumi amounts to an unpardonable breach of professional integrity, and lewd fantasies with the shy female mentor at their center, Manabu typically ends up behaving like a kid beset by the pangs of his first crush whenever he tries to decide how to deal with the young woman in a sensible manner. Manabu is a great example of the extent to which *Nichijou*, in spite of the tone of farcical two-dimensionality it may at times evoke, is able to deliver complex and multifaceted psychologies within its multihued character gallery.

The most distinctive feature of the series' structure consists of its use of sets of skits with recurring themes as interludes between any two longer bits of drama. Some of the most remarkable of these recurring sketches deserve attention as illustrative cases. The skipping rope skits, for example, feature two figures wearing headpieces which are initially reminiscent of eggs but eventually turn out to be giant pieces of *daifuku* (a Japanese confection consisting of rice cakes with a sweet filling). This discovery is enabled by the action's foregrounding of the same peculiar head accessory in the context of the installment in which Mio has to wear a costume including said accessory in an attempt to attract potential customers to a *daifuku* stall. This episode is itself part of a strand of the series chronicling a *daifuku* manufacturer's obsessive efforts to boost his business by means of increasingly inappropriate, and therefore offputting, promotional strategies. The entrepreneur's son, Tsuyoshi, is occasionally inveigled much against his will into his father's preposterous initiatives in this constituent of the series, while also featuring as the hapless centerpiece of the skits focusing on the science teacher Kana Nakamura's labors to capture Nano — of which Tsuyoshi, by the unfathomable logic of chaos theory, is invariably the unintended victim. The most exquisitely unfathomable of *Nichijou*'s occasionally obscure skits are those which go by the title of "Helvetica Standard": this is a totally random self-contained comical short without any obvious link with *Nichijou*'s main story, except for the fact that the supporting character of Yuria is insistently depicted as an avid reader of this title. A true jewel of KyoAni's ability to diversify the content of its sketches with unpredictable results comes in the form of an exquisitely crafted ministory which capitalizes on the genius of the absurd at its most narratively adventurous. This consists of a space saga chronicling a tale of political strife, abuse and power hunger and pivoting on the possession of two small wooden cubes which, if joined together, can deliver the means of ascending to kingship. These fall into the hands of a menial soldier who, uncertain as to how to use them, procrastinates by opening one of the spaceship's windows to have a smoke (without, needless to say, affecting the airworthiness of the vessel), and hence causes the objects to plunge into the void. At this point — and this is where the story's true magic resides — the cubes land straight into Yuuko and Mio's classroom and nest themselves into Mio's hair, there to become her trademark hair ties. This embedded drama turns out to be Yuuko's dream, which indicates that even though the girl may not be the brightest chisel in the toolbox, to stay with the carpentry motif, she unquestionably harbors a pretty rich unconscious.

As Kimlinger persuasively argues, *Nichijou*'s most memorable aspect ultimately resides with the quality of the animation itself. "The series is alive with movement, displaying a genuine love for animation that is rare in anime," the critic maintains. "Strange that a directionless, ultimately inconsequential comedy should be the strongest expression in some time of the love of the art for its own sake.... Even the series' lamest, tamest sketches are full of animated inventions and elevated by the joy of pure movement.... A good deal of effort went into individualizing [the characters'] body language, expressions, and locomotion." It is when *Nichijou* allows its flair for dynamism free rein so as to deliver unrestrained "physical comedy," according to the critic, that the show "enters the rarefied realm of the truly inspired. And even when it isn't, it is so well-executed and unfailingly interesting just to watch that it's pretty easy to forget that it's essentially an empty comedic spectacle. That's the power of love for you" (Kimlinger). *Nichijou*'s singularly high production values ensure that its animation is unswervingly fluid, and that the artwork sustaining the motion never fails to come across as vivacious, polished and varied, even when the palette it adopts relies on a sparing range of hues, rough crayon marks replace regular coloration, or the actors' physiognomies are desaturated to a stylized grayscale for metaphorical purposes. Motion and artwork join hands in the evocation of a visually mellow tone which contrasts ironically with the frenzied rhythm of the many explosive sequences which give shape to the characters' innermost emotions and mental processes with utter gusto. A good example is provided by the series of fishing images offered in the OVA. These are intended to embody Mio's hidden thoughts as she struggles to praise Yuuko without allowing any negative remarks accidentally to creep into her discourse, as though she were sneaking her way through an obstacle course littered with lethal traps. By deftly deploying the technique of frame juxtaposition, the OVA resorts to a totally unpredictable analogy, and depicts Mio's verbal labors as comparable to those of a person patiently endeavoring to reel in a huge fish without ever losing control of the longed-for prey.

Further illustrations of the series' exuberant approach to movement are supplied by the sequences where the degree of dynamism and drama fueled into the animation equals — and even rivals — the most action-oriented moments in a *shounen* anime. A case in point is the scene in which Yuuko frantically struggles to save a sausage she is about to eat from falling on the floor; the one in which Mio endeavors to rescue the math notebook which could reveal her most intimate secrets; and the one in which Yuuko, stuck in the hall for misconduct, finds herself witnessing an out-of-this-world wrestling match between the Principal and a stray deer, powerless to do anything about this obvious aberration from the routine though she senses she should because there is obviously no way anybody — even people far more resourceful than Yuuko — would be ready to respond to such a phenomenon on the basis of empirical wisdom. Another superb example of *Nichijou*'s bodily comedy in the sequence centered on Mio as she goes berserk after seeing her romantic dreams shattered and, at the end of a superhumanly manic run, ends up rescuing a drowning kid: an incongruous yet touching exploit which regales the show with a blissfully cathartic moment. The review posted on *Rossman Reviews and Ratings* felicitously describes this sequence as "the time Mio witnesses her worst fear and runs away from it at full-tilt-speed, breaking the school break-out record, flinging herself over the school gates after spinning around the uneven bars 30 times, becoming the best shadow boxer Mr. Gentleman has ever seen, and giving that old lady a piggy back ride while carrying a tour guide flag before jumping into the river for a power swim and rescuing that drowning boy" ("*Nichijou—My Ordinary Life*").

As the *Polychromium* review of the show emphasizes, another defining attribute of *Nichijou*'s approach to animation consists of its repeated intimations that visual language often holds expressive capacities which far exceed the power of verbal communication. "Pictures speak louder than words," the review proposes. "Silence is deafening. None of these strategies escapes use in this show, as *Nichijou* sometimes uses jokes that [do not] include spoken words, but only grunts, visuals and music" ("*Nichijou* Review: An Outside-The-Box Comedy"). A paradigmatic instance of the extent to which *Nichijou* is capable of relying on pictures as its primary artistic tool with scarce concern for the putative authority of verbal communication is provided by the entirely wordless — altogether soundless in fact — segment in which Mio and Yuuko strive to build a house of cards with heroic zeal, while Nano and Mai insistently threaten the success of this epic enterprise with their inadvertently destructive movements. The exceptional caliber of *Nichijou*'s animation, compounded with the passion for experimentation to which its many adventurous gestures attest, is such that there are times when "one can't help but wonder," as RYHZUO observes, "if KyoAni isn't deliberately showing off their workmanship with this anime. Many originally very short panels from the manga are translated into incredibly imaginative and stunning sequences of animation that simply scream 'because we can'" (RYHZUO). However, whether or not KyoAni has used *Nichijou* at least partly as an arena to flaunt its competence, there can be no doubt as to the series' cinematographical ingenuity, graphic liveliness, and overall technical excellence.

Undeniably, some KyoAni fans who have been typically drawn to the studio's anime by their narrative vitality might have been disappointed by *Nichijou*'s flagrant eschewal of anything one could call narrative in the conventional sense of the term. Nevertheless, devout admirers who regard the studio's experimentative flair as its most appealing quality will feasibly commend this eccentric series as the epitome of KyoAni's daring and, more specifically, of its ability to play imaginatively with the relationship between appearance and reality to challenge the audience and elicit its mindful responses. In *Nichijou*, that relationship is articulated as an ironical tension: whereas at face value, nothing about the show seems in the least delicate or elegant, a patient scrutiny of its internal dynamics discloses unexpected levels of complexity and brilliance. *Nichijou*'s ostensible lack of refinement is suggested, for example, by its use of simple palettes in the depiction of both characters and settings, and by its insistent reliance on brief explosions of madcap action, surreal blunders, and zany quips of circusy bluntness. The show's sophistication reveals itself as we gradually familiarize ourselves with their recurring personae's long-term aspirations: often concealed or disguised by those characters' involvement in humorous vignettes, such contents are by no means immediately obvious, and it would be therefore easy for a viewer unwilling to give the series a chance to unfurl to miss them altogether. However, those who do allow *Nichijou* to draw them into its quirky folds will be most likely not only to take cognizance of its characters' dreams and objectives but also to empathize with the often complex emotions which KyoAni has tactfully woven into their fabrics. It is enough to observe closely the robot Nano's desperate efforts to fit into normality, on the one hand, and the all-too-human Yuuko's equally desperate efforts to transcend normality, on the other, to form an adequate impression of the anime's underlying dramatic potential.

As jel x has pointed out, *Nichijou*'s embedded treasures include a degree of emotional richness one would not initially associate with its colorful and hyperactive façade. It is at these hidden levels of the show that KyoAni's unique talent announces itself with characteristically judicious restraint. "Right beneath the surface," argues the reviewer, "is a surprising amount of heart and emotion that kind of creeps up on you. That heart begins spilling out in the second half of the series with the 'Like Love' segments. Almost entirely unrelated to the main story, these little portions of cavity-inducing sweetness manage to be very effective with hardly any dialogue or context. Take a look at the first, and probably best, segment.... It's a love story told entirely with facial expressions and movement, telling us more in 30 seconds than hours of love letter mix-ups and accidental gropings ever could" (jel x). The full measure of *Nichijou*'s elusive artistic refinement is borne out by the stylized and almost minimalist terseness of its design at both the graphic and the performative levels. RYHZUO has captured this quality in memorable terms, arguing that "as the modern entertainment sector continues to emphasize excess and surplus, *Nichijou* is a much welcome, and frankly much needed throwback to a more old-school approach to entertainment. *Nichijou*'s frugal yet distinct style reminds us that something is perfect, not because there's nothing more to add to it, but because there is nothing more to take away ... behind all the technicalities and production values, lies a very simple ideal. Everything about *Nichijou* revolves around this central principle of being enjoyable. All that it does, every scene, every character, every line of dialogue alludes back to this principle. Because at the end of the day, all *Nichijou* wants you to do is one thing; it wants you to enjoy yourself.... Fun is the only thing that matters, and it's this frugality, this ingenious simplicity, that allows everything to just click together like magic" (RYHZUO).

As anticipated in Chapter 1, the latest expression of KyoAni's enthusiastic commitment to experimentation — a corollary of its belief that learning never ends — is the TV series *Hyouka*. This anime signals the studio's first foray into the realm of mystery fiction through the adaptation to the screen of a popular novel by Honobu Yonezawa. As G. J. Demko reminds us, "the mystery genre has been, and is, enormously popular in Japan. A major newspaper survey in 1999 revealed that the most popular author in the country was a mystery writer — Jiro Akagawa — and three of the top four were also writers of detective stories. One of the most popular TV shows in 2000 was a detective program — Hagure Keiji — in which a hero named Yasura solves crimes in 27 exciting episodes! In a country where guns are strictly regulated and rare and the crime rate is relatively low (but there are organized crime groups known as the Yakuza), crime fiction is universally admired and avidly consumed.... In Japan the mystery genre is remarkably vigorous and always changing.... The genre is enormously popular and the output of mystery literature is prodigious. And, if one wants a lively, accurate and imaginative peek into a society that is rapidly changing and dealing with social pathologies once thought to be uniquely 'western,' the Japanese mystery field is one of the most entertaining and effective entryways" (Demko). For the sake of contextual accuracy, it should also be recalled that in the specific domain of Japanese literature, the word which has loosely come to designate both the mystery and the detective genres is *suirishōsetsu*: a term which in fact translates literally as "deductive reasoning fiction" (*suiri* [推理] = "reasoning," "inference" + *shousetsu* [小説] = "novel," "story"). This etymology underscores the central role played by conjecture, logic and analytical interpretation in the indigenous understanding of the genre. Demko has highlighted this distinctive preference, noting that the typical Japanese mystery story evinces a somewhat "old fashioned tendency to emphasize the puzzle-solving dimension of the genre," and amusingly adding that most mystery yarns are in fact "police procedurals" characterized by "a dearth of flashy and flamboyant private eyes, no doubt a reflection of the Japanese penchant for order and predictability" (Demko). *Hyouka* is faithful to this traditional legacy by focusing on the efforts made by a bunch of amateur detectives to delve into the circumstances surrounding a buried crime by recourse to ambiguous clues. Most importantly, *Hyouka* sets great store throughout by its protagonists' mental agility, industriousness, deductive skills and nasal intuition, while also highlighting their struggles to differentiate between genuinely telling signs and deceptive diversions. In the process, it pays homage to the original sense of *suirishōsetsu* with its sustained commitment to the art of reasoning — and, relatedly, to the art of fiction-making, which it repeatedly posits as a somewhat inevitable concomitant of inferential thinking and detection. In order to situate *Hyouka* in its cultural milieu, it is also worth noting, as Satomi Saito explains, that "the detective fiction genre has been one of the most popular in Japanese popular literature since its introduction in Japan in the late nineteenth century.... Japanese detective fiction delineated its generic border as a modern popular literature differentiating itself from serious literature (*junbungaku*) as well as from other genres of popular fiction, such as *tsuuzoku shōsetsu kōdan*, and *taishuu shōsetsu*" (Saito, p. v).

Hyouka's formal and generic novelty in the context of KyoAni's oeuvre to date has been underlined by the writer responsible for the series' composition, Shoji Gatoh, best known as the creator of *The Full Metal Panic* saga: "this work was a type that I haven't had much opportunity to work with before, and it's full of new things for me, so it's been very rewarding to use my head and face the challenges it's thrown at me" (cited in "Anime Spotlight: *Hyouka*"). The story chronicles the eerie adventures of high-school freshman Houtarou Oreki, a youth whose most distinctive personality trait is a deeply ingrained propensity to save up energy, and hence refrain from engaging in any strength-consuming activity unless he is left with no choice. Nagged by his elder sister Tomoe into joining Kamiyama High School's waning Classics Club (*Kotenbu*), Houtarou uncharacteristically embarks on a course of action destined to draw him into a chain of enigmatic events. Yonezawa's novel highlights the centrality of the Classics Club from the inceptive stages of the narrative, introducing it as a major topic of the letter sent by Tomoe to Houtarou from Benares. Although the letter does not go into any exciting detail about *Kotenbu*'s history, the urgent and vaguely ominous tone carried by Tomoe's words gives it a rather solemn aura. "As your big-sis," writes Tomoe, "let me give you, someone who has safely become a high school student, a piece of advice. Enter the Classics Club. The Classics Club is a humanities club in Kami-High with a long tradition. Also, I am not sure if you already know it or not, but I also belonged to the club in the past. I heard of this from someone else, but it seems that our tradition-rich club has had no newcomer for three years and is currently with no member at all. If no one joins the club this year it will be disbanded. As an old girl of the club it is certainly not something I can stand. However, if there are newcomers in April then the situation will turn out differently. Houtarou, safeguard the Classics Club, the youth of your big-sis" ("*Hyouka*: Volume 1, Chapter 1, 1—Letter from Benares").

Having thus been inveigled into the moribund association somewhat in spite of himself, the protagonist becomes increasingly entangled with three other key personae: the attractive and passionately inquisitive Eru Chitanda, the sole daughter of an affluent family who appears to have joined the society to pursue a quest originating in a dark incident from the past; Satoshi Fukube, Houtarou's best friend since middle school and an insatiable collector of data endowed with a phenomenal memory; and

Mayaka Ibara, another close mate who has been in Houtarou's class since elementary education, and is led to join the Classics Club by her attraction to Satoshi. At the core of these characters' adventures lies a mysterious case held to have occurred thirty-three years prior to the present-day story. The club itself does not constitute merely a convenient narrative device for drawing the key personae together and magnetizing them toward a common cause. In effect, it soon transpires that a potentially invaluable source of pointers to the solution of the puzzle is nested precisely in a long forgotten collection of works left behind by the former members of the Classic Club: a compilation titled "Hyouka" (氷菓—literally, "ice candy"). The series thus invites critical reflection on the story it dramatizes as a story *about* textuality. To be more precise, it thematizes textuality as a threefold phenomenon: a problem (the act of deciphering a cluster of musty texts); a procedure (the act of encoding meaning into texts through writing and the act of processing that meaning through reading); and a goal (the final outcome of the problem and the procedure in tandem). Furthermore, *Hyouka* forges a potent bond between detection and textuality as Houtarou progressively realizes that Eru's appetite for mysteries is so intense that the only way to keep her satisfied is to *appear* to be treating an event as a major riddle even if it is really only a marginal conundrum, and hence to act *as if* the event was truly capable of mobilizing one's full intellectual capacities. With this discovery, Houtarou reaches the conclusion that "what's important isn't the truth, but whether or not [he] can appease Chitanda's curiosity." This statement epitomizes one of the series' most important, though understated, themes by exposing the nebulous nature of the boundary separating the notion of detection as the empirical search for right answers, and detection as the speculative art of fiction-making. It thereby invites reflection on the collusion of investigative skill and storytelling flair—of logic and narration. Houtarou's ability to weave a story around a perceived mystery ultimately surpasses the significance of the mystery itself—and indeed its veracity. Hence, it could be argued that *Hyouka* uses the legion riddles strewn over its fabric as the raw materials providing Houtarou-the-storyteller with themes around which he may construct compelling narratives. Eru's obsession with puzzles requires Houtarou to act as a versatile improviser, and concoct satisfying fables out of the blue and from one second to the next. This renders his role analogous to that of the street entertainer of old, expected to weave engaging yarns out of a repertoire of motifs determined by custom and popular taste—and Eru's function, in turn, akin to that of the story-addicted marketplace crowd.

If *Hyouka* confirms KyoAni's unquenchable thirst for new challenges and for fresh opportunities to enhance its technical and narrative expertise, it should be noted that it concomitantly marks an important moment in the developmental trajectory of the story's original creator. Yonezawa indeed appears to have also been driven by a keen desire to learn something new in his contribution to the execution of the anime in the capacity of composition cooperator. "My first intentions were to leave everything to the Animation Staff, because 'every man to his trade,'" Yonezawa has commented, "and I hardly know anything about film. But I had second thoughts, that maybe there was something even I could do to help bring out the atmosphere and the feel of the classic club in film. There were several things that changed my mind, but the greatest reason was probably because I could trust Kyoto Animation as a work partner. If I confront them, they'll grapple with me. They won't just toss my ideas aside. Even if I jump in when it's not my trade, they'll add my ideas where they should be added, and turn them down when need be. I believed they would do that, and set about working on a new 'HYOUKA'" (cited in "Anime Spotlight: *Hyouka*"). These observations confirm KyoAni's commitment to the value of collaboration as a key component of creativity in all its manifestations, demonstrating that the cooperative spirit governing its in-studio practices is commodious enough to extend — to no less generous a degree — to its relationship with external influences. The vital importance of collaboration has also been emphasized by Gatoh with these telling remarks: "this time I've been working more behind the shadows as a staff member, like a catcher trying to firmly catch all of the balls being thrown his way by everyone" (cited in "Anime Spotlight: *Hyouka*").

The series' director, Yasuhiro Takemoto, has described KyoAni's adaptation as something of a coming-of-age story, which suggests that the mystery aspect, crucial though it is to *Hyouka*'s overall mood, does not exhaust its potentialities but can in fact be regarded as a vehicle for the exploration of a more far-reaching drama. "Thorns of Youth" is therefore the topos prioritized by Takemoto in his interpretation of *Hyouka*'s plot. "This is what I wanted to depict," he continues." When we're in school, that special time in our lives, we experience many things. Fun things and interesting things, of course, but also events that prick at our hearts, and I believe that all of these become very bright, precious memories to us. I wanted to depict how such thorns leave their scabs, causing our hearts to grow stronger and mature" (cited in "Anime Spotlight: *Hyouka*"). As noted earlier in this discussion, *Hyouka*'s presentation of extraordinary events is imbued with irony, which has the effect of making them look as if they were quite ordinary and thus invests them with arrestingly uncanny connotations. It is in its treatment of the bildungsroman element that the anime's ironical take on the relationship between the ordinary and the extraordinary can be best appreciated. The coming-of-age quality with which Takemoto and his team have sought to impart the series' development situates its mysteries and weird fables in a thoroughly ordinary world. This is by no means tantamount to saying that it thereby trivializes or mocks them — in effect, it invests them with uncommon dramatic verve by making them seem unexceptional elements in the daily experiences of a bunch of budding adolescents, but then allowing them to take us by surprise as their lurking extraordinariness is gradually disclosed.

The evocation of dramatic intensity through a rampant sense of trepidation and suspense abets the mystery plot's distinctive trajectory, and on this count too, KyoAni's show does not fail to fulfill the requirements of its parent genre. In fact, like many cinematic gems in that field, it deploys camera angles, sound effects, and the play of light and shadow to excellent effect in the service of cunning plot twists and bizarre revelations. However, though indubitably grounded in a rich generic substratum, *Hyouka* makes an original contribution to the mystery tale. Indeed, its deployment of an impromptu detective team consisting exclusively of teenagers adds a further dimension to the show's generic dimension since, in keeping with director Takemoto's focus on the "Thorns of Youth," the anime compounds the mystery at the heart of the investigation proper with the mysteries of self-discovery and self-understanding: that is to say, dilemmas which all developing human must at some point confront, and negotiate with varying degrees of angst or aplomb. In the process, the art-play partnership comes to the fore in two interrelated forms. On the one hand, the series' generic affiliations posit the art of detection as its central concern. This art is handled in an eminently playful terms as the self-appointed sleuths fumble their way through hints, whispers and red herrings while also juggling at every turn the enigmas thrown into their path by as yet inchoate emotions. At this level, *Hyouka* uses its thematically pivotal art as an exciting pretext for play. On the other hand, *Hyouka* foregrounds its play — i.e., its dramatic performance — as a quest in which investigative duties and the vicissitudes of personal growth jointly compel the characters to devise artful strategies for dealing with both. At this level, *Hyouka* deploys its formal identity as a play to establish a context in which art can be discovered and enjoyed.

As indicated, the series elevates textuality to the status of both the structural catalyst triggering its characters' interactions and the potential repository of vital answers to the mystery whose solution motivates those characters' collaborative quest. In so doing, *Hyouka* obliquely proposes an analogy between the act of reading and the art of detection. It thereby suggests that the reader hunting for meaning and the detective in search of clues to a mystery are figuratively comparable agencies. If the reader can be regarded as a detective, and vice versa, then it is also possible, by extension, to conceive of the viewer as a reader-detective whose task is to treat the signs transmitted by visuals and words as clues to variable and ambiguous meanings, and not as potted messages unamenable to examination. In the specific case of *Hyouka*, viewers are drawn into the action as reader-detectives to the extent that they are encouraged to decipher the cryptic traces proffered both by the anime's story itself and by the old texts embedded within it as signs open to interpretation rather than as predetermined truths. This entails that the audience is afforded a substantial degree of freedom in the performance of its decoding moves. In fact, it could be argued that the anime's semiotic flexibility fosters the audience's active participation both in its play and in its art, and thus signals a sparkling apotheosis for KyoAni's commitment to cooperation.

Hyouka ushers the audience into its characteristic ambience right from the start, delivering a solid and beautifully written first episode sustained throughout by sharp dialogue, whose mood in many ways anticipates the tenor of what is to follow. A slightly ominous sense of mystery is almost immediately evoked by the protagonist's internal reflections. "The fourth floor of the auxiliary building. It's the end of the world," mulls Houtarou as he approaches the Classics Club room, expecting to find it empty and lured by the prospect of a secluded corner of the school all to himself — an ideal lair for someone who seems naturally inclined to maintain "a low profile." As it happens, a beautiful girl is already in the room, standing by a window and dreamily surveying the school grounds. The eerie tone introduced by the protagonist's words is now intensified by his unexpected meeting with Eru — an encounter rendered poignant by well-chosen cinematographical ruses, and especially the employment of unusually intense close-ups of individual eyes. The series also uses its initial installment to foreground its departure from the *moe*-oriented slice-of-life formula deployed by KyoAni in its most recent anime in the direction of the suspense thriller. However, it does not plunge its audience into the deep end of that generic pool, choosing instead to shepherd it into the action gracefully through a bundle of relatively trivial mysteries which can be quite easily unraveled by recourse to ordinary logic and common sense. The conundrums dramatized in the opening installment might seem fairly insignificant compared to the axial mystery on which the main body of the drama revolves. Yet, they serve to indicate in an unequivocal fashion that the show's introductory drama is building up to something of greater and graver magnitude. This impression is abetted by the quality of their execution. In spite of their either trivial or fabricated nature, those minor incidents are constructed with great care and with the same painstaking attention to detail which regular viewers have instinctively come to associate with KyoAni's productions. At the same time as this strategy makes them dramatically enticing in themselves, it also serves an additional purpose: whetting the audience's appetite for things to come. In infusing its hors d'oeuvre with succulent ingredients, *Hyouka* unobtrusively invites us to wonder just what kind of gourmet fare it will be able to dispense upon its real and central mystery. Moreover, the first episode's minor mysteries function as structural devices capable of bringing the pivotal personae together in a convincing and natural manner, and thus enable KyoAni to pave the way to the articulation of multifaceted character interactions. There is a sense in which the content of the enigmas themselves is relatively negligible in comparison with the richness of the interpersonal dynamics which they tangentially disclose. In this respect, *Hyouka*'s initial minimysteries could be seen to serve a purpose analogous to the one served by music in *K-ON!* franchise.

The accumulation of peculiar incidents which give rise to the show's initial brainteasers is predicated upon the bizarre notion, keenly voiced by Satoshi, that "the best way to tame a mystery is with another mystery." The small mysteries include a classic closed-room riddle, a horror-tinged enigma centered on a ghost pianist and, most notably, the case of a "secret club." The first of these mysteries holds a major function in setting the series' character dynamics in motion by giving Houtarou an opportunity to show off effortlessly his deductive flair. At the same time, Eru finds a perfect excuse for indulging her hearty appetite for riddles, as well as a chance to warm further to Houtarou — in whom she seems to have already developed an interest unbeknownst to the boy himself — as a prospective Classics Club associate (and possibly more than that). The ghost-pianist puzzle serves a different dramatic role, working mainly as a leitmotif for Satoshi to tap into in order to flaunt his knack of storytelling. The last — and most elaborate — of the mysteries introduced in the first installment pivots on the yearly appearance on the school's bulleting board of a poster supposedly not belonging to any association within the aegis of the Student Council. The elusive society goes by the charismatic name of "The Golden Web." In his unraveling of the secret-club puzzle, which actually turns out to be a mystery of Houtarou's own invention, the protagonist evinces a talent for a kind of investigative logic redolent of Edgar Allan Poe, and specifically of the reasoning followed by his detective, Dupin, in "The Purloined Letter." In this renowned tale, Dupin avers that a truly sophisticated criminal would hide a valuable booty in the place where common minds would be least likely to search for it — namely, in full view. Only a mediocre wrongdoer would elect a remote nook as his secret place. Thus, while Eru and Satoshi automatically assume that the notice advertising the secret club is bound to be hidden in some obscure spot, Houtarou insists that the main bulletin board is in fact its most plausible location. The youth argues that only a naive person would choose an unsubtle strategy to make an impression, and deems the picking of an out-of-the-way corner as a clear marker of lack of subtlety. However, "if you were clever enough to run a secret club," Houtarou avers, "you'd try to outwit people in a more dignified way." The irony in all of this is that even though Houtarou has no compunction in deriding callow people, he is in fact acting like a very inexperienced guy himself vis-à-vis Eru. The girl's proximity, as Satoshi is quick to observe, is enough to cause Houtarou to behave pointedly out of character. In focusing on the self-effacing Houtarou as he relinquishes his comfort zone, and engages in activities he would not habitually contemplate just for the sake of pleasing a member of the other sex, *Hyouka* already reveals, even at this unripe stage in its development, a remarkable flair for sensitively nuanced characterization.

Finally, the secret-club riddle is notable on the purely aesthetic front as a gorgeous example of the sorts of stylistic flourishes with which KyoAni occasionally regales its action in the passionate pursuit of experiment. This can be witnessed in the form of a cascading mass of typographic characters, seemingly issuing from the bulletin board itself, which crowd around Houtarou as though they sought to suffocate him. The youth interprets the notices on the board as enthusiastic expressions of energy and, being proverbially averse to unnecessary action, instinctively perceives them as an oppressive force. Therefore, the portentous horde of characters inundating him constitutes a visible embodiment of the flow of energy coursing the board, which to Houtarou can only signify an annoying or even inimical agency. Though amusing in virtue of its psychological message, the scene is made most memorable by its technical quality, as the dark letters detaching themselves from the wall to bear down on the protagonist evoke a world in which *everything* is inherently animate, and in which the signs making up human discourse are certainly no exception. As the story progresses, the aliveness of the written word is reproposed as an important visual motif at various junctures. In a particularly entertaining instance of this trend, made most striking by its association with an elegantly spooky ambience and by its hallucinatory nature, the characters which come to life are the entries in two dinner menus proffered to Houtarou by an imaginary version of Eru decked out as a Gothic Lolita waitress. In scenes such as these, the ideograms appear to detach themselves from the surfaces on which they have been inscribed, and to acquire not merely animate but exuberantly dynamic existence. By throwing into relief the vitality of typographic characters, *Hyouka* palpably elevates language to the status of a protagonist. The portrayal of the written word as the embodiment of pulsating energy functions as a metaphor for the materiality, vibrancy and inherent aliveness of language at large.

At the same time, the idea that typographic characters are intrinsically endowed with vitality also operates as a striking metaphor for the essence of animation itself as an art capable of bringing inert matter to life. KyoAni's desire to convey this essential aesthetic message is confirmed by its virtuoso performance, and assiduous deployment of original technical flourishes, not only in the dramatization of climactic sequences which could be automatically considered worthy of such an investment but also in the chronicling of peripheral or purely anecdotal occurrences. A case in point is the sequence in which Mayaka recounts the circumstances surrounding the loan of a book held in the school library. Though somewhat baffling, these events certainly do not belong in the category of the extraordinary, yet derive undeniable dramatic substance from the imaginativeness with which they are recorded, especially in the manipulation of proportions and colors. Likewise engaging are the schematic visuals accompanying Houtarou's conjectures in the face of this minor enigma, whose quasi-mathematical seriousness stands out as rather incongruous with the triviality of the case, and therefore serves to underline the ironical disparity between the so-called mystery itself and the sophistication of the reasoning devoted to his solution by Houtarou. This, as seen, is largely meant to satisfy Eru's addiction to strange tales, and hence consolidate the series' preoccupation with storytelling, and its relationship with both fiction and truth.

While *Hyouka* is not doubt appealing to audiences with a liking for high-school comedy or a taste for adolescent romance, it is likely that many of the series' viewers have been drawn to it by a preference for mystery yarns, and by curiosity about KyoAni's approach to a genre it had never explored before. Aficionados of the mystery genre are known to be pointedly adverse to spoilers, notwithstanding the medium or format in which the story is couched. In examining *Hyouka*, therefore, it is necessary to resist the temptation to divulge information which many viewers would rather learn at their own pace. This is especially true of decisive details pertaining to the nature of the pivotal mystery, and to each of the key characters' individual relation to, and perspective upon, that narrative core. Without indulging in spoilers, it is safe to surmise that the one factor which makes the series potentially intriguing for any audience, regardless of individual generic predilections, is *Hyouka*'s emphasis on the centrality of language. As suggested in the preceding pages, this message is conveyed in two forms, insofar as it is encapsulated by both the collusion of detection and textuality, and the presentation of the written word as an animate reality. Taken in tandem, these two manifestations of the centrality of language to *Hyouka*'s world picture enable the show to foreground the value of the unexceptional, since both phenomena are effectively inscribed in everyday human interactions. As we have seen, *Hyouka* does not present the everyday as its one and only priority but actually intermeshes it persistently with scattered allusions to the extraordinary. In addition, even though *Hyouka* focuses on its protagonists' ordinary experiences, its action is woven around a decidedly exceptional occurrence. Nevertheless, it would be hard to refute that in spite its substantial concessions to the extraordinary, the series in fact locates life's most intriguing mysteries and most affecting marvels not with unusual events but rather with the rhythms of common existence. The series' stress on the centrality of language underscores this axial proposition. After all, language forms such a substantial part of our daily activities that we rarely pause to reflect on either the mysteries surrounding its origins or the aporias plaguing its clumsy mediation between expression and meaning. Yet, taking language for granted as an essential but purely functional component of our existence does not erase its irreducible inscrutability. Language remains *both* common *and* mysterious, *both* humdrum *and* wondrous. By positing language as a pivotal preoccupation throughout, *Hyouka* perpetuates KyoAni's commitment to the wonders of the mundane in an original and thought-provoking style. Besides, it is through its *play* on the relationship between the ordinary and the exceptional that the show elaborates its individual interpretation of the *art* of detection, its chief theme, and the *art* of animation, its mechanical and yet magical vehicle.

As argued in this study's first chapter, and as reiterated in the opening segment of the present chapter, one of KyoAni's most intriguing qualities lies with its capacity to imbue unexceptional circumstances with special pathos and verve. Without pandering to the trite conventions of soap opera, while also refraining from slavish adherence to the formulae of sit com pure and simple, the studio has progressively refined its flair for bringing out not only the dramatic intensity latent in the most commonplace scenarios but also the unique sense of wonder which pervades people's lives when they least suspect that this may be the case. It is by paying heed to the minutest facets of ordinary existence that KyoAni has time and again accomplished this feat. Furthermore, its preparedness to combine a rare eye for detail with a penchant for the quirky and the absurd has enabled the studio to leave its distinctive mark on the contemporary anime scene where other companies have concentrated on the overtly spectacular as the most direct route to success. The close analyses of anime produced by KyoAni over the past decade have hopefully corroborated the contention advanced in Chapter 1.

In *Munto*, as we have seen, KyoAni appears to pay homage to the preference for the extraordinary characteristic of much (though by no means all) mainstream anime by chronicling a cosmic saga of mythological magnitude. However, even in that context, the values it seeks to uphold most alacritously turn out not to be nested in interstellar grandeur but to issue instead from regular human intercourse in a run-of-the-mill environment. With *Full Metal Panic? Fumoffu* and *Full Metal Panic! The Second Raid*, KyoAni proclaims its unflinching commitment to the hidden treasures of everyday life by treating the story's action adventure and sci fi materials not as ends in themselves but rather as solid and finely crafted frames for the staging of a resolutely down-to-earth human drama. *The Melancholy of Haruhi Suzumiya* and *The Disappearance of Haruhi Suzumiya* can be regarded as KyoAni's boldest exploration of the dramatic possibilities inherent in science fiction of the universe-bending variety. Nevertheless, it would be hard to deny that it is from its tantalizingly eccentric take on the slice-of-life recipe — interspersed with generous helpings of comedy and tongue-in-cheek romance — that the franchise derives the unmistakable tone which has gained it worldwide acclaim. Addressed as a triad, KyoAni's adaptations of visual novels by Visual Art's/Key point to a further, and related, skill which the studio has consistently demonstrated over time: an uncommon knack of distilling the wonders of the ordinary from ostensibly extraordinary events. *Air*, *Kanon* and *Clannad* undoubtedly abound with mystical and otherworldly motifs, yet the truly magical elixir extracted by KyoAni from their multilayered yarns consists of essentially mundane situations and acts redolent of Wordsworth's "little, nameless, unremembered acts of kindness and of love." It is with the anime studied in this final chapter that KyoAni's dedication to the ordinary reaches an effervescent culmination, now bolstered by a philosophical message of immense potential: namely, a paean to the inextricability of humanity's creative and ludic drives.

Homage to Kyoto Animation

> "One of Kyoto Animation's greatest strengths is, simply, the quality of their actual animation.... Sometimes when an anime tries to have one or more of its characters look cute, or moe, it goes too far, and the character no longer looks realistic because of it. Poor anatomy frequently results, and this can kind of drag the viewer out of the story. Poorly drawn characters, or characters that don't have realistic body types, can quickly sever the viewer's suspension of disbelief, or at least the viewer's ability and willingness to become immersed within the story. Kyoto Animation largely avoids this pitfall. Yes, Lucky Star's art style is not very realistic, but it's not meant to be; no more than Crayon Shin-Chan or South Park's art style is meant to be ... years after I watch an anime, what I remember most are specific scenes that really captured the imagination and left me feeling like I was watching something larger than life. So, on the whole, I very much like Kyoto Animation's approach to putting an added special dash of soaring sparkling stupendousness into the key scenes of the material that they adapt.... In some ways, Kyoto Animation is to anime [what] CLAMP is to manga artistry."— Triple_R

Filmography

Air (2004–2005)

Original Title: *Air*. **Status:** TV Series (12 episodes + 1 recap episode). **Episode Length:** 24 minutes. **Director:** Tatsuya Ishihara. **Original Creator:** Visual Art's/Key. **Series Composition:** Fumihiko Shimo. **Music:** Jun Maeda, Magome Togoshi, Shinji Orito. **Original Character Designer:** Itaru Hinoue (Visual Art's). **Character Designer:** Tomoe Aratani. **Art Director:** Jouji Unoguchi. **Chief Animation Director:** Tomoe Aratani. **Background Art:** Emi Kesamaru, Miyuki Hiratoko, Miyuki Tsukazaki, Mutsuo Shinohara, Naoki Hosokawa. **Chief Editor:** Seiji Morita. **Sound Director:** Yota Tsuruoka. **Special Effects:** Rina Miura. **Color Key:** Akiyo Takeda. **Animation Production:** Kyoto Animation. **Production:** Kyoto Animation (Yokujin Denshou Kai), Mubik (Yokujin Denshou Kai), Pony Canyon (Yokujin Denshou Kai), TBS (Yokujin Denshou Kai). **Sound Effects Production:** Gakuonsha.

Air in Summer (2005)

Original Title: *Air in Summer*. **Status:** TV Special (2 episodes). **Episode Length:** 24 minutes. **Director:** Tatsuya Ishihara. **Original Creator:** Visual Art's/Key. **Series Composition:** Fumihiko Shimo. **Screenplay:** Fumihiko Shimo. **Music:** Jun Maeda, Magome Togoshi, Shinji Orito. **Original Character Designer:** Itaru Hinoue (Visual Art's). **Character Designer:** Tomoe Aratani. **Art Director:** Jouji Unoguchi. **Chief Animation Director:** Tomoe Aratani. **Producers:** Shinichi Nakamura, Yoko Hatta, Yoshihisa Nakayama. **Background Art:** Chioi Hosokawa, Emi Kesamaru, Miyuki Hiratoko, Mutsuo Shinohara. **Sound Director:** Yota Tsuruoka. **Sound Effects:** Eiko Morikawa. **Color Designer:** Akiyo Takeda. **Animation Production:** Kyoto Animation. **Production:** Kyoto Animation, Pony Canyon, TBS.

Clannad (2007)

Original Title: *Clannad*. **Status:** TV Series (24 episodes). **Episode Length:** 25 minutes. **Director:** Tatsuya Ishihara. **Original Creator:** Visual Art's/Key. **Series Composition:** Fumihiko Shimo. **Screenplay:** Fumihiko Shimo. **Music:** Jun Maeda, Magome Togoshi, Shinji Orito. **Original Character Designer:** Itaru Hinoue. **Character Designer:** Kazumi Ikeda. **Art Director:** Mutsuo Shinohara. **Chief Animation

Director: Kazumi Ikeda. **Animation Directors:** Chiyoko Ueno, Fumio Tada, Futoshi Nishiya, Hiroyuki Takahashi, Kazumi Ikeda, Kazuya Sakamoto, Mariko Takahashi, Shoko Ikeda, Yukiko Horiguchi. **Producers:** Naohiro Futono, Shinichi Nakamura, Yoko Hatta, Yoshihisa Nakayama. **Background Art:** Anime Workshop Basara. **Editor:** Kengo Shigemura. **Sound Director:** Yota Tsuruoka. **Color Designer:** Akiyo Takeda. **Animation Production:** Kyoto Animation. **Production:** TBS.

Clannad After Story (2008–2009)

Original Title: *Clannad After Story*. **Status:** TV Series (24 episodes). **Episode Length:** 30 minutes. **Director:** Tatsuya Ishihara. **Original Creator:** Visual Art's/Key. **Series Composition:** Fumihiko Shimo. **Screenplay:** Fumihiko Shimo. **Music:** Jun Maeda, Magome Togoshi, Shinji Orito. **Original Character Designer:** Itaru Hinoue. **Character Designer:** Kazumi Ikeda. **Art Director:** Mutsuo Shinohara. **Chief Animation Director:** Kazumi Ikeda. **Animation Directors:** Chiyoko Ueno, Futoshi Nishiya, Hiroyuki Takahashi, Kazumi Ikeda, Mariko Takahashi, Saiichi Akitake, Yukiko Horiguchi. **Sound Director:** Yota Tsuruoka. **Color Designer:** Akiyo Takeda. **Animation Production:** Kyoto Animation.

The Disappearance of Haruhi Suzumiya (2010)

Original Title: *Suzumiya Haruhi no Shōshitsu*. **Status:** movie. **Length:** 163 minutes. **Chief Director:** Tatsuya Ishihara. **Director:** Yasuhiro Takemoto. **Screenplay:** Fumihiko Shimo. **Storyboard:** Tatsuya Ishihara, Touko Takao, Yasuhiro Takemoto. **Unit Director:** Hiroko Utsumi, Kazuya Sakamoto, Mitsuyoshi Yoneda, Naoko Yamada, Noriyuki Kitanohara, Touko Takao. **Music:** Satoru Kousaki (monaca). **Original Creator:** Nagaru Tanigawa. **Original Character Design:** Noizi Ito. **Character Design:** Shoko Ikeda. **Art Director:** Seiki Tamura. **Chief Animation Directors:** Futoshi Nishiya, Shoko Ikeda (Ultra Chief Animation Director). **Animation Directors:** Chiyoko Ueno, Hiroyuki Takahashi, Kazumi Ikeda, Mariko Takahashi, Miku Kadowaki, Seiichi Akitake, Yukiko Horiguchi. **Sound Director:** Yota Tsuruoka (Rakuonsha). **Director of Photography:** Natsumi Hamada (assistant), Ryuuta Nakagami. **Producers:** Atsushi Itou, Hideaki Hatta. **Assistant Art Director:** Naoki Hosokawa. **Assistant Producer:** Mayumi Yamaguchi. **Color Design:** Mayumi Nagayasu (assistant), Naomi Ishida. **Color Key:** Mayumi Nagayasu, Naomi Ishida, Rie Takagi. **Editing:** Kengo Shigemura (Studio Gong). **Planning:** Nobuhiko Sakawa, Satoshi Arashi, Shunji Inoue, Takeshi Yasuda, Yoko Hatta. **Sound Effects:** Eiko Morikawa (Churasound). **Sound Production Manager:** Yoshimi Sugiyama (Rakuonsha). **Special Effects:** Rina Miura, Yukie Tsuda.

Full Metal Panic? Fumoffu (2003)

Original Title: *Full Metal Panic? Fumoffu*. **Status:** TV Series (12 episodes). **Episode Length:** 24 minutes. **Director:** Yasuhiro Takemoto. **Screenplay:** Fumihiko Shimo, Shoji Gatoh, Yasuhiro Takemoto. **Storyboards:** Hiroshi Matsuzono, Ichirou Miyoshi, Jun'ichi Sakata, Noriyuki Kitanohara, Sumio Watanabe, Tatsuya Ishihara, Tomihiko Ohkubo, Yasuhiro Takemoto, Yutaka Yamamoto. **Music:** Toshihiko Sahashi. **Original Creator:** Shoji Gatoh. **Original Character Design:** Shikidouji. **Character Design:** Osamu Horiuchi. **Art Directors:** Jouji Unoguchi, Kikuko Tada. **Animation Directors:** Akira Takata, Fumio Tada, Kazumi Ikeda, Kensuke Ishikawa, Manabu Nakatake, Mitsuyoshi Yoneda, Osamu Horiuchi, Shoko Ikeda, Shuji Ono. **Sound Director:** Yota Tsuruoka. **Director of Photography:** Ryuuta Nakagami. **Producers:** Hiroshi Ogawa, Masafumi Fukui, Michio Suzuki, Nobuhiko Sakoh, Shigeaki Tomioka, Takatoshi Hamano, Takeshi Yasuda, Toshio Hatanaka, Tsuneo Takechi. **Animation Producer:** Yoko Hatta. **Art Setting:** Kikuko Tada. **Chief Manager:** Nagaharu Ohashi. **Color Coordination:** Rie Takagi. **Editing:** Seiji Morita. **Music Producer:** Takashi Watanabe. **Music Selection:** Satoshi Yano. **Planning Producers:** Atsushi Itou, Hideaki Hatta. **Production Assistant:** Yoshimi Nakajima. **Setting:** Hiroyuki Takahashi. **Sound Effects:** Hiromune Kurahashi (Soundbox). **Animation Production:** Kyoto Animation.

Full Metal Panic! The Second Raid (2005)

Original Title: *Full Metal Panic! The Second Raid*. **Status:** TV Series (13 episodes). **Episode Length:** 24 minutes. **Director:** Yasuhiro Takemoto. **Series Composition:** Shoji Gatoh. **Script:** Fumihiko Shimo, Shoji Gatoh. Yasuhiro Takemoto, Yutaka Yamamoto. **Storyboards:** Ichirou Miyoshi, Noriyuki Kitanohara, Shinobu Yoshioka, Yasuhiro Takemoto, Yutaka Yamamoto. **Original Creators:** Shikidouji, Shoji Gatoh. **Character Design:** Osamu Horiuchi. **Art Director:** Jouji Unoguchi. **Chief Animation Director:** Osamu Horiuchi. **Sound Director:** Yota Tsuruoka. **Director of Photography:** Ryuuta Nakagami. **Animation Producer:** Yoko Hatta. **Color Design:** Rie Takagi. **Editing:** Kengo Shigemura (Studio GONG). **Layout:** Hiroyuki Takahashi. **Music Director:** Tomoko Shibuya (Scitron Digital Contents). **Music Producer:** Takashi Watabe. **Sound Effect Director:** Yota Tsuruoka (Gakuon-sha). **Animation Production:** Kyoto Animation.

Full Metal Panic! The Second Raid (2006)

Original Title: *Full Metal Panic! The Second Raid*. **Status:** OVA (1 episode). **Episode Length:** 30 minutes. **Director:** Yasuhiro Takemoto. **Screenplay:** Shoji Gatoh. **Storyboards:** Yasuhiro Takemoto. **Music:** Toshihiko Sahashi. **Original Creators:** Shikidouji, Shoji Gatoh. **Character Design:** Osamu Horiuchi. **Art Director:** Jouji Unoguchi. **Animation Director:** Osamu Horiuchi. **Mechanical Design:** Kanetake Ebikawa. **Sound Director:** Yota Tsuruoka. **Executive Producer:** Nobuhiko Sakoh, Shouji Udagawa, Takeshi Yasuda, Yoko Hatta. **Producers:** Tomoko Suzuki, Tsuneo Takechi. **Art Setting:** Jouji Unoguchi. **Background Art:** Emi Kesamaru, Miyuki Hiratoko, Naoki Hosokawa, Natsumi Katou, Shinji Matsuura, Yoshinory Kawauchi, Yutaka Ito. **Color Design:** Rie Takagi. **Editing:** Gen Itakura, Kengo Shigemura. **Logo Design:** Jin Ichikawa (HY). **Music Director:** Tomoko Shibuya. **Music Producer:** Takashi Watanabe. **Planning:** Hiroshi Ogawa, Shinichiro Inoue. **Production Managers:** Atsushi Itou, Hideaki Hatta, Mayumi Yamaguchi. **Setting:** Hiroyuki Takahashi. **Setting Manager:** Kazuki Kurihara. **Sound Effects:** Hiromune Kurahashi. **Animation Production:** Kyoto Animation.

Hyouka (2012)

Original Title: *Hyouka*. **Status:** TV Series (24 episodes). **Director:** Yasuhiro Takemoto. **Series Composition:** Shoji Gatoh. **Script:** Shoji Gatoh. **Music:** Kouhei Tanaka. **Original Creator:** Honobu Yonezawa. **Character Design:** Futoshi Nishiya. **Art Director:** Shūhei Okude. **Animation Director:** Futoshi Nishiya. **Sound Director:** Yota Tsuruoka (Rakuonsha). **Director of Photography:** Ryuuta Nakagami. **Executive Producer:** Takeshi Yasuda. **Producers:** Hideaki Hatta, Makoto Ito (AC²). **Animation Producer:** Riri Senami. **Associate Producers:** Fumihiko Shinozaki (Kadokawa Media House), Isao Ishikawa (Quaras), Mitsuhiro Ogata (Kadokawa Media House), Yoshimi Nakajima (Quaras). **Background Art:** Ikuko Tamine, Jouji Unoguchi, Kouji Maruyama, Manae Yamatogi, Mikiko Watanabe, Miyuki Hiratoko, Momoka Nagatani, Mutsuo Shinohara, Naoki Hosokawa, Nozomi Ōishi, Shingo Kasai, Tomoki Hiraishi, Yukiko Takeuchi, Yumi Okada. **Character Setting:** Hiroshi Karata. **Color Design:** Naomi Ishida. **Editing:** Gen Itakura, Haruka Yasumoto, Kengo Shigemura (Rakuonsha). **Logo Design:** Jin Ichikawa. **Music Producer:** Shigeru Saitō (Lantis). **Online Editing Manager:** Takayuki Tabata. **Original Work Assistance:** Hideyuki Hitomi (Shonen Ace Editorial Dept.), Hiroshi Mizuno (Newtype Editorial Dept.), Shin Ueno (Kadokawa Sneaker Bunko Editorial Dept.), Tomomi Kaizu (Newtype Editorial Dept.), Yoshihito Utsumi (Shonen Ace Editorial Dept.), Yoshinori Mino (Shonen Ace Editorial Dept.). **Photography:** Akihiro Ura, Hiroki Ueda, Kazuya Takao, Norihiro Tomiita, Rin Yamamoto, Tetsuro Umezu, Yoshiko Tanaka, Yuji Shibata. **Planning:** Shunji Inoue, Takeshi Yasuda, Tsuneo Takechi, Yoko Hatta. **Series Composition Cooperation:** Honobu Yonezawa. **Setting Manager:** Ikuna Ōhashi. **Sound Effects:** Eiko Morikawa. **Sound Production Manager:** Yoshimi Sugiyama. **Special Effects:** Rina Miura. **Animation Production:** Kyoto Animation.

K-ON! (2009)

Original Title: *K-ON!* **Status:** TV Series (14 episodes). **Episode Length:** 24 minutes. **Director:** Naoko Yamada. **Series Composition:** Reiko Yoshida. **Screenplay:** Jukki Hanada, Katsuhiko Muramoto, Reiko Yoshida. **Storyboards:** Kazuya Sakamoto, Mitsuyoshi Yoneda, Naoko Yamada, Noriyuki Kitanohara, Taichi Ishidate, Tatsuya Ishihara, Touko Takao. **Music:** Hajime Hyakkoku. **Original Creator:** kakifly. **Character Design:** Yukiko Horiguchi. **Art Director:** Seiki Tamura. **Chief Animation Director:** Yukiko Horiguchi. **Sound Director:** Yota Tsuruoka. **Director of Photography:** Rin Yamamoto. **Producers:** Naohiro Futono, Shinichi Nakamura, Yoko Hatta, Yoshihisa Nakayama. **Advisor:** Tatsuya Ishihara. **Animation Producer:** Eharu Oohashi. **Background Art:** Harumi Ike, Hiroyuki Tsubaki, Jouji Unoguchi, Mikiko Watanabe, Miyuki Hiratoko, Mutsuo Shinohara, Naoki Hosokawa, Nozomi Ōishi, Sagako Itakura, Shingo Kasai, Shūhei Okude, Tomoki Hiraishi, Yoshikatsu Matsumoto, Yukiko Takeuchi. **Color Design:** Akiyo Takeda. **Insert Song Composition:** Hiroyuki Maezawa ("Curry nochi rice"; "Fude pen ~bōru pen~"), Kunihiko Murai ("Tsubasa o Kudasai"; episode 1), Miki Fujisue ("My love is a stapler"), Shigeo Komori ("Maddy Candy"; episode 4). **Insert Song Lyrics:** Emi Inaba ("Curry nochi rice"; "Fude pen ~bōru pen~"; "My love is a stapler"), KANATA ("Maddy Candy"; episode

4), Michio Yamagami ("Tsubasa o Kudasai"; episode 1). **Music Producer:** Shigeo Komori. **Musical Instrument Design:** Hiroyuki Takahashi. **Photography:** Hiroki Ueda, Kazuya Takao, Kōhei Funamoto, Natsumi Hamada, Norihiro Tomiita, Rin Yamamoto, Ryuuta Nakagami, Shin'ya Tomofuji, Tetsuro Umezu, Yoshiko Tanaka, Yuji Shibata. **Special Effects:** Rina Miura. **Animation Production:** Kyoto Animation.

K-ON! Season 2 (a.k.a. *K-ON!!*, 2010)

Original Title: *K-ON!!* **Status:** TV Series (26 episodes). **Episode Length:** 24 minutes. **Director:** Naoko Yamada. **Series Composition:** Reiko Yoshida. **Screenplay:** Jukki Hanada, Katsuhiko Muramoto, Masashi Yokotani, Reiko Yoshida. **Storyboards:** Hiroko Utsumi, Ichirou Miyoshi, Kazuya Sakamoto, Mitsuyoshi Yoneda, Naoko Yamada, Noriyuki Kitanohara, Taichi Ishidate, Tatsuya Ishihara, Touko Takao, Yasuhiro Takemoto. **Music:** Hajime Hyakkoku (F.M.F). **Original Creator:** kakifly. **Character Design:** Yukiko Horiguchi. **Art Director:** Seiki Tamura. **Animation Directors:** Chiyoko Ueno, Futoshi Nishiya, Kazumi Ikeda, Miku Kadowaki, Seiichi Akitake, Shoko Ikeda, Yukiko Horiguchi. **Sound Director:** Yota Tsuruoka. **Director of Photography:** Rin Yamamoto. **Producers:** Naohiro Futono, Shinichi Nakamura, Yoko Hatta, Yoshihisa Nakayama. **Animation Producer:** Eharu Oohashi. **Background Art:** Mikiko Watanabe. **Color Design:** Akiyo Takeda, Kana Miyata. **Editing:** Kengo Shigemura. **Music Producer:** Shigeo Komori (F.M.F). **Musical Instrument Design:** Hiroyuki Takahashi. **Photography:** Akihiro Ura, Kazuya Takao, Kōhei Funamoto, Natsumi Hamada, Ryuta Nakagami, Tetsuro Umezu, Yuji Shibata. **Special Effects:** Rina Miura. **Animation Production:** Kyoto Animation.

K-ON! (2011)

Original Title: *K-ON!* **Status:** movie. **Length:** 115 minutes. **Director:** Naoko Yamada. **Screenplay:** Reiko Yoshida. **Storyboards:** Naoko Yamada, Tatsuya Ishihara. **Unit Directors:** Hiroko Utsumi, Naoko Yamada, Tatsuya Ishihara. **Original Creator:** kakifly. **Character Design:** Yukiko Horiguchi. **Art Director:** Seiki Tamura. **Chief Animation Director:** Yukiko Horiguchi. **Assistant Animation Directors:** Chise Kamoi, Chiyoko Ueno, Futoshi Nishiya, Kayo Hikiyama, Nao Naitō, Nobuaki Maruki. **Color Coordination:** Akiyo Takeda, Kana Miyata. **Color Design:** Akiyo Takeda. **Insert Song Arrangement:** Tom-H@ck. **Insert Song Composition:** Tom-H@ck. **Insert Song Lyrics:** Shoko Omori. **Insert Song Performance:** Aki Toyosaki. **Layout Supervisor:** Yoshiji Kigami. **Musical Instrument Design:** Hiroyuki Takahashi. **Production Managers:** Keisuke Yokota, Yōtarō Satō. **Production Producer:** Shin'ichirou Hatta. **Setting Managers:** Fumina Ōhashi, Riri Senami. **Special Effects:** Rina Miura, Shizuka Uno. **Theme Song Arrangement:** Hajime Hyakkoku (OP), Shigeo Komori (ED). **Theme Song Composition:** Hiroyuki Maezawa (ED), Tom-H@ck (OP). **Theme Song Lyrics:** Shoko Omori (OP; ED). **Theme Song Performance:** Aki Toyosaki (OP), Yōko Hikasa (ED), Hiroki Ueda, Ikuko Tamine, Kana Miyata. **3DCG:** Tetsuro Umezu, Yuji Shibata. **Animation Production:** Kyoto Animation. **Distributor:** Shochiku Film.

Kanon (2006–2007)

Original Title: *Kanon*. **Status:** TV Series (24 episodes). **Episode Length:** 24 minutes. **Director:** Tatsuya Ishihara. **Original Creator:** Visual Art's/Key. **Series Composition:** Fumihiko Shimo. **Screenplay:** Fumihiko Shimo. **Music:** Jun Maeda, OdiakeS, Shinji Orito. **Original Character Designer:** Itaru Hinoue (Visual Art's). **Character Designer:** Kazumi Ikeda. **Art Designer:** Mutsuo Shinohara. **Art Director:** Mutsuo Shinohara. **Chief Animation Director:** Kazumi Ikeda. **Animation Directors:** Chiyoko Ueno, Futoshi Nishiya, Hiroyuki Takahashi, Kazumi Ikeda, Mitsuyoshi Yoneda, Satoshi Kadowaki, Shoko Ikeda, Yukiko Horiguchi. **Producers:** Naohiro Futono, Shinichi Nakamura, Yoko Hatta, Yoshihisa Nakayama. **Sound Director:** Yota Tsuruoka. **Sound Effects:** Eiko Morikawa. **Color Designer:** Akiyo Takeda. **Special Effects:** Rina Miura. **Animation Production:** Kyoto Animation.

Last War of Heavenloids and Akutoloids (2009)

Original Title: *Tenjou-nin to Akuto-nin Saigo no Tatakai*. **Status:** movie. **Length:** 83 minutes. **Director:** Yoshiji Kigami. **Series Composition:** Yoshiji Kigami. **Script:** Yoshiji Kigami. **Storyboard:** Yoshiji Kigami. **Unit Director:** Yoshiji Kigami. **Music:** Satoru Kousaki. **Character Design:** Tomoe Aratani. **Art Director:** Seiki Tamura. **Animation Director:** Tomoe Aratani. **Sound Director:** Yota Tsuruoka. **Director of Photography:** Ryuuta Nakagami. **Producer:** Atsushi Itou, Hideaki Hatta. **Art Setting:** Hiroyuki Takahashi. **Assistant Animation Director:** Futoshi Nishiya, Kazumi Ikeda, Seiichi Akitake. **Chief Producer:** Takeshi Yasuda. **Color Setting:** Rie Takagi. **Editing:** Kengo Shigemura. **Music Producer:** Shigeru Saitō. **Planning:** Yoko Hatta. **Animation Production:** Kyoto Animation.

Lucky☆Star (2007)

Original Title: *Lucky☆Star*. **Status:** TV Series (24 episodes). **Episode Length:** 24 minutes. **Directors:** Yasuhiro Takemoto, Yutaka Yamamoto. **Series Composition:** Touko Machida. **Script:** Kagami Yoshimizu, Katsuhiko Muramoto, Shoji Gatoh, Tomoe Aratani, Touko Machida, Yūko Okabe, Yutaka Yamamoto. **Storyboards:** Ichirou Miyoshi, Kazuya Sakamoto, Satoshi Kadowaki, Shinobu Yoshioka, Taichi Ishidate, Tatsuya Ishihara, Tomoe Aratani, Touko Takao, Yasuhiro, Yutaka Yamamoto. **Music:** Satoru Kousaki (MoNACA). **Original Creator:** Kagami Yoshimizu. **Original Character Design:** Kagami Yoshimizu. **Character Design:** Yukiko Horiguchi. **Art Directors:** Emi Kesamaru (assistant), Seiki Tamura. **Chief Animation Director:** Yukiko Horiguchi. **Sound Director:** Yota Tsuruoka. **Director of Photography:** Kazuya Takao. **Executive Producers:** Masao Kawano, Nobuhiko Sakawa, Takeshi Yasuda, Yoko Hatta. **Animation Producer:** Eharu Oohashi. **Background Art:** Ikuko Tamine, Joji Unoguchi, Miyuki Hiratoko, Shinji Matsuura. **Color Design:** Ayumi Shimoura. **Composition Cooperation:** Kagami Yoshimizu. **Editing:** Gen Sakakura, Kengo Shigemura (Studio Gong), Tomoko Sato (Studio Gong). **Layout Manager:** Ken Senami. **Logo Design:** Kiyoyuki Hirano, Tsutomu Yamaguchi, Yumi Yukinori (On Graphics). **Music Producer:** Shigeru Saitō (Lantis). **Photography:** Hiroki Ueda, Kazuya Takao, Natsumi Hamada, Rin Yamamoto, Ryuta Nakagami, Shinya

Tomafuji, Tetsuo Umetsu, Yoshiko Tanaka. **Planning:** Shinichiro Inoue. **Planning Producers:** Atsushi Itou, Hideaki Hatta. **Production Assistant:** Shin'ichirou Hatta. **Production Manager:** Hisataka Sakahara. **Setting:** Hiroyuki Takahashi. **Sound Effects:** Eiko Morikawa (Chuura Sound). **Sound Manager:** Yoshimi Sugiyama (Rakuonsha). **Sound Producer:** Yota Tsuruoka. **Special Effects:** Sachie Tsuda. **Animation Production:** Kyoto Animation.

Lucky☆Star (2008)

Original Title: *Lucky☆Star*. **Status:** OVA (1 episode). **Episode Length:** 42 minutes. **Director:** Yasuhiro Takemoto. **Storyboards:** Yasuhiro Takemoto. **Music:** Satoru Kousaki. **Original Creator:** Kagami Yoshimizu. **Character Design:** Yukiko Horiguchi. **Art Director:** Seiki Tamura. **Chief Animation Director:** Yukiko Horiguchi. **Director of Photography:** Kazuya Takao. **Color Setting:** Ayumi Shimoura. **Editing:** Kengo Shigemura. **Animation Production:** Kyoto Animation.

The Melancholy of Haruhi Suzumiya (2006)

Original Title: *Suzumiya Haruhi no Yuutsu*. **Status:** TV Series (14 episodes). **Episode Length:** 24 minutes. **Director:** Tatsuya Ishihara. **Script:** Fumihiko Shimo, Joe Itou, Katsuhiko Muramoto, Nagaru Tanigawa, Shoji Gatoh, Tatsuya Ishihara, Yutaka Yamamoto. **Storyboards:** Kazuya Sakamoto, Noriyuki Kitanohara, Satoshi Kadowaki, Shinobu Yoshioka, Taichi Ishidate, Tatsuya Ishihara, Tomoe Aratani, Yasuhiro Takemoto, Yutaka Yamamoto. **Music:** Satoru Kousaki. **Original Creator:** Nagaru Tanigawa. **Original Character Design:** Noizi Ito. **Character Design:** Shoko Ikeda. **Art Directors:** Miyuki Hiratoko (assistant), Seiki Tamura. **Chief Animation Director:** Shoko Ikeda. **Mechanical Design:** Kanetake Ebikawa. **Sound Director:** Yota Tsuruoka (Rakuonsha). **Director of Photography:** Yoshiko Tanaka. **Executive Producers:** Nobuhiko Sakawa, Shouji Utagawa, Takeshi Yasuda, Yoko Hatta. **Color Design:** Naomi Ishida. **Editing:** Kengo Shigemura (Super Editor Kyon). **Planning:** Naohisa Yamashita, Shinichiro Inoue. **Planning Producers:** Atsushi Itou, Hideaki Hatta. **Recording:** Satoshi Yano. **Recording Assistant:** Fumiaki Tanaka. **Series Production Director:** Yutaka Yamamoto. **Setting:** Hiroyuki Takahashi. **Setting Manager:** Kazuki Awara. **Sound Effects:** Eiko Morikawa (Sound Garden). **Sound Manager:** Yoshimi Sugiyama (Rakuonsha). **Special Effects:** Rina Miura. **Animation Production:** Kyoto Animation.

The Melancholy of Haruhi Suzumiya (2009)

Original Title: *Suzumiya Haruhi no Yuutsu*. **Status:** TV Series (28 episode). **Episode Length:** 25 minutes. **Director:** Tatsuya Ishihara. **Screenplay:** Fumihiko Shimo, Joe Itou, Katsuhiko Muramoto, Nagaru Tanigawa, Shoji Gatoh, Tatsuya Ishihara, Yasuhiro Takemoto. **Storyboards:** Ichirou Miyoshi, Mitsuyoshi Yoneda, Naoko Yamada, Noriyuki Kitanohara, Taichi Ishidate, Tatsuya Ishihara, Tomoe Aratani, Touko Takao, Yasuhiro Takemoto. **Music:** Satoru Kousaki (monaca). **Original Creator:** Nagaru Tanigawa. **Original Character Design:** Noizi Ito. **Character Design:** Shoko Ikeda. **Art Director:** Seiki Tamura. **Chief Animation Director:** Futoshi

Nishiya. **Sound Director:** Yota Tsuruoka. **Director of Photography:** Ryuuta Nakagami. **Producer:** Atsushi Itou. **Assistant Animation Directors:** Chiyoko Ueno, Kazumi Ikeda, Mariko Takahashi. **Color Design:** Naomi Ishida. **Editing:** Kengo Shigemura. **Logo Design Assistance:** Jin Ichikawa (sun graphic). **Music Producer:** Shigeru Saitō (Lantis). **Setting:** Hiroyuki Takahashi. **Animation Production:** Kyoto Animation.

The Melancholy of Haruhi-chan Suzumiya (2009)

Original Title: *Suzumiya Haruhi-chan no Yuutsu.* **Status:** ONA Series (25 episodes). **Episode Length:** 5 minutes. **Director:** Yasuhiro Takemoto. **Original Creator:** Nagaru Tanigawa. **Original Manga:** Puyo. **Original Character Design:** Noizi Ito. **Character Design:** Futoshi Nishiya. **Animation Production:** Kyoto Animation.

Munto (2003)

Original Title: *Munto.* **Status:** OVA (1 episode). **Episode Length:** 52 minutes. **Director:** Yoshiji Kigami. **Art Director:** Seiki Tamura. **Producer:** Yoko Hatta. **Animation Supervisor:** Yoshiji Kigami. **Chief Animator:** Tomoe Aratani. **Director of Models:** Tomoe Aratani. **Script Director:** Yoshiji Kigami. **Production:** Kyoto Animation.

Munto 2: Beyond the Walls of Time (2004)

Original Title: *Munto: Toki no Kabe o Koete.* **Status:** OVA (1 episode). **Episode Length:** 58 minutes. **Director:** Yoshiji Kigami. **Script:** Yoshiji Kigami. **Storyboard:** Yoshiji Kigami. **Music:** Shinji Ikeda. **Character Design:** Tomoe Aratani. **Art Director:** Seiki Tamura. **Animation Director:** Tomoe Aratani. **Sound Director:** Yota Tsuruoka. **Director of Photography:** Ryuuta Nakagami. **Producer:** Yoko Hatta. **Assistant Animation Director:** Satoshi Kadowaki. **Assistant Director:** Yutaka Yamamoto. **Color Coordination:** Rie Takaki. **Editing:** Chieko Takayama, Seiji Morita. **Sound Effects:** Eiko Morikawa. **Sound Production Manager:** Yoshimi Sugiyama. **Special Effects:** Rina Miura. **Production:** Kyoto Animation. **Animation:** Kyoto Animation. **Backgrounds:** Ani Village.

Nichijou (a.k.a. *My Ordinary Life*, 2011)

Original Title: *Nichijō.* **Status:** TV Series (26 episodes). **Episode Length:** 24 minutes. **Director:** Tatsuya Ishihara. **Series Composition:** Jukki Hanada. **Script:** Chizuru Segawa, Joe Itou, Jukki Hanada, Katsuhiko Muramoto, Keiichi Arawi, Maiko Nishioka, Taichi Ishidate, Tatsuya Ishihara. **Storyboards:** Eisaku Kawanami, Hiroko Utsumi, Ichirou Miyoshi, Kazuya Sakamoto, Mitsuyoshi Yoneda, Naoko Yamada, Noriyuki Kitanohara, Taichi Ishidate, Tatsuya Ishihara, Yasuhiro Takemoto. **Music:** Yuuji Nomi. **Original Creator:** Keiichi Arawi. **Character Design:** Futoshi Nishiya. **Art Director:** Jouji Unoguchi. **Animation Directors:** Chise Kamoi, Chiyoko Ueno, Futoshi Nishiya, Hiroyuki Takahashi, Kazumi Ikeda, Miku Kadowaki, Nobuaki Maruki, Seiichi Akitake, Shoko Ikeda, Yukiko Horiguchi. **Sound**

Director: Yota Tsuruoka (Rakuonsha). **Director of Photography:** Kazuya Takao. **Producers:** Atsushi Itou, Hideaki Hatta. **Background Art:** Ayami Hidaka (Anime Workshop Basara), Ayumi Takasaki, Cheon Bok Lee (Studio Blue), Hiroyuki Tsubaki (Anime Workshop Basara), Ikuko Tamine, Ji Hye Kim (Studio Blue), Jouji Unoguchi, Manae Yamatogi, Masaki Yoshizaki, Mi Jin Lee (Studio Blue), Mikiko Watanabe, Miyuki Hiratoko, Mutsuo Shinohara, Naoki Hosokawa, Nozomi Ōishi, Sagako Itakura (Anime Workshop Basara), Seiji Watabe (Anime Workshop Basara), Shingo Kasai, Shūhei Okude, So Jeong An (Studio Blue), Tomoki Hiraishi, Yoshikatsu Matsumoto (Anime Workshop Basara), Yukiko Takeuchi, Yumi Okada. **Chief Production Supervisor:** Takeshi Yasuda. **Color Key:** Akiyo Takeda, Kana Miyata, Mayumi Nagayasu, Naomi Ishida, Rie Takagi, Yūka Yoneda. **Editing:** Kengo Shigemura (Studio Gong). **Music Producer:** Shigeru Saitō (Lantis). **Photography:** Akihiro Ura, Hiroki Ueda, Kazuya Takao, Kōhei Funamoto, Natsumi Hamada, Norihiro Tomiita, Rin Yamamoto, Ryuuta Nakagami, Tetsuro Umezu, Yoshiko Tanaka, Yuji Shibata. **Planning:** Naohiro Futono, Shunji Inoue, Takafumi Ishibashi, Takeshi Yasuda, Tsuneo Takechi, Yoko Hatta. **Production Managers:** Keisuke Yokota, Nagaharu Ohashi, Shin'ichirou Hatta, Sōta Kawano. **Series Composition Cooperation:** Keiichi Arawi. **Setting:** Hiroyuki Takahashi. **Special Effects:** Rina Miura. **Shizuka Uno Production:** Kyoto Animation.

Nyoron Churuya-san (2009)

Original Title: *Nyoron☆Churuya-san*. **Status:** ONA Series (13 episodes). **Episode Length:** 2 minutes. **Director:** Yasuhiro Takemoto. **Original Creator:** Nagaru Tanigawa. **Original Manga:** Eretto. **Original Character Design:** Noizi Ito. **Animation Production:** Kyoto Animation.

The World Reflected in the Eyes of the Girl Looking at the Sky (2009)

Original Title: *Sora o Miageru Shoujo no Hitomi ni Utsuru Sekai*. **Status:** TV Series (9 episodes). **Episode Length:** 30 minutes. **Director:** Yoshiji Kigami. **Series Composition:** Yoshiji Kigami. **Screenplay:** Yoshiji Kigami. **Episode Director:** Yoshiji Kigami. **Music:** monaca, Satoru Kousaki. **Character Design:** Tomoe Aratani. **Art Director:** Jouji Unoguchi, Seiki Tamura. **Animation Director:** Tomoe Aratani. **Sound Director:** Yota Tsuruoka. **Director of Photography:** Ryuuta Nakagami. **Producer:** Atsushi Itou, Hideaki Hatta. **Art Setting:** Hiroyuki Takahashi. **Assistant producer:** Shin'ichirou Hatta. **Color Setting:** Rie Takagi. **Editing:** Gen Itakura (Studio Gong), Kengo Shigemura. **HD Editing:** Kengo Shigemura, Tomoko Sato. Logo Design: Hiroaki Kamihara. **Music Producer:** Shigeru Saitō. **Online Editing Producer:** Takayuki Tabata. **Online Home Page Producer:** Kazuki Kurihara. **Planning:** Yoko Hatta. **Promotion:** Yosuke Nishiyama (Kadokawa Shoten). **Recording:** Yasushi Nagura. **Recording Assistant:** Mika Kamemoto. **Sound Effects:** Eiko Morikawa. **Animation Production:** Kyoto Animation.

Bibliography

Adams, S. "Scott Adams Quotes." *ThinkExist*. http://thinkexist.com/quotes/scott_adams/.

Addison, J. "Imagination Quotes." *BrainyQuote*. http://www.brainyquote.com/quotes/topics/topic_imagination.html.

Adorno, T. "Creative Quotations for Brainstorming and Lateral Thinking." http://www.brainstorming.co.uk/quotes/creativequotations.html.

"Anime Spotlight: *Hyouka*." *Anime News Network*. http://www.animenewsnetwork.co.uk/anime-spotlight/2012/spring/hyouka.

The Asahi Shimbun. 2011. "Anime News: Kyoto Tram Features Comic Protagonists' Images." *The Asahi Shimbun*. September 19. Translated by *The Asahi Shimbun* from the website of *Anime Anime Japan Ltd*. http://ajw.asahi.com/article/cool_japan/anime_news/AJ2011091911066.

Ascaloth. 2009. "*Clannad: After Story*." *The Nihon Review*. http://www.nihonreview.com/anime/clannad-after-story/.

Banks, J. 2009. "[Review] *Full Metal Panic: The Second Raid*." *Anime 3000*. http://www.anime3000.com/articles/anime/405-review-full-metal-panic-the-second-raid.html.

Barron, F. "Creative Quotations for Brainstorming and Lateral Thinking." http://www.brainstorming.co.uk/quotes/creativequotations.html.

Baudrillard, J. 1988. "Simulacra and Simulations." In *Selected Writings*, edited by M. Poster. Stanford, CA: Stanford University Press.

Besen, E. (2003a). "Analogy and Animation: A Special Relationship: Part 1— Show and Tell." http://www.awn.com/articles/analogyani/analogy-and-animation-special-relationship-part-1-show-and-tell/page/2%2C1.

Besen, E. (2003b). "Analogy and Animation: A Special Relationship: Part 2 — Think Like an Animator, Walk Like a Duck." http://www.awn.com/articles/analogyani/analogy-and-animation-special-relationship-part-2-think-animator-walk-duck/page/2%2C1.

Besen, E. (2003c). "Analogy and Animation: A Special Relationship: Part 3 — Good Studios, Bad Films, v. 1." http://www.awn.com/articles/analogyani/analogy-and-animation-special-relationship-part-3-good-studios-bad-films-v1/page/1%2C1.

Bourdieu, P. 1991. *Outline of a Theory of Practice*. Cambridge: Cambridge University Press.

Buber, M. "10 Quotes on the Importance of Play." *Planning with Kids*.

http://planningwithkids.com/2009/04/14/10-quotes-on-the-importance-of-play/.

The Captain. 2011. "This Is Why *K-ON* Is Worth Your Time." *Cosplay Fun*. http://cosplayfun.wordpress.com/tag/kyoto-animation/.

Cavallaro, D. 2010. *Anime and the Visual Novel: Narrative Structure, Design and Play at the Crossroads of Animation and Computer Games*. Jefferson, NC: McFarland.

"A Close Look at an Anime Production House Part 1." 2008. *Kanon* DVD, vol. 1. ADV Films.

"A Close Look at an Anime Production House Part 2." 2008. *Kanon* DVD, vol. 2. ADV Films.

"A Close Look at an Anime Production House Part 3." 2008. *Kanon* DVD, vol. 2. ADV Films.

"A Close Look at an Anime Production House Part 4." 2008. *Kanon* DVD, vol. 3. ADV Films.

"A Close Look at an Anime Production House Part 5." 2008. *Kanon* DVD, vol. 4. ADV Films.

"A Close Look at an Anime Production House Part 6." 2008. *Kanon* DVD, vol. 5. ADV Films.

"A Close Look at an Anime Production House Part 7." 2008. *Kanon* DVD, vol. 5. ADV Films.

"A Close Look at an Anime Production House Part 8." 2008. *Kanon* DVD, vol. 6. Funimation.

Confucius. "Confucius Quotes." *BrainyQuote*. http://www.brainyquote.com/quotes/authors/c/confucius.html.

Cytrus. 2011. "*K-ON! Movie Review*." *Yaranakya*. http://yaranakya.wordpress.com/2011/12/27/k-on-movie-review-spoiler-free/.

Dahmen-Ingenhoven, R. 2004. *Animation: Form Follows Fun*. Basel: Birkhauser.

De Mente, B. L. 2006. *Elements of Japanese Design*. Tokyo, Rutland, VT, and Singapore: Tuttle. Kindle Edition.

Demko, G. J. "Mysteries in the Land of the Rising Sun." *G. J. Demko's Landscapes of Crime*. http://www.dartmouth.edu/~gjdemko/japan.htm.

Drazen, P. 2011. *A Gathering of Spirits: Japan's Ghost Story Tradition From Folklore and Kabuki to Anime and Manga*. Bloomington, IN: iUniverse, Inc. Kindle Edition.

Einstein, A. "Creative Quotations for Brainstorming and Lateral Thinking." http://www.brainstorming.co.uk/quotes/creativequotations.html.

"Explanation of the Heisei 22 National Census." 2010. *Kyoto Prefecture Website*. http://www.webcitation.org/5sanOdvNM.

Fargo, P. 2004. "*Full Metal Panic? Fumoffu*— Preview." *Anime News Network*. http://www.animenewsnetwork.co.uk/review/full-metal-panic-Fumoffu.

Fearn, H. 2011. "Lessons from Japan: Investing in Local Identities." *The Guardian*. Monday 8 August. http://www.guardian.co.uk/local-government-network/2011/aug/08/lessons-from-japan-local-identities.

Gordon, A. F. 2007. *Ghostly Matters: Haunting and the Sociological Imagination*. Minneapolis and London: University of Minnesota Press. Kindle Edition.

Grant, P. B. 2011. "Nabokov and the Art of Play." Review of Thomas Karshan. *Nabokov and the Art of Play*. *British Journal of Aesthetics*. Vol. 15, Issue 4; pp. 446–449.

Haruhi Suzumiya Illustrations: Autumn & Winter. 2010. Tokyo: Kadokawa Shoten.

Hu, T. G. 2010. *Frames of Anime: Culture and Image Building*. Hong Kong:

Hong Kong University Press. Kindle Edition.

"*Hyouka*: Volume 1, Chapter 1, 1— Letter from Benares." 2012. Translated by Baka-Tsuki. *Baka-Tsuki*. http://www.baka-tsuki.org/project/index.php?title=Hyouka:Volume_1_Chapter_1.

Ibuka, M. "Masaru Ibuka Quotes." *BrainyQuote*. http://www.brainyquote.com/quotes/quotes/m/masaruibuk311883.html.

Ishida, N. 2007. "The Director Was Haruhi." *Newtype USA*, August.

Ishihara, T. 2007. "The Director Was Haruhi." *Newtype USA*, August.

Ishihara, T. 2011. "Director Roundtable." http://ultimatemegax.files.wordpress.com/2011/11/director-roundtable1.pdf.

Iwasaka, M., and Toelken, B. 1994. *Ghosts and the Japanese: Cultural Experience in Japanese Death Legends*. Logan: Utah State University Press.

Japan Media Arts Festival in Kyoto. 2011. http://plaza.bunka.go.jp/kyoto/english.html.

"Japanese Box Office, February 6–7." 2010. *Anime News Network*. February 11.

"Japanese Retro Fashion." 2010. *Country Facts: The World at Your Fingertips*. http://www.kwintessential.co.uk/articles/japan/japanese-retro-fashion/1498.

jel x. 2011. "Promoted Story: KyoAni and the Power of Suggestion." *Japanator*. http://www.japanator.com/promoted-story-kyoani-and-the-power-of-suggestion-20289.phtml.

"Kadokawa: *Haruhi* Film Earns 200 Million Yen in 1st Week." 2010. *Anime News Network*. February 12.

Kadowaki, S. 2007. "The Director Was Haruhi." *Newtype USA*, August.

Kawasumi, H. 2008. "Anime Review: Kanon." http://hirito.blogspot.co.uk/2008/03/anime-review-kanon.html.

Keionbu Colorful Memories!! 2011. Kyoto: Kyoto Animation Original Goods.

Kidd. 2011. "The Rise and Rise of Kyoto Animation." *Anime Addicts Anonymous Podcast*. http://www.aaapodcast.com/archives/4640/.

Kimlinger, C. 2011. "*My Ordinary Life*. Episodes 1–7 Streaming." *Anime News Network*. http://www.animenewsnetwork.co.uk/review/my-ordinary-life/episodes-1.

"*K-ON!* Is #3 in December/January Box Office in Japan." 2012. *Anime News Network*. January 11.

"*K-ON!* School Anime Pilgrimage Part 1." 2010. *Moé Passion—An Adventure and Anime Culture Blog by a US Sailor*. http://punynari.wordpress.com/2010/09/25/k-on-school-anime-pilgrimage-part-1/.

"*K-ON!* (TV)." *Anime News Network*. http://www.animenewsnetwork.co.uk/encyclopedia/anime.php?id=10562&page=22.

Kyoto Animation. http://www.kyotoanimation.co.jp/.

"Kyoto Animation Plans *Chū-2 Byō Demo Koi ga Shitai!* Anime." 2011. *Anime News Network*. 28 December. http://www.animenewsnetwork.co.uk/news/2011-12-27/kyoto-animation-plans-chuni-byo-demo-koi-shitai-anime.

Lankoski, P. 2003. "Character Design Fundamentals for Role-Playing Games." http://www.ropecon.fi/brap/ch12.pdf.

Lau, E. 2003. "*Full Metal Panic? Fumoffu*." *T.H.E.M. Anime Reviews*. http://www.themanime.org/viewreview.php?id=590.

Leon. "Japanese Aesthetics in Design." http://vehicle4change.wordpress.com/japanese-aesthetics-in-design/.

Lim, S. 2007. *Japanese Style: Designing with Nature's Beauty*. Layton, UT: Gibbs Smith.

Lonsdale, S. 2008. *Japanese Style*. London: Carlton.

Lyttle, P. 2012. *Japanese Street Style*. London: A&C Black.

Ma, T. "*Full Metal Panic Fumoffu.*" Magikumo. http://www.makigumo.com/reviews.php?id=9.

Martin. 2009. "Marcel Theroux Goes in Search of Wabi-Sabi." *Mono no aware*. http://mononoaware.concretebadger.net/2009/03/21/marcel-theroux-goes-in-search-of-wabi-sabi/.

Martin, T. 2006. "*Full Metal Panic! The Second Raid*— DVD 1." *Anime News Network*. http://www.animenewsnetwork.co.uk/review/full-metal-panic-the-second-raid/dvd-1.

Martin, T. 2007a. "*Full Metal Panic! The Second Raid*— DVD 2." *Anime News Network*. http://www.animenewsnetwork.co.uk/review/full-metal-panic-the-second-raid/dvd-2.

Martin, T. 2007b. "*Air*— DVD 1." *Anime News Network*. http://www.animenewsnetwork.co.uk/review/air/dvd-1.

Martin, T. 2007c. "*Air*— DVD 3." *Anime News Network*. http://www.animenewsnetwork.co.uk/review/air/dvd-3.

Meek, B. 2007. "*Lucky Star.*" *T.H.E.M. Anime Reviews*. http://www.themanime.org/viewreview.php?id=1129.

The Melancholy of Haruhi Suzumiya Official Fanbook. 2006. Tokyo: Kadokawa Shoten.

Morris, I. 1994. *The World of the Shining Prince: Court Life in Ancient Japan*. New York, Tokyo and London: Kodansha International.

"*Nichijou: My Ordinary Life.*" 2011. *Rossman Reviews and Ratings*. http://www.therossman.com/rrr/anime/nichijou.html.

"*Nichijou* Review: An Outside-The-Box Comedy." 2011. *Polychromium*. http://polychromium.wordpress.com/2011/10/03/nichijou-review/.

Paz, O. "Art Quotes." *BrainyQuote*. http://www.brainyquote.com/quotes/topics/topic_art2.html.

Ransom, K. 2012. "Review — *K-ON! The Movie.*" *Anime News Network*. http://www.animenewsnetwork.co.uk/review/k-on/the-movie.

Richie, D. 2011. *Viewed Sideways: Writings on Culture and Style in Contemporary Japan*. Berkeley, CA: Stone Bridge.

Ross, C. 2006. "*The Melancholy of Haruhi Suzumiya.*" *T.H.E.M. Anime Reviews*. http://www.themanime.org/viewreview.php?id=942.

Russell, B. *The Quotations Page*. http://www.quotationspage.com/quotes/Bertrand_Russell.

RYHZUO. 2011. "Review — *Nichijou.*" *Blickwinkel*. http://imperialx.wordpress.com/2011/09/28/review-nichijou/.

Saito, Satomi. 2007. "Culture and Authenticity: The Discursive Space of Japanese Detective Fiction and the Formation of the Natrional Imaginary." Dissertation, University of Iowa, 2007. http://ir.uiowa.edu/etd/145.

"7 Japanese Aesthetic Principles to Change Your Thinking." 2009. *Presentation Zen*. http://www.presentationzen.com/presentationzen/2009/09/exposing-ourselves-to-traditional-japanese-aesthetic-ideas-notions-that-may-seem-quite-foreign-to-most-of-us-is-a-goo.html.

Shadowmage. "*Full Metal Panic? Fumoffu.*" *The Nihon Review*. http://

www.nihonreview.com/anime/full-metal-panic-fumoffu/.

Shiraishi, M. 2011. *The Disappearance of Haruhi Suzumiya* DVD, Disc 2. Manga Entertainment.

Takaii. 2011a. "*Nichijou*—07." *Random Curiosity.* http://randomc.net/2011/05/15/nichijou-07/.

Takaii. 2011b. "*Nichijou*— 26 (END)." *Random Curiosity.* http://randomc.net/category/nichijou/.

Takao, T. 2011. "Director Roundtable." http://ultimatemegax.files.wordpress.com/2011/11/director-roundtable1.pdf.

Takemoto, Y. 2011. "Director Roundtable." http://ultimatemegax.files.wordpress.com/2011/11/director-roundtable1.pdf.

therik. 2009. "*Kanon* (2006) Review." *Anime-Planet.* http://www.anime-planet.com/reviews/a560.html.

Tierney, P. L. "The Nature of Japanese Garden Art: Seijaku." *Kyyriolexy.* http://kyriolexy.wordpress.com/gemme-di-talento-larte-ed-il-bonsai/il-giardino-in-10-semplici-regole/the-nature-of-japanese-garden-art-seijaku-l-tierney/.

Triple_R. 2010. "Kyoto Animation: My Take On It." *Assessing the Anime.* http://assessingtheanime.blogspot.com/2010/02/kyoto-animation-my-take-on-it.html.

Ueda, M. 1967. *Literary and Art Theories in Japan.* Ann Arbor: Center for Japanese Studies, University of Michigan.

Wordsworth, W. "Quotations by Author: William Wordsworth." *The Quotations Page.* http://www.quotationspage.com/quotes/William_Wordsworth/.

Yi. 2010. "*K-On!!* Going Retro — Fashion in Listen!! and No, Thank You!" *Listles Ink.* http://listlessink.wordpress.com/2010/08/19/k-on-going-retro-fashion-in-listen-and-no-thank-you/.

Yoshida, M. 1984. *The Hybrid Culture— What Happened When East and West Met.* Hiroshima: Mazda.

"Zen Buddhism." *Gaiam life.*" http://blog.gaiam.com/quotes/authors/zen-buddhism.

Index

Adams, S. 3
Addison, J. 24
Adorno, T. 78
Air (game) 84–85
Air (movie) 89
Air (TV series) 2, 13, 88–95, 105, 174
Air in Summer 93–94
Ando, T. 5
Ascaloth 111

Banks, J. 39
Barron, F. 78
Battles Without Honor and Humanity 36
Baudrillard, J. 15
Beckett, S. 151
Besen, E. 81, 82
Blade Runner 57
Bourdieu, P. 117
Buber, M. 119
Bullit 40

The Captain 23, 29, 125, 134
Carter, B. 56
Castle, N. 36
Cavallaro, D. 95–96
Chigira, K. 27, 30
CLAMP 174
Clannad (game) 86–87, 109
Clannad (movie) 86
Clannad (OVA) 109–110
Clannad (TV series) 2, 14, 92, 105–109, 174
Clannad After Story 2, 86, 108, 110–111
Confucius 1
Cytrus 143, 145

Dahmen-Ingenhoven, R. 15
De Mente, B.L. 4, 5, 13, 123
Demko, G.J. 162–163
Descartes, R. 27
Dezaki, O. 86, 89

The Disappearance of Haruhi Suzumiya 2, 13, 63–76, 142–143, 173
Drazen, P. 101

Einstein, A. 3

Fargo, P. 32–33
Fearn, H. 11
Fukasaku, K. 36
Fukuda, M. 36
Full Metal Jacket 36
Full Metal Panic! 27–29
Full Metal Panic? Fumoffu 1–2, 13, 27, 29–37, 152, 173
Full Metal Panic! The Second Raid (OVA) 27
Full Metal Panic! The Second Raid (TV series) 2, 13, 29, 37–44, 173
Fushimi Inari Taisha 14
Fushimi-ku 14
Fushimi-Momoyama Castle 14–16

Gatoh, S. 27, 164, 166
Gonzo 3, 27, 29, 32, 33, 37, 40, 77
Gordon, A.F. 102–103
Grant, P.B. 119
Gundam SEED 36

Haruhi Suzumiya Illustrations — Autumn & Winter 75–76
Hatta, H. 11, 23
Hatta, Y. 11
Hideyoshi, T. 14
Hu, T.G. 13
Hyouka (novel) 164
Hyouka (TV series) 2, 120, 162

Ibuka, M. 1
Ikehata, T. 126
Ishida, N. 48
Ishihara, T. 47–48, 66, 67, 72, 73, 80, 81, 96

Ito, N. 44
Iwasaka, M. 101–102

jel x 54, 118, 162

K-ON! (movie) 2, 14, 120, 129, 142–148
K-ON! (OVA) 129
K-ON! (TV series) 2, 14, 120, 129–142
Kadowaki, S. 48
Kanon (game) 85
Kanon (TV series) 2, 13, 80, 81, 92, 95–105, 111, 174
Kawasumi, H. 104
Keionbu Colorful Memories!! 138
Kidd 77
Kimlinger, C. 148, 159
Kubrick, S. 36

Lankoski, P. 117
The Last Starfighter 36
Last War of Heavenloids and Akutoloids 24
Lau, E. 31
Leon 18–19
Lim, S. 5
Lonsdale, S. 5
Lucky☆Star (OVA) 128
Lucky☆Star (TV series) 2, 14, 27, 81, 120, 121, 125–129, 131
Lyttle, P. 138–139

Ma, T. 33
Machiavelli, N. 37
Mann, T. 37
Martin 123
Martin, T. 91, 95
Meek, B. 126
The Melancholy of Haruhi-chan Suzumiya 2, 62
The Melancholy of Haruhi Suzumiya (2006) 2, 13, 44–59, 173
The Melancholy of Haruhi Suzumiya (2009) 2, 13, 59–61
The Melancholy of Haruhi Suzumiya Official Fanbook 61–62
Momoyama-cho 14
Mori, T. 126
Morris, I. 89–90
Munto 1, 24–27, 173

Munto 2: Beyond the Walls of Time 1, 24–27
My Ordinary Life please see *Nichijou*

Nichijou (OVA) 159–160
Nichijou (TV series) 2, 14, 81, 148–162
Nietzsche, F. 61
Nyoron Churuya-san 2, 62

Otaku no Video 126

Paz, O. 121
Poe, E.A. 170

Ransom, K. 148
Richie, D. 22, 23
Russell, B. 24
RYHZUO 156, 161, 162

Saito, S. 163–164
Schopenhauer, A. 61
Schulze, G. 15
Shadowmage 33
Shiraishi, M. 71
Sora o Miageru Shoujo no Hitomi ni Utsuru Sekai 24

Takaii 152, 155
Takao, T. 66, 67, 68, 70, 74
Takemoto, Y. 27, 67, 68, 72, 74, 166, 167
Tanigawa, T. 44
Tenjou-nin to Akuto-nin Saigo no Tatakai 24
therik 104, 105
Tierney, P.L. 9, 123
Toelken, B. 101–102
Triple_R 53, 174

Ueda, M. 6, 7, 23

Visual Art's/Key 78, 80, 81, 83, 84, 92, 116, 117, 174

Wordsworth, W. 174
The World Reflected in the Eye of the Girl Looking at the Sky 24

Yi 138, 141, 142
Yonezawa, H. 162, 164, 166
Yoshida, M. 15
Yoshimoto, K. 126
Yuushou, O. 6–7

www.ingramcontent.com/pod-product-compliance
Ingram Content Group UK Ltd.
Pitfield, Milton Keynes, MK11 3LW, UK
UKHW042010140426
5217IPUK00015B/1095